FROM YELLOW STAR TO
POP STAR

DORIT OLIVER-WOLFF

Published by RedDoor
www.reddoorpublishing.com

ISBN 978-1-910453-09-4

A CIP catalogue record for this book is available from the British Library

Cover design: Rawshock design
Typesetting: www.typesetter.org.uk
Printed and bound in Great Britain by Clays Ltd, St Ives plc.

Writing this book caused me to re-live my early life, a mixture of extreme pain and great joy. I dedicate it to my family.

AUTHOR NOTE

I am a Holocaust survivor and international recording artist. I am an author and experienced public speaker. My talks are not a historical account of events, but focus on my experiences of the Holocaust, seen through the eyes of a five-year-old Jewish girl, and my life beyond that. I survived against all the odds.

My talks are educational, inspiring (hopefully), at times unbelievable, sometimes funny, and they are suitable for people of all ages! I give my talks at schools, colleges, hotel venues, literary gatherings, ladies' luncheons, educational conferences – any venue where people wish to hear about my true life account, that of a Holocaust survivor.

My passion is to build bridges between different religions. I am convinced that if people would listen to each other and compare their similarities rather than their differences, nations would learn to get along far better. Nobody has the right to persecute or kill others for being a different religion, race, creed or colour. Everybody has the same right for *living* and for *life*. It's not that I want to remember the Holocaust, but I simply cannot forget. This is part of my story. These are my memories.

FOREWORD

This book is a song of survival and success. It deals in resilience and resourcefulness on a grand scale. It traces the author's life through times of persecution, fright, rebuilding, international singing success and betrayal. At every stage the author's intelligence and quick-wittedness shine like the searchlights she used to evade; like the spotlights she later sang beneath.

Dorit Oliver-Wolff is Jewish by birth. For her, Jewishness is a thing neither to defend nor celebrate. It is just fact. To Dorit, many things are, and always were, more important than her racial identity. In wartime Europe, others felt differently. In the later stages of World War II, Jews were rounded up on an industrial scale and transported from their homelands to camps in Germany and Poland. From Hungary, where Dorit lived in hiding with her mother until the Russian liberation, almost two thirds of the Jewish population of some 725,000 was transported in the early months of 1944 to Auschwitz II-Birkenau. The vast majority perished. Dorit and her remarkable mother, through a mix of bravery, guile, ingenuity, intelligence and luck, evaded capture. They survived the Holocaust. But their troubles were far from over.

After having survived in Budapest on scraps of food stolen or begged for, and having lived in a series of safe houses, consulates or convents, Dorit's mother took herself and her vulnerable charges to Novi Sad in what is now Serbia (then part of Yugoslavia), where the Communist regime had newly occupied the political void. They were behind the Iron Curtain where life remained difficult, especially for Jews. It was not long before Dorit's resolute mother arranged for them to emigrate from Yugoslavia to Israel under the bilateral treaty for ethnic migration.

Although Dorit had received a music scholarship in Yugoslavia, it was in Israel that her formal education really began. It was a place where she felt at peace but not a place where she was destined to remain. Her mother (by now remarried) took the family to Turkey. It was under her mother's tutelage that Dorit learned to dance. She became a member of her mother's dance troupe and toured throughout Turkey, Greece and Cyprus, not only dancing but also taking on singing solos. Her encounters with entertainers, showgirls, prostitutes and pimps provided great life-experience for a young teenager. It was in Cyprus that Dorit married and gained British citizenship: a decision that was to have a profound effect on the course of her life.

There followed years of singing, touring, recording, increasing fame and of motherhood. Dorit became sought after for singing engagements in Monte Carlo and Nice as well as throughout her adopted home country of Germany. Eventually, she was betrayed by those closest to her and lost almost everything. She kept possession only of her daughter. And then they found Frank.

When Dorit asked me to help with her book, I expressed some concerns. I was aware that the early drafts had been dictated and that Dorit's first language was not English; I feared the task would be all consuming. However, after agreeing to read the first three chapters there was no going back: I was captivated. It was immediately clear that her skill as a narrator would do justice to her remarkable story. Dorit's fluency in several European languages helps to create a writing voice and style which brings to life the nomadic existence of her early years.

This book traces the author's experiences of deepest hatred and unexpected compassion; her encounters with new languages, cultures and customs. It charts her journey from Holocaust survivor to educated young woman and highly talented singer, performing throughout Europe and making successful records with celebrated musicians. Most of us know of people who have survived difficult times only to come through stronger. But the mountainous scale of Dorit Oliver-Wolff's lows and highs leaves one in awe.

Michael J Fleming

THE CONCERT

I could hear the compère announcing my name. The orchestra struck up my signature tune and even before I appeared on the stage, there was a standing ovation. All sorts of feelings flashed through my mind. Was I not that little Jewish girl who used to break out into a cold sweat and hide at the sight of a German soldier in uniform?

This concert in Bremerhaven was, for me, the most emotional and strange show business experience. The annual Dinner Dance was a spectacular event for the German air force. The organisers had insisted I should sing at this gala evening. It was a very special occasion. The ladies were in beautiful ball gowns and the gentlemen had on their best greyish blue uniforms. Many were wearing their medals. Some had so many they almost covered the left side of their jackets.

The seats were all taken, with the higher-ranking officers being seated in the first and second rows. The auditorium was decorated with the most amazing flower arrangements. When I arrived, I had walked the red carpet leading from the pavement where the chauffeur-driven limousines would stop at the entrance. I had never seen so much pomp and glitter before.

It was not surprising that the sight of so many German uniforms brought up a strange feeling inside of me, especially when the house lights were switched off and only the spotlight and footlights came on. I suddenly felt panic. Why had they insisted I should be the one who should entertain them? Why me?

Although I had hesitated I could not refuse this engagement. This would not have been professional. The fact that these were men in German uniforms spooked me. The memories just overwhelmed me. Here I was, standing on stage and the men in uniform were applauding me. I felt a lump in my throat. For a moment I could not move. I did not think I could sing. My smile must have looked like a mask. Suddenly my mood changed. I had this immense feeling of triumph.

My performance was very emotional. I knew it was good. I sang my little Jewish heart out. I was overwhelmed by the thought, yes, I have made it! I am alive. I have not perished in a gas chamber. Who would ever have imagined, out of all the other singers in Germany, it was I who had been requested to sing here tonight?

I did not finish with my usual song, but I chose 'Havanagilla', a Hebrew song. They all stood up and clapped in rhythm with the song. I cannot find words to describe my feelings that night. But I felt that I had made it, I had reached my dream. This was what it was all about. The irony! Many members of my family had been killed during the Holocaust and yet here I was a survivor, standing on the stage before the very people, whose parents, grandparents or uncles could have been responsible. That I could be here, alive, famous and successful and applauded; this satisfying, triumphant feeling will stay with me forever!

But I could never forget the dark days of my childhood. Time spent being hunted like an animal. That is the other side of my story.

AGAINST ALL ODDS

It was not until my mother and I went for a stroll in the park in Budapest on a beautiful sunny day when a big, fat, blonde woman approached us, spat at me and shouted *'büdös zsidó'* (stinking Jew) that I realised that I was Jewish. This was my instant introduction into Judaism. I was only six years old. Now that I am 79 I can write about my memories. Not that I want to remember. I simply cannot forget.

WAR – The bombing of Belgrade 1941
A horrendous noise woke us. The walls were shaking and the smell of smoke seeped through the windowpane. The room was filled with smoke. We could hardly see. My eyes were burning and itching. Tears were rolling down my cheeks. My mother and I, we both jumped out of the bed trying to look out of the window to find out what this noise was all about. Fire and black smoke were blinding us and the thuds and the horrible growling noises were deafening. We knew instinctively we had to get out.

We ran down the corridor, down the steps only to find other people trying to escape the burning house. We were all heading towards the front door of the building. People were shoving, screaming and shouting, calling out the names of their children, mothers or relatives to see if they managed to escape. A bomb must have hit the adjoining building as part of our block had big gaps in the wall. I could see the black sky through the hole. There was a lot of grey dust falling on us, like ash. Surprisingly no one got injured on the stairs. It was utter chaos. No one knew what was happening. The front door of the building was jammed, as everyone was attacking it trying to get out.

Eventually, somebody managed to open the front door and we were on the street which was full of people in their nighties or pyjamas with horrible grimaces on their faces. One could see the panic and fear. As we looked up we could see black smoke amongst the red flames that looked like furious red tongues licking anything in their reach, burning and destroying everything with fury, without mercy. Parts of bodies were hanging from the tram line wires which ran parallel above the houses as if they were washing on the clothes line: legs, arms, all still with the blood dripping down from them. This must have been the result of the bombs hitting the houses. People whose bodies were torn apart from the explosions had landed on the tram wires. Blood was dripping from the body parts onto the rubble on the ground. People trod in the puddles. Many people who walked underneath those limbs were unaware what was hanging from the tram wire above them; they too were drenched with dripping blood. We did not have time to stop as the people were simply pushing along in one direction all trying to get out of the burning town.

It really turned the stomach. You just wanted to be sick, unimaginably horrendous. A real horror film, except that it was reality.

But you couldn't stop even if you wanted to, or look back. There was only one way and that was in the direction that everybody else was heading. You had to be careful not to fall because you would never get up. People would just trample you to death. I could not see all that much because everybody was much taller than me. Everybody was panic stricken and running for their lives.

Such chaos.

I could see people's feet. Some had shoes or boots on but many had nothing but bare feet; Mum and I had slippers on. It was very difficult to run and not lose the slippers.

My mother had grabbed me by my hand and told me not to let go whatever happened. People were trying to get back into the houses, trying to break the doors, trying to get inside to rescue other people who were trapped inside the burning buildings.

Every few minutes an aeroplane dived onto the crowd and mowed the running people down with machine-gun fire. Every time the aeroplanes dived the people threw themselves onto the ground covering their heads with their arms and hands to protect themselves. Usually, the parents threw themselves over their children shielding them from the bullets with their own bodies.

I was petrified I was going to lose my mother or become separated from her or be trampled on. Mother kept on saying, 'Don't let go of my hand. Try not to fall down. Don't look back and keep close to me.' The running people were so close together that their bodies formed a solid moving wall.

In the middle of this chaos there was a horse making a terrible noise kicking in all directions, stamping on people and turning round and round. Its mane and tail were on fire and blood was coming out of its eyes and nostrils. That horse was standing on his hind legs, whilst thrashing uncontrollably in all directions with its front legs. Such a terrible noise, which I have never heard before or since. Some people tried to get hold of the horse but it was impossible. It was big, strong, in terrible agony and blind.

The Stukas dived down again from the skies and the horse was the victim of their bullets, at least saving some people from being trampled to death. Everybody dived onto the pavement. People threw themselves on top of me and I could not move my arms or legs. I could not get up, I could hardly breathe. Someone was lying on top of me. A warm and wet sticky substance with a funny sweet smell was dripping all over me. I could not shout or maybe I did but I could not hear my own voice. The body was so heavy and once the bombs stopped the body on top of me did not move. I was too little and too weak to be able to free myself from the dead heavy weight. Whose hand was I holding onto? Some people must have realised what happened. The weight was lifted. I was on my feet again.

There was no time to stop and inspect whether I was injured. As I was not crying or limping and continued to run with my mother, she took it for granted that I must have been unharmed. I was covered in red thick sticky blood but no one took any notice. My mother wiped some of the blood off and we continued moving.

By this time we were very tired, very hungry and very frightened. There was nowhere we could stop and rest. We did not have any food or drink. It was unsafe to take shelter, the bombed houses were collapsing. By now it was dark and there were no more houses around. We had left the city of Belgrade. We reached the woods where we were welcomed by the partisans.

They gave us food and drink. These woods were on high ground and we could see fire, red fire. The sky was burning, this was Belgrade in flames. It was really quite beautiful. I liked the look of it. As a five-year-old little girl how could I realise the monstrous atrocity and horror of this situation? How could I have known at that moment our whole life had changed and we had nothing, no home, no security, no money, no friends and no possessions except the nighties that we were wearing? Luckily we had each other.

By now people had formed into little groups. Some people took charge of others. People were looking for each other's relatives and friends asking strangers whether they had seen such and such. Hoping their loved ones had escaped.

I was so tired; all I wanted was to sleep. We were given blankets and hot soup with a slice of bread. We were told to stay in groups and not move from the spot which we were allocated.

I was so cold. I was shivering. I could hear my teeth chatter. I was so very frightened. I have never known or seen anything like I experienced that day.

April in Yugoslavia was still very cold. I was given a blanket where they cut out a space for my head and arms; a thick leather belt which was placed around my waist went around me three times. New holes had to be punched into the belt so that the buckle could hold it. Needless to say it was much too long for me. My mother found some scissors somehow and cut this blanket so that it could fit me. She and most of the others had the same outfit. She was shivering too. The blanket smelled quite horrible but we stopped shivering and this was nice, smell or no smell.

* * *　　* * *　　* * *

Just four months previously I had been dancing and singing at the Yugoslav court in front of the young King Peter of Yugoslavia. This was at the Gala Concert in aid of orphans which my Mother organised for the Red Cross. The Royal family was hosting it. This was a fantastic party, lots of food, hot chocolate with whipped cream, lots of cakes, colourful balloons and clowns. There were long, long tables set with white tablecloths where the children were sitting and enjoying this lavish party. The Royal family and members of the Court were acting as waiters and waitresses.

I wore a white satin dress, the skirt was trimmed with white marabou feathers, and so was the neckline. I wore a little glittering tiara on my head. I danced a Russian *kazacok* and sang accompanied by a 15-piece band. I was a little show-off. Everyone made such a big fuss of me. At the end of my performance even the young King gave me a kiss on my cheek. I was a little star, having so much fun. My whole family and friends were proud of me and I enjoyed every minute of it. I was such a happy little girl. And now, four months later, everything had changed. Never before had I known what fear was.

* * *   * * *   * * *

The woods were full of trenches and this is where we had to stay, where the partisans had established their headquarters.

My mother cuddled me in her arms and everybody was asleep. I could not sleep as there had been too much excitement. In the distance I saw pretty little lights not too far from where we were. These lights were going on and off. It was fascinating to watch. I woke my mother up to show her. She did not think it was so funny and asked me to stay and not to move or make any noise no matter what: she would come back for me. Mother crawled away like a snake on her tummy. She was very clever. How could she move without making any noise? I was very impressed. There were some more lights going on and off at different times but these lights were so near they were almost next to our hide-out. I could almost touch them. Then some lights shimmered far away. They were going on and off as though as if they were talking to each other. I was all alone in the dark. I knew I must not cry and must not be heard. I must not be discovered. Mother would come back for me. It was not so difficult not to be afraid because I do not really think I knew what it felt like to be afraid. I had nothing to compare this feeling with. How could I foresee that the next four years would be fear and more fear?

It is amazing how much one can see in the pitch dark as your eyes become accustomed to it. By now I was used to the quiet and I could hear any faint movement. My mother was suddenly holding me very close to her and a few men in uniform continued to crawl towards the place where the pretty lights came from. The little group which we were a part of were instructed to crawl, without making any noise, to another place allocated to us. Mother stroked my hair and kissed my eyes, put her arms around me. The bombings, the horrors and the tears of the last few days disappeared for a little while.

As we were moving towards the new place we saw an underground passage which looked like a bunker. There was a candle burning inside. We caught a glimpse of three soldiers and a pretty young woman in the middle of the group. Her hands were tied. She was holding a torch. I heard the soldiers talking very angrily to her but it did not make much sense to me. She spat into the face of one of the soldiers. In turn he slapped her face. They took the young woman away. She tried to wriggle out to no avail – they were bigger and stronger than her. After a short while there was a short sound of a bang. At that time I did not know what the bang was. I know now that this was her being shot.

Later the soldiers came and were very nice to me. They hugged and kissed me on both cheeks and shook me by my hand and told me I was a good little partisan, a little hero. I had saved many lives by noticing the lights. They were signals from a spy. The pretty girl turned out to be a traitor. She was signalling to the enemy to tell them where we were and how many people were hiding. If I hadn't alerted them we would all be dead by now. I felt very important and proud. The soldiers also rewarded me and my mother by moving us from our hiding place under the trees into a barn where there were many more soldiers and it was much warmer. They gave us more food. I was the only child amongst all these men.

From that day on I became the little mascot of the partisans. I was spoiled and given bits and pieces of food whenever they could find some. They treated me with respect and as an equal. The woods were full of families with children hiding from the bombs and the Germans.

* *　　* * *　　* * *

Somehow we became reunited with my auntie Hedi, Zorica her two-month-old baby, and my grandmother. They must have also escaped from Belgrade taking a different route to get to these woods. It was a miracle that we all found each other and were reunited. A true miracle. We were all crying and hugging each other. Our happiness was indescribable. The only person who was not short of food was Zorica, my little baby cousin. Her food was ready on demand. As food was very short my aunt would sometimes press out some of her breast milk into a little beaker and I had to drink it. They said it was good for me and it would save my life. It tasted horrible and it also smelled terrible. But as my cousin Zorica was drinking it and liked it – it must have been good enough for her, so it must have been good enough for me.

Hedi was the wife of my mother's brother Nicola, called Miki. He was separated from us and had joined the partisans. Unfortunately he was caught and captured. He was deported to Budapest to a depot – some kind of a sorting place where the Jews were divided and transported to various concentration camps depending on their usefulness. This is where he was united with my father before they were separated again and sent to different concentration camps.

Oma, my grandmother, was very, very frightened and forever praying, her hands clasped and her fingers entwined together rolling her eyes to the sky towards Almighty God. She had lengthy conversations with this God who must have been up in the sky. 'Why oh why have you forsaken us? Please Almighty God have mercy on us. On my little family; save my little family.' Sometimes I could hear her clearly and loudly, but sometimes I could only see her lips moving and hear a mumbling sound often made with her eyes shut; the same words with a few variations. My grandma assured me that her God always hears her prayers and He acts in the most mysterious way and I must trust in God and that all prayers are heard and answered. I never heard any answer.

Our aim was to get to Budapest, as the Germans had not occupied Hungary yet where my mother and grandmother were both born and thus spoke fluent Hungarian. We thought we should be safe there. My aunt Hedi came from Vienna. She fled to Yugoslavia because the anti-Semitism and the persecution of Jews had started in Austria.

* * *   * * *   * * *

Arriving in Budapest my mother found a small apartment on the city outskirts, which consisted of one room, a bathroom and a kitchenette which only had two electric hobs. There were three adults and two children and we were so happy to have found a roof over our heads. We had no money, no possessions, just each other. The three beds were shared. Huddling together was warmer and we felt safer. Food was very scarce and as we did not have any proof of residency we did not get food coupons. I was not allowed to go out or play with any other children, as it was too risky. People asked questions and everybody was suspicious of everybody else.

If the police or one of the members of the Nazi party were to discover us and know we were Jewish we would be taken into a concentration camp or into one of those houses where the Jews were forced to live. On the doors of these houses was a big yellow star showing everyone that there were only Jews living there. It was a JEW HOUSE. Soldiers were at liberty to come and pick up anyone and deport them to a concentration camp or simply throw them into the Danube. The Jews were not allowed to shop in non-Jewish shops. The newspapers were all full of anti-Semitic propaganda with ugly caricatures of Jews grabbing money. Now it was punishable to employ them, even befriend them.

Jews were the enemy who were responsible for the war. Anyone who helped or harboured a Jew would be taken to a concentration camp. The Danube was said to have turned red from all the bodies of the Jewish people who were shot point blank and thrown into the river. Many Hungarians witnessed this but dared not do anything about it.

We mostly slept in our clothes. We only took our shoes off when we were in bed. We had to be ready to run into the air-raid shelter, fast. One time the sirens were sounded when the Russian bombers were already above us. No time to waste on getting dressed. We often ran with our shoes in our hands to the air-raid shelter.

We all had our usual places in the cellar; everyone respected each other's places. Somehow there was an order in the midst of this chaos. As we lived in a side road, strangers never came to our shelter, not like in the centre of Budapest where anyone caught in the air raid could get shelter wherever they happened to be at the time. We had only our regular people who lived in this block of 12 flats.

I can remember one old fat lady who had asthma and a weak

heart. She was coughing nonstop, holding her white handkerchief which she pressed against her mouth every time she had a coughing attack. She was very nice and I really liked her. She would always smile at me and talk to me. Sometimes she would bring an apple with her and give it to me. We had to stay in the air raid shelter often for a very long time until we heard the all-clear sound.

As there was no radio or any kind of entertainment I suddenly took it upon myself to start singing and entertain everybody. Surprisingly, nobody asked me to keep quiet. On the contrary, they encouraged me by applauding. They even placed a little wooden box in the middle, for me to stand on. I had requests and people started bringing me little bits of goodies like a piece of sugar, a biscuit. This was my pay.

They called me the little angel of the air-raid shelter. I knew I was destined to sing. When I was singing the fear disappeared. I was not even very hungry. I realised I made people happy. Some of the people, whom I had never seen smiling, suddenly had a little twinkle in their eyes and a little smile.

And then one by one they came and thanked me, giving me a little hug or a little kiss, sometimes on the top of my head. It was a wonderful feeling to be able to make other people happy. I don't think anybody realised we were Jewish or in hiding or if they did they kept it very quiet.

My mother was the only one who was the bread winner in our family. She had many jobs. When asked from where we came, the answer was: my uncle has been called up into the army and we came up from a small village to be nearer to him. We could not let anybody know, of course, that he had been caught by the SS and deported to a concentration camp.

* * *   * * *   * * *

13

When the Nazis separated my father and uncle they were assembled into a group and asked who had a trade. According to the answer they were separated into two different groups. Electricians, plumbers, builders were in one group and in the other those who were doctors, teachers, engineers and musicians. Miki being an electrician and useful to the Nazis was in one group and my father, who was an architect and a brilliant pianist, was put with the other people like doctors, solicitors, accountants in another group. We never heard or knew what happened to them or to which concentration camp they were transported.

* * *   * * *   * * *

When my grandmother went shopping I would go with her. We would always have to stand in long queues. People started queuing just after midnight for a loaf of bread, to be there early in the morning when the bakery opened. Once you established your place in the queue this was yours. If anyone tried to jump the queue or slowly wriggle through, terrible fights would erupt. Often it would not end with just verbal abuse. More than once it ended up similar to a mob lynching.

Some people from the same family or friends would change or take turns whilst queuing. Nothing but nothing was more important than this queue for bread. When the sirens were screeching, warning the bombers were approaching and everybody should go to the nearest shelter, only very few people would leave their place in the queue and run for shelter. The majority of us stayed and took the risk of being killed rather than losing our place. Bread was life. Some people humorously commented: 'At least we die with a full stomach.'

Often the only food we had was bread. If we were lucky we

had a little bit of cooking oil and a clove of garlic which would be chopped into tiny pieces and mixed with the oil. We would then dip the bread into the oil. How wonderful this tasted. We ate very small pieces so it lasted longer.

Some days my mother would take me with her into town. It was very cold and the ground was covered with snow. In the distance, on one occasion, I saw some men, maybe fifteen or sixteen of them, dressed in long black coats and black hats.

Some had beards, some were only young, and some were really old, doubled up and very shaky. They were in a group sweeping the snow from the pavement. They all had a big yellow star on the front of their coats. Some also wore a yellow band on their sleeves. They were guarded by two soldiers in grey uniform with bayonets on the rifles hanging from their shoulders. Mother would cross the road to avoid these people. Some people who were passing them would turn and spit at them. But they never tried to defend themselves or to spit back.

Not only did people spit at these men in black but they shouted at them: 'büdös zsidó' (stinking Jew). The soldiers who guarded them only laughed but never stopped the attackers.

By this time I did know that I too was a stinking Jew; however, I did not know what a Jew was supposed to look like. In Yugoslavia only the very religious Jews were known as Jewish. The rest of the people like my family who were not religious, were never made to feel anything other than a local person. Religion was never an issue.

As we were approaching the group of men in black my Mother hissed through her teeth: 'Don't look, don't turn, and don't ask any questions', gripping my hands even stronger. She walked on as if nothing unusual had happened. I could not believe when I heard myself asking her: 'Anyuci (mommy) could we go over to the other side of the road and spit at those people, too? My mother squeezed my hand so hard, as if she wanted to break it. 'No, darling. It is not polite to spit.' And she quickened her steps and I was very disappointed. How come everybody else was allowed to spit but not me?

Remembering this incident much later in life I felt mortified by this urge and deeply ashamed. But then again how could I understand what was happening? How unforgivable and undignified it must have been for those poor people to be spat at for no fault of their own – who happened to be born Jewish?

The newspapers were full of warnings saying every Jew must wear a yellow Star of David. If caught without it, this was punishable by death. Huge posters were everywhere, all with the same threat. When we got back home my mother, Hedi and Oma had a very serious conversation. I overheard my mother saying; 'Under no circumstances is any of us going to sew a yellow star on our cloths. I cannot understand' – my Mother said – 'why these Jews are so stupid and make it so easy for those bastards. They are so timid and frightened. No, we are not joining this mass suicide. We must keep a low profile and not let anyone know that we are Jewish.' Although it was a law punishable by death if you did not wear the yellow star – it was sure suicide if you did wear one. We did not move into the Jewish quarters, which were the ghettos.

We just mingled, hid, kept a low profile and hoped nobody would notice us; always a step ahead of the Hungarian police who were called the Nyilas – the Arrows. The Hungarian 'Arrows' killed more Jews in Hungary than the Germans did.

Our little family unit was multilingual. We all spoke German. Auntie Hedi had an Austrian accent as she came from Vienna. My mother and grandmother were both Hungarian. I spoke Hungarian, German and Serbo-Croatian, as in Novi Sad where I was born people were brought up speaking three languages, because at various times Novi Sad was occupied by Austria or Hungary.

Later in life I often wondered why my mother and grandmother ever left Hungary. I suppose my mother met my father, got married and the rest is history. From the stories I can remember my father was a tall, handsome, talented, spoiled young man from a very wealthy intellectual family. Unfortunately, he did not live with us. Come to think of it, I only remember seeing my mother at the weekends. She was working in Belgrade, teaching dance in the Yugoslav palace. During the week I lived with my grandma, Miki and Hedi. The night when the war broke out in Yugoslavia it was my weekend to spend with my mother. That is how we were together that night. God knows how our lives would have turned out if it had happened during the week when I was with my grandma.

I never had a chance to get to know my father because he was killed at the age of 28 or 29. My family often commented how very similar I was to my dad in my mannerisms, my phraseology, and the love and talent for music. I would have so much loved to have a father. For years every time there was a picture in the magazines or newspapers writing about the Holocaust survivors, I searched and hoped to find him. I could never find out anything about him or learn about his life because all those who could have given me this information have been killed.

From such a big family, I am the only survivor.

THE JUMP

One day without any warning we packed our very few belongings and moved from this little haven of ours. We just knew we had to go – a gut feeling? Probably a neighbour or a friend had hinted about our existence. We did not all leave together. Mother and I left first, and then Grandma, Hedi and Zorica followed.

The place where we moved to was on the fifth floor and we had to share it with another family. This was a 'safe house' protected by the Swiss Flag. There was an old couple with their son and daughter-in-law, and her mother. So, there were the five of them. The old gentleman, who hardly ever moved, but coughed and coughed day and night, had a very pale skin and deep lines on his cheeks and very thin grey hair. There must have been something very wrong with him. Sometimes he would spit into his handkerchief, but other times he just swallowed. I was very frightened of him. His fingers were long and thin like matchsticks. His eyes just stared at one spot. His breathing made a whistling noise. He never spoke to me or to anyone else. One day he just stopped coughing, all of his family cried, but most of all his wife. She said it was a blessing because at least he went peacefully. He would have never survived a camp.

We shared the kitchen, bathroom and the toilet. Grandmother, mother, Zorica and I shared one room. Hedi was in a tiny little room scarcely big enough for a single bed.

She was very ill. She had dysentery. This was highly contagious. We could not send her to any hospital so we put her in that little room in quarantine and only my mother would go in and out to look after her, feed and wash her. Besides, even if we were to call a doctor, they would not come to visit Jews. We could not chance reporting Hedi's condition as for sure they would remove and dispose of her.

The families kept very much to themselves. We just tolerated one another. We did not complain about the old man constantly coughing and they did not report Hedi to the authorities, so we were quits.

From the bedroom, although it was very high up, one could see the very busy high street with trams, buses, taxis and horse drawn carriages. I spent a lot of time looking out of this window, which kept me and my imagination busy. I was allowed to do this freely because it was so high up that nobody could detect me. The big building opposite was a Jew House with a big yellow star on the door. The house we were in had none of this, only the Swiss flag. When the sirens sounded to warn us that the bombers were approaching we hardly ever bothered to go down to the cellar as we knew to go amongst strangers was more dangerous than staying put.

* * * * * * * * *

In Budapest it was a daily routine to hear the ear-piercing sounds of the whistles, short long short, and one day from nowhere men in grey uniforms appeared. Some had Alsatian dogs on a leash with them. They formed a big circle, first they were about three metres apart but systematically the circle got smaller and smaller. People who were trapped within the grey uniforms had to produce identity papers. If the soldiers were satisfied with their documents then those people were allowed out of the circle. Those without papers were taken away. Usually they were pushed into a van which was waiting nearby. This time it was different. Those men who had no papers were escorted by two soldiers who pointed guns at the frightened creatures. They were led into a doorway and from where I stood, fortunately outside of the circle, all I could see was how the men had to undo the front of their trousers and for some reason unknown to me some of them got shot on the spot in the doorway.

Some people were protesting, some people were released and it was not until much, much later that I learned why they singled out certain men and not others. This incident will haunt me as long as I live. When I was much older and learned that the Jewish boys were circumcised, only then did I realise how inhuman and brutal was this behaviour carried out by the Nazi bastards.

I was too young to understand why it was necessary for people to deliberately make their sons distinguishable from other men so that they can be recognised as Jews. At this time I was glad I was a girl.

I learned later that this procedure was a part of the Jewish religion. This was the wish of God. But can God justify saying this to his so-called chosen people? If I had a choice I would rather not be circumcised and live than be circumcised and die. Once I found out the reason why these people were shot on the spot I made up my mind that if I ever had a son I would never have him circumcised.

After this unforgettable horror everybody dispersed as if nothing had happened. Except the people who were shot were thrown into wheelbarrows and pushed to the vans that were waiting on the side of the road. Then they disposed of them into the parked vans. On the way home I remember that we did not talk much. When I tried to ask questions, my mother would say: 'Not now, I will explain when we get home.'

My grandmother, whom I loved so very much, was still praying and praising the Almighty God and thanking Him. Why did He not stop these Nazis from killing all those people and letting us starve? If He had such power, why did He not stop all this? Why did He allow those soldiers to kill those poor men just because they saw in those men's trousers something they did not like? And why did not my grandmother stop praying? What was she thanking Him for? On Friday nights when it started to get a bit darker, she would light a candle, if she had one. If not she would pierce a match box and place two matches into the holes and light the matches. She would put a shawl onto her head and she would clasp her hands together and close her eyes. She looked so very special and severe.

She mumbled words which I did not understand and then just before this ritual was over, she would unfold her hands as if she was collecting the smoke and the light from the flames of that little flickering candle. She would then put her hands on my head and say, 'Be blessed my child – just like your ancestors Rachel, Rebecca and Leah'. Then she kissed me on my head. She then proceeded to give the same blessing to my cousin Zorica. And then we would have something to eat if we were lucky. Eating was one of the most important parts of our day.

If we were not queuing up for bread, then we were queuing for vegetables. At meal times we only had black tea – which was not really black but pale yellow due to the very little amount of tea mixed with hot water and a bit of sugar – followed by a slice of bread.

Toast was a special delicacy and making it was a performance of itself. We had a wrought iron stove with one ring. The slice of bread was simply held with the fork or the tip of a knife. The bread was held over the ring. This was a very skilled job. If the flames were too high the bread would burn and the person who was holding the fork would also burn their fingers. We were rationed. Therefore we could not take the chance to burn it. The toasted bread was then flavoured with a clove of garlic. If we were extremely lucky, a few drops of oil would be dribbled onto the toast. This was a tasty meal!

My grandmother was very inventive. For somebody who had never cooked in her life, as before the war she had a cook, it was quite remarkable what she could produce from potato skins, beans, onions and paprika. I remember when Grandma once got hold of a piece of smoked rind. This she put into boiling water for a maximum of five minutes. This made the hot water with potato skins a very tasty hot soup.

She must have used this piece of rind for weeks. This rind was no bigger than 8 cm by 5 cm. We never had set meal times. We ate when we had something to eat and everything was shared. We were always on the move. Often just as we sat down for a well-deserved meal, sirens would sound and we would have to run down to an air-raid shelter. This would happen three or four times a day but mostly at night.

There were some funny situations as well. Once Mother got hold of potatoes, not just the potato skins as usual, which we always retrieved from the dustbins behind big hotels. Mother also brought home some sausages. Grandmother cooked the most magnificent thick potato and bean soup with sausages. The smell was wonderful. Just as we were sitting down to eat came the usual routine sirens. Prepared to leave everything, we rushed to the door, down four flights of stairs, down to the shelter.

But this time a woman stood in the door and did not want to let us into the shelter. She said we were contaminating the air. She did not want to breathe the same air with us, filthy stinking Jews. We went back. We had actually been quite

22

reluctant to leave this wonderful feast in the first place. The soup was still in the plates untouched, quite warm.

To our great surprise Grandmother had not rushed down with us. She had grabbed her plate of soup and dived under the bed to eat it. She swore that even if the bombs were coming through the roof she would not leave her soup. She would rather die with a full stomach. Who knows when we would have another chance to have such a wonderful meal?

As a consequence of the terrible encounter with this bitch of a woman (may she rot in hell) we never went to the shelter again. It was a big block of flats. We never saw this woman again. Who knows, my prayers might have been answered?

* * *　* * *　* * *

The block of flats was built around a square courtyard which had mustard-coloured mosaic tiles and a fountain in the centre. As you came up the stairs there was a high concrete wall and a balustrade. There was a stone railing which was as high as my chin. As usual I went to my favourite place at the window. A big open truck stopped opposite the house with the star. About ten soldiers in uniform jumped out of the truck, with bayonets fixed on their rifles, rushed into the house and a short while later lots of people were rushing out through the doorway; some had suitcases, and some had nothing.

The soldiers were shouting and pushing them on to the lorry with the sides of their bayonets. A little old lady with white hair and a black scarf on her head, with two walking sticks, walked very slowly and could not get onto the truck. So, one of the soldiers kicked her as she was trying to climb up, she fell down to the pavement. A man and a woman wanted to get out of the truck to help her but were hit with the butt of a rifle and fell

23

back into the lorry. Two of those soldiers picked up the little old lady and threw her into the lorry, like a sack of potatoes.

I was an incredibly inquisitive child. I ran out of the flat although I knew I was not allowed out. I wanted to have a closer look at what was happening across the road. Like a shot I was running down the steps. Then I heard a tremendous noise coming up towards me. A beautiful young girl, she must have been ten years older than me, with the most fabulous curly, dark hair down her shoulders, was running, completely breathless, taking two steps at a time, trying to reach the top. When she saw me, hardly being able to talk, she asked me where I lived. I pointed out to her: 'There!' She asked me to hurry and get her a glass of water. 'Hurry, hurry,' she said she had to take her pill. It was a question of life and death and she needed water. She was in a real panic. She had time to stroke my hair and to push me hurriedly towards the door. She had tears running down her cheeks. She was so beautiful. She practically pushed me inside through the front door. Then out of the corner of my eyes I saw her climb onto the central rail at the top of the stairs and jump off. All I could hear was a dull thud, no screaming, just a thud.

She just wanted to get me out of her way, to save me witnessing this brave act.

By this time, two soldiers who were pursuing her had almost caught up with the girl but as they reached out the girl jumped. They tried to stop her but luckily they were too late. She must have escaped from the lorry opposite.

Rather than be taken to the concentration camp or even worse, taken to a whore house where girls as young as twelve have been known to be taken, where they were used for sex by the soldiers, she jumped to her death. Innocent little Jewish girls were raped regularly by these heartless brutal men. It makes you wonder how many of them have daughters at home the same age as these poor innocent little girls who they used as sex objects.

The two soldiers were also out of breath. They just looked over the balustrade. They must have seen her falling. The two soldiers just shrugged their shoulders – 'oh shit' was their comment. They turned around and left down the steps, not a glimpse of remorse or a sigh, nothing.

They did not notice me. When I heard the footsteps coming up the stairs, I hid behind the door. When they were gone I went back and looked over the railing. She just laid there on the mustard-coloured mosaic floor, like a rag doll, her limbs all distorted and twisted. Her legs spreading in different directions, one arm over her shoulder, the other next to her side. Her face to one side, her beautiful long black hair was covering part of her face which lay in a deep red pool of blood. Still, so motionless, she never screamed, not a sound. I just stood there gazing at the girl, who only a few minutes ago was alive and talking to me. How can anyone comprehend what courage, what strength at such an early age this girl displayed? What was going on in her mind? What was she thinking of that last moment when she jumped? I could not stop crying. I felt as if my heart was squeezed by an iron hand. I cannot recall any time before having cried so much. This was physically painful.

Soon after the girl landed on the ground many people gathered around her. Some were horrified. Others looked at the dead body as if nothing had happened. Some people must have seen the lorry opposite. Some could have even watched the girl being chased by the two soldiers. Who knows?

After a lot of toing and froing, it was established that the girl did not live in this block of flats. No one seems to have missed her or claimed her crumpled little body. By nightfall the body was gone. The soldiers took it. There was a slight depression on

25

the mosaic floor. Almost all of the blood was cleaned up. Only a smidgen, a very faded pinkish colour, was the giveaway that there had been a large pool of blood there only the day before.

That night I could not sleep. I had recurring dreams about this girl for many years. Eventually, other horrible dreams took over from the old ones. But in time many of those dreams crept back into my mind. For a while they stayed hidden, dormant in the folds of my memory. I almost think they are gone, but they never ever go away. They never leave me completely. They just have a little rest for a while. It is not that I want to remember, it is just that I cannot forget.

MOTHER

Mother was in charge of our family. There were three adults and two little girls. She was the only bread winner and all this at the age of twenty seven. Zita Magda was her name. Magda or Magdus – or even Magduska. She was clever, very brave, and inventive and above all she could think and act spontaneously. Magda was petit and slim. She had even, pearl white teeth; big, pale brown eyes with a green tinge; well-shaped eyebrows and wavy long dark brown hair. Her feet were tiny, 3.5 shoe size. Her hands were so small and beautifully kept. She had the habit of raising one of her eyebrows when she disapproved of something. This habit stayed with her to the end of her life.

During the war, my little mother was a real hero. She had many jobs. With each job she created new names for us; new identities. She chose jobs where I could go with her. One of her jobs was outside Budapest in a small village, in a boy's boarding school. The matron was a very large and fat woman. Her nickname was 'Madárka' – which meant 'Birdie' in English. She told everyone she had never had a proper meal, only nibbled like a little bird. How come she was so obese? Nobody believed her but laughed and giggled when she referred to herself as a little birdie.

The school was set in the most beautiful wooded grounds, flowering shrubs, flowers, three houses. One of the houses was called 'Bagolyvár', in English 'owl castle'. The boys had their own song. I still remember some of the lyrics:

'Bagolyvári legények hullárihaj
Aki velünk szembeszáll
Öklünk orrába talál hullárihaj' etc.

27

Our castles young men hulary hoy
They who challenge us
Our fists would find their noses hulary hoy etc.

There were several variations of the song, but this is all I can remember. After seventy-eight years, I am quite surprised that, out of the blue, these words came to me.

Mother was teaching gymnastics and music. She was very popular and well-liked by the boys. We lived in the staff quarters. I was allowed to roam freely, to play and had regular meals. It is here where I learned how to read and write Hungarian. I was a fast learner. I had an inquisitive mind. I picked up very easily anything that was taught to me. I was like a thirsty blotting paper that soaked up knowledge.

Many of my mother's jobs ended very abruptly. Even in this time before Germans occupied Hungary, the anti-Semitism was very strong. The Hungarians treated the Jews worse than the Germans. They wanted to gather brownie points from the Germans. They must have been competing with each other, to see who could get rid of the most Jews the quickest.

On one occasion, probably my mother felt it was time to disappear again as we had had to so many times before. It was always without warning. I cannot remember the name of the place where we went next. We lived in a very pretty village in a ground floor flat. A gravel footpath led to the front door of the little white-washed cottage. It had black wooden shutters with little hearts carved into them. There were lots of flowers, mainly roses. We had a large bedroom, large kitchen. It even had a table and two chairs and our own bathroom. I clearly remember colouring on this table. I would draw dolls on thick cardboard, painting faces, and then on a much thinner paper I would paint dresses which I could fasten to the dolls.

These dresses would have little tags on the shoulders and on the waist. When it was cut out, great care had to be taken not to cut the tags off, because without them the outfits would not stay on the doll. Colouring these creations was the best part. Red, green, blue. I only had a few colours. Sometimes stripes would be added or maybe spots, even flowers could be dotted here and there. I could even produce furniture such as beds and a table, and all these from cardboard. All I needed was a pair of scissors, pencil, colouring crayons. The scope was endless.

By now I could read and I loved to read. My mother worked as a dancing teacher and also gave private lessons on dancing. Again I was not allowed to go outside to play. One day though I saw a little girl outside the house playing. She had two dolls, real dolls, not made out of paper, and a real dolls' pram. I had never seen such beautiful creatures ever before in my life. This girl must have been a little bit older than me.

I must have been staring from behind the curtains. She noticed me and after a while she came to the window. Each of us standing, parted by the window and the curtain. We looked at each other. We smiled at each other. She picked up one doll like a puppeteer, then the other and performed a little show with the two dolls. It was very funny. She looked at me, awaiting my approval. I applauded and was very impressed.

I opened the window and we started talking. I had to be careful to remember what my name was at this time in this place. I had to remember where we came from, what my mummy's job was. I had to memorise this exactly so if caught and questioned we would both tell the same story. Mother explained to me that we had to play different games at different times. No one must find out that this was a game. We had to be perfect like real actors. We would rehearse for hours until we got our story just right! It was fun: how boring it would have been to have the same name all the time, to have lived in the same place. But once we decided on who we were, what our names were, we were not permitted to change or vary anything; until such time as we went to another place and my mum and I would choose a new game. These were the strict rules. So when I opened the window and talked to the little girl I was well prepared with my new identity.

I was mesmerised by those beautiful dolls. Not having one of my own, except the cardboard ones I had created, to see and be able to touch such beautiful things and the real doll's pram was something I always dreamt of. The girl was very pretty too, with white blond ringlets and a big pink bow on the side of her head. She was very friendly and wanted to play and share the dolls with me.

I told her I was not well and that my mum had told me to stay indoors so that I could get better soon. This little girl was very persuasive. It made sense when she told me that we would play with the dolls just inside the door and that when we had a glimpse of my mother coming I could quickly run inside, shut the door, and she would never find out.

Playing with the dolls and my newfound best friend I really enjoyed myself. Never before had I had a girlfriend that I could play with. Most of the time I was alone or in the company of grown-ups. My cousin Zorica was five years younger and not much fun to play with. She did not understand, she was just a baby. I did love her, though. I did help to look after her but she was not someone I could play properly with, not that I knew many games that girls of my age played. I had seen girls of my age playing hopscotch, hide-and-seek and playing with dolls. But I had always been an onlooker. This time I was a co-player, so much better, so different.

I did feel a strange feeling in my tummy when my mother became visible. Turning around the corner of the house I jumped inside, shut the door, sat at the table continuing with my drawing as if nothing happened. I did feel, though, as if my heart was going to jump out through my mouth. My mother gave me a big cuddle, kissed me, more hugs, she was so happy to see me. How peculiar this felt, so different.

Never did I forget the new name, never did I falter about any new changes. This feeling in my tummy got worse and worse, I started to cry. I did not want to keep a secret from her. I never did before. I did not want to disobey her. I was a good girl. I always did as I was told. As for my defence I had such a good time playing with my new best friend, my only ever friend. I wanted this game to last forever. I never wanted to stop. The guilt and the pain were greater than my enjoyment. The guilt of not telling my mother what I had done, how could I not tell her? We never had secrets from each other before.

My mother got very worried when she saw me crying. I hardly ever cried. I had to tell her about the game, about my best friend, the dolls, the pram, how much nicer it was to hold a real doll not just a cardboard one. My mother joined me in crying. I don't remember when or if I had ever seen my mother crying. She was not angry. We hugged each other for a long time and we both cried, probably for different reasons. I was glad to have shared my secret.

Not long after this episode we moved again. My mother had a cousin in Buda, which was on the other side from Pest, which was separated by the blue Danube. Gitta was a lot older than my mum. She lived in a beautiful big house. It was a corner property surrounded with wrought-iron double fencing and high green hedges. This was in the elegant part in a tree-lined district. We stayed there from time to time.

31

She loved my mother and she spoiled her. When we stayed with her we had clean sheets on our beds, Gitta would run a hot bath for my mother and me. We could use her perfumed soap, soft towels and talcum powder. It felt so good. There was a white tablecloth on the table at meal times and proper food to eat. She even had a maid, but not for long. The anti-Semitism became worse, Jewish people were not allowed to employ non-Jews, and the Gentiles were forbidden to work for the Jews. Gitta's maid-cum-housekeeper had worked for her for about thirty-five years. By now she was a member of her family. She nursed Gitta's son when he was born. She had her own accommodation in part of the house, which, incidentally, was far superior to where mother and I had to live. Now the maid had to leave.

Mother's cousin Gitta had a beautiful big garden. She turned the rose beds into a vegetable garden. She also had some tame rabbits, in individual little hutches at the bottom of the garden. Food was very scarce. When we came to stay she would serve rabbit stew. She was always very hospitable and generous. Above all she and my mother adored each other. I have never seen my mum being so warm and affectionate with anybody else but me. I only wished we could stay and live there for ever. Each time we had to say goodbye they hugged each other and stood still as if they wanted to capture this moment for ever. How wonderful it would be if we could stay and live here, but there must have been a very good reason why we only came for short periods.

Mother never mentioned why we never went back. When the German SS came and occupied Hungary – I believe it must have been around 1944 – Gitta and her family were deported to a concentration camp. They confiscated the house with all its contents. Probably a high-ranking German officer moved in. This is what usually happened.

I believe that deep down my mother wanted to be like Gitta. I think she was my mother's role model. Only after the war did my mother talk about Gitta, with such admiration and respect.

* * *   * * *   * * *

Mother was involved with the Red Cross. She was a very active and respected member of the organisation. The Red Cross were responsible for saving hundreds of Jewish children. The children were often separated from their parents and put into houses where they were guarded by soldiers. These children were never seen or heard of again.

During the war my mother's favourite disguise was her white nurse's uniform and a starched scarf that was tied at the back of her neck under her dark hair. In the front, in the middle of the headgear, was a large Red Cross badge. On her lapel was another Red Cross badge.

A white bus with a Swiss flag and emblem on either side was used for rescue operations. Besides the driver there was my mother, 'the nurse in charge', and the man in a white doctor's overall, with the stethoscope around his neck. On his lapel he also had a Red Cross badge. He was carrying a doctor's bag which was filled with bandages, plasters and various boxes.

At the main entrance to a building holding the children there were usually two uniformed men. All vehicles were stopped. My mother would produce a document from the Swiss Consulate and demand that children were immediately released into her custody to be passed to the Swiss authorities. The consulates had diplomatic immunity and the soldiers respected this for a while. The Swiss Consulate fed the children, dressed them and reassured them they were safe. It is hard to imagine what those little children must have felt to be suddenly separated from their parents and put under lock and key by men in uniform without explanation. These children were all under thirteen years old. This was because all children under thirteen were automatically put to death.

* * *   * * *   * * *

The secret underground organisation was very active throughout occupied Europe. They found places for people to stay who were on the run. Mother and I received help from these people, too. They smuggled people out of captivity, from Jew Houses, from wherever there was an opportunity. The nurse's uniform was a perfect cover for my mother. I was often the little stooge who played the role of a 'little girl' patient who has to be taken to the hospital. Sometimes I had a bandage around my head or nose, sometimes on my hands. She never referred to me as 'my daughter' – but 'this little girl'. I must have been a useful cover for mother. She must have been less conspicuous having a young child with her.

Even before the Germans occupied Hungary, the Hungarians were very keen to fulfil to perfection ethnic cleansing without the help of anyone else. It seems so unbelievable; Hungarian people are well known to have produced famous and talented people, painters and musicians like Liszt and Bartok, also famous scientists and poets. Yet this nation has also been capable of genocide. How can this make sense?

* * *   * * *   * * *

My mother met up with an old boyfriend, Béla, her childhood love. They had lost contact. Here they were together again. My mother had left Hungary and moved to Yugoslavia where she married my father. I noticed she smiled a lot more when Béla was around. He was very kind and loving to me too. We used to go to the park together, the three of us. He used to push the swing and held my mother's hand. These were happy times. Béla even treated us to a horse-drawn sledge ride. The snow covered the landscape. We had thick blankets over our knees. I sat in between the two of them. It was freezing cold but we were warm and snug under the blankets. It was so cold that as we breathed a white cloud came out of our noses and out of our mouths. The ride in Buda on Shwáb Hegy was a very happy memory. At times I wondered whether Béla was my dad.

By now I was already very thin and undernourished. Béla sold his gold cigarette case which his parents had given him for his bar mitzvah when he was fourteen years old. This is the Jewish ceremony when a boy becomes a man. He sold this precious possession so I could go to a children's sanatorium and be fed properly for a few weeks. I was seriously undernourished, only skin and bones.

There was this sanatorium in Buda where they specialised in children's ailments. It was known to be a safe and secure place, where I could recover. It had been founded by a Hungarian aristocrat, who was still its patron. It was a building surrounded by lots of trees. We were received by a very friendly man and woman. The place was very light and warm and I could see lots of little girls and boys playing and laughing in a big room. However, I could not bear the thought of being parted from my mother even for a day. Even if it was to save my life.

After we said our goodbyes, we all cried and they said they would come in a week's time and collect me. They assured me that this lady and gentleman would take care of me. I would have a nice warm room, plenty of food, and it would be really good for me. I did not like the sound of any of it. As mother and Béla closed the front door behind them I could feel my heart stop. I wanted to scream. I was panic stricken. I spotted an open window on the ground floor at the end of a long corridor. I ran towards the opening which was a large glass door opening onto a veranda. Without thinking I simply jumped out.

How lucky for me that this was on the ground floor and the ground was covered with deep snow which was at least a metre deep. I did not think about hurting myself. I just ran towards mother and Béla who had not quite reached the front gates. I did not know I could run so fast, especially in such deep snow. I think I was jumping like a rabbit more than running. Panic was driving me. The thought that I might never see my mother again was unbearable.

Despite the freezing conditions, I could feel the palms of my hands sweating. I could hardly breathe. I was shivering and my body felt like all the blood had been frozen. All this was beyond my comprehension. As I was running and hopping towards the big iron gates, the only thing that I could think of was: 'Please God don't let me be too late, don't let me miss her!'

When my mother reached the gates I screamed at the top of my voice. Mother turned back and she saw me. With open arms she ran towards me. I could see her face, she was crying, too. She bent down and wrapped her arms around me; she could not bear being parted from me either. None of us spoke as we walked through the tall iron gates. The man and the woman from the sanatorium ran after us and tried to catch up with us but the waiting *fiaker* (horse-drawn carriage) was waiting for mother and Béla. This was very handy as we jumped into it as fast as we could and drove off. I did not have to go back. Poor Béla and his cigarette case, we never talked about it ever again. I did promise Béla when I grew up I would buy him a gold cigarette case.

* * *   * * *   * * *

Things changed from day to day, even from hour to hour. Nothing was predictable, no one knew what would happen, and maybe it was for the best.

Béla disappeared. There were no goodbyes or tears. My mother was not too upset when Béla did not show up. I am convinced that my mother and he had an understanding and knew exactly the situation. I think he belonged to a secret organisation. But I think she did miss him. He made her smile and we both felt safe when he was around.

Shortly after I ran away from the children's sanatorium my mother told me that the place was raided. Somebody must have informed the police that the sanatorium was harbouring Jewish children and as a result they came and all who were there at the time were deported to concentration camps. I must have had a guardian angel somewhere. If I had stayed there I too would have been taken away.

Many years later, after the war, mother had a letter from him. Béla had changed his surname into a non-Jewish sounding name. He joined the Russian army, which later occupied Hungary after the Germans were defeated. He was promoted to a high-ranking officer. I am sure that my mum and Béla had made a promise to each other that after the war was over they would seek out one another and get married. Some years later my mother confessed to me that they had promised this to each other when they were still in elementary school.

After the war was over they each tried to find one another. There were no records, no possibility to find out who was dead or who was alive. Only hope. Béla was told that mother and I were transported to the gas chambers in Germany and were no more. Thus Béla married and had two boys. It turned out that

37

it was Béla's new wife, a childhood friend of both of them, who gave him this false information. She told him she had seen us being put onto the train which was known to be destined for the gas chambers. She knew that only if my mother was dead would he marry her.

A few years after the war, he and my mother found that their feelings for each other had never changed. They had been childhood sweethearts, soul mates. Béla wanted a divorce but how could he leave two little boys, one aged three and the other five? His wife threatened him if he left her she would take her life. What a hopeless situation. My mother would never agree or encourage him in any way to leave his wife with two little children, although it was an unforgivable dirty trick that she had played on both of them.

Ibolya (Violet), Béla's wife, started drinking heavily, and spent lots of time in sanatoriums, we were later told. What a lot of pain and heartache she caused! How could she live with this on her conscience? This treachery obviously did not bring her the happiness that she expected.

SAFE HAVENS

For a time the Hungarians respected the diplomatic immunity of various foreign consulates. One day we sought refuge in the Yugoslav Consulate in Budapest. The Yugoslavs were very nice and they did help us and many other Jewish people. As the consulate was under diplomatic immunity it was a safe refuge. During the day we were hidden behind piles of furniture in an office which acted as a storeroom for unused desks and chairs. These were very cleverly piled on top of each other, so when you opened the door it was obviously a storeroom, but behind, there was a gap left for people to hide. The number of people varied from day to day; sometimes there were several families. Sometimes there were as many as 20 or 25 people. There was only enough room to squat. Now and then we had to change to a different room so as not to be found. During the night we were allowed to walk in the corridors freely to stretch our legs, but only two or three at a time, not to raise any suspicion. At night the consulate was closed and only the night staff would be on duty. It was very difficult to know who to trust. There were lots of people who felt it was their duty to inform the secret police about any Jews that were hiding.

There was a constant change of faces. Some left in the middle of the night, others arrived. This is where we met Erwin Gruenberg. He too came to seek refuge in the Yugoslav Consulate as he was from Novi Sad like us. He was about thirteen years old. He had been on a train being transported to a concentration camp with many other Jews. Erwin went to the WC, locked the door and somehow managed to unscrew the toilet and escaped through the hole whilst the train was still moving. He told me he just lay there face down, waiting for the train to disappear. Then he walked and somehow found his way to Budapest. What a brave boy he was. He attached himself to mother and me. I was very pleased to have someone to talk to. He stayed with us for quite a while.

One afternoon whilst in the consulate I was desperate to go to the toilet and was allowed out of hiding but was told to act in a way so as not to draw any attention to myself. We had to be invisible. This was easy because as a six-year-old girl nobody took any notice of me. We had been in the consulate for a few weeks so I knew the place quite well. It was a large building. It had thick blue carpets, long corridors, with lots of rooms, and people were coming and going all the time. I remembered most of the employees who worked at the consulate. Some knew of our existence and they were very helpful.

As I was walking towards the toilet at the far end of the long hallway I saw Mr Fischer, the doorman, a tall slim grey-haired man. He always wore a tweed jacket. He had two small wire-haired fox-terrier dogs, which had bright red leather collars. He was standing facing three men who wore long black leather coats, long boots and black hats. Mr Fischer did most of the talking and the three men in black were nodding. I saw how Mr Fischer pointed towards the door out of which I had just come. There were a dozen or more people of different ages hidden in there. I could feel my heart almost jumping out of my throat. 'Don't panic,' I told myself, hoping they had not noticed from which room I had come. 'Don't run,' I kept on telling myself. I knew I had to get back to warn my mother and all the people who were hidden in that room.

The three men walked away, towards the steps. They walked fast. They were almost running. I then walked into the room where the people were hidden and told them what I had just seen.

Immediately the people dispersed, some climbed through the window and shimmied down the pipes. These were the young and fit ones. Some left through the front door. Others stayed but hid in a different room. Mother, Erwin and I walked towards one of the other offices and mingled with the other Yugoslavs, pretending to be visiting. Just as we reached the other side of the corridor, about eight men all dressed in black, rushed towards the room where we had been a few minutes earlier, blowing their whistles. They did arrest a few people who were not quick enough. The three of us stood amongst the rest of the visitors watching how these poor people were marched down the corridor out of the consulate. I saw Mr Fischer standing on top of the stairs with his two dogs and their red leather leashes. I swore to myself that one day I would find this swine Mr Fischer and kill him. I hated this man with such intensity for many years. How could I have had such feelings of hate so young?

* * *   * * *   * * *

Shortly after this episode the consulates' immunities were not respected any longer. The black uniforms would do spot checks at random whenever they felt like it, which made hiding in the consulates or embassies very dangerous, almost impossible.

After the shocking episode in the Yugoslav Consulate we found ourselves in one of the houses under Swedish protection. This was a place mainly for children. There were fifty other children of all ages in this building. These were the children who had been saved, whose parents had been taken away to camps. Here they were sorted out for transfer to other countries. My mother was one of the people helping. There was also a man and a woman. He was supposed to be a doctor. They had two little dachshunds.

Whenever someone was ill, all they had to give them was an aspirin. We all slept on the shiny parquet floor. We each had a blanket for cover. We were like sardines all lined up next to each other. This room was very large with a double door and a balcony at the end. I made friends with a little boy of my age who had lots of freckles and glowing red hair. Needless to say, we had very little to eat. One night we were all in the dark supposed to be sleeping when this little boy out of nowhere appeared under my blanket and gave me an apple. We both pulled the blanket over our heads and shared the apple. Suddenly my mother, who was in charge as usual, pulled the blanket off, made a horrible spectacle, accusing me of stealing the apple and as a punishment I had to sit outside the door in the dark and cold and was made an example of to all the other children. The little boy out of friendship admitted it was he who stole the apple so he came and sat with me. I never told her that I had nothing to do with stealing the apple. For the first time in my life I felt hate and anger towards my mother.

She explained later she had to punish whoever was stealing because if everyone would steal there would be no food left to share out. As I was her daughter I should give a good example. She had to treat everyone the same way. I understood this, forgave her but have never forgotten it. Especially as she never asked me or let me explain, although I would never have told her that the little boy had given the apple to me. It was his apple and he saved it to give it to me.

Not long after this a big lorry arrived and we all had to leave in a hurry. I never saw or heard about the little boy with red hair again. God help him, I hope he survived and remembers and also tells his story.

* * *   * * *   * * *

Time for a new game. This time mother worked in a military hospital as a nurse. It was one of my mother's many jobs. She could hide me in this place. I was hidden in so many places and ways. But this was quite a new way. My mother made a game out of our daily adventures; therefore I did not realise the severity of the situation. In the hospital mother had a room in the nurses' quarters. When she was on duty, instead of hiding in the cupboard or under the bed, I was to lie on my tummy face down on the springs. The mattress and the bed would then be made up on top of me. In this position I could breathe and the soldiers could not find me when they came to inspect the room. As I was so little, the bed was made up perfectly on top of me and no one could see there was a little person inside.

There were four beds in this room. I was in one and Erwin was in the next bed. Erwin was the boy who we met in the Yugoslav Consulate when we were hiding from the SS. Somehow he attached himself to us. When we left, he came, too.

I was very happy to have him around. He was with us for quite a long while. He was put in the bedding in the same position in the next bed. When no one was nearby, we would whisper to each other. This made the time pass so much faster. Every now and then my mother would come and lock the door from the inside and we were able to get out and stretch our limbs. Other times she would give us some water to drink through a straw. During the day we had to lie on our bellies for hours and hours. At night when mum came off duty we would be able to stretch our legs and sneak out to the toilet. If it was too urgent we had to pee into the sink at the same time as running the tap water, so that the smell could not be detected. It was very uncomfortable and boring just to lie there, never knowing for how long. But it was a lot better than being gassed or taken away God knows where.

Out of pity, mother took in a dark-haired lady with a very swollen stomach. She used the fourth bed. We were told there was a baby in her tummy, although we did not hear it cry. She was in the bed pretending to be a patient.

When my mother came off duty she would lock the door behind her and she would always bring some food with her, which we shared equally amongst us. Sometimes she would have bread, sometimes it was just raw potato peels, carrots, whatever she could scrape together and was edible. We ate it. The lady had an equal share. After some weeks a big parcel arrived for this woman. She unpacked it. The smell was wonderful. I had never seen such a big piece of food. I was told it was a turkey. This lady with the baby in her tummy opened her parcel and tore out a big piece of meat and started to eat it all by herself; not sharing it with any of us. We just looked at it. The saliva was running down from our mouths and we could not believe she did not make any attempt to share any of the turkey with us. For a few minutes my mother was watching the woman finishing her chunk of meat. When she started to pack the remains up to put it away, my mother jumped and yanked the parcel out of this woman's hands, unwrapping the paper. The woman started to pull the meat back. This was a proper tug of war. My mother was furious with her. I thought for a moment she was going to hit her or pull her hair. 'You selfish bitch,' my Mother screamed, 'are you not ashamed of yourself? We shared with you every scrap of food we could find. I gave you shelter, jeopardizing my own children because I felt sorry for you and your unborn child, and you sit here amongst these poor children, who are starving. How can you just sit here, stuff your mouth, and let them watch you? What kind of a human are you?' I had never seen my mother so furious.

By now my mother was in possession of the rest of the roast

turkey. She pulled three pieces of meat from the turkey, with bare hands, one piece for Erwin, one for me, one for herself. The remains of the turkey she packed up and put in a safe place. The woman was sitting in a chair, shaking, obviously petrified from my mother's outburst. My mother said, this meat will be shared out tomorrow between all of us. Now the woman protested and became very nasty. So my mother took the wrapped up turkey, pushed it into the woman's hands, pulled her out of the chair, opened the door and threw the woman out.

ESCAPING FROM THE NUNS

Mother had one of her special talks with me. The one I had to listen to very, very, carefully! This was all about how I had to get out of Budapest. It was becoming very dangerous. The bombing was worsening. Food was harder to get hold of and the soldiers were receiving more help from the civilians, who were informants and helping them to locate hidden Jews. I must go to a safe place outside of Budapest, for a short time, until the situation improved. This is a school run by nuns. She explained, we have to always be a step ahead of the Nazi police, who will put us into a concentration camp if we are caught. If we were separated for a short while it would be easier to be invisible.

I felt a lump in my throat, panic stricken, but mother knew best. She always made the right decision. I must not show how frightened I am. This would make her extremely sad. It must be just as hard for her to be apart from me as it is for me. It will be only for a short time. I was just a little girl. Mother always explained to me the plan, which I had to follow or we would not still be alive.

There will be lots of other little girls my age and older at the school. The soldiers would not be looking into a school run by Catholic Sisters. There would be food and I could learn how to read and write; maybe even dancing lessons. She tried to make it sound really nice. Not that I had a say in the matter. Once my mother made a decision that was it. She was clever by making me feel I had a choice but in reality this was just a game. A game of life or death, one wrong decision and we would be caught, as we had so nearly been many times.

Next morning we set off early in the morning to catch a train. Arriving at a small village, about two hours' train journey from Budapest, there were only the two of us getting off the train. Mother asked the man in the little cubicle, inside the station, how we could get to the Convent school? He pointed with his finger towards the road. There was no transport. We had to walk. The road was dusty and not made up like in Budapest. We walked for ages.

It must have been very difficult to find a safe place for me to hide. The nunnery was in the middle of a farm. There were cows in the fields, chickens in the yard and lots of other animals which I had not seen before. There it was! Open fields surrounded this imposing, dominant building. It seemed to be taller than any of the other houses. This was a grey forbidding place.

As we approached the front door, which towered above us, I could hear the church bells. The big wooden door was opened by a grey-faced unfriendly looking nun. Her black habit was fastened with a thick leather belt on the side of which a long black rosary was attached. She had her hands clasped in front of her and her bony fingers gave me the creeps. She greeted us, nodded her head first to my mother then to me. Then she said, 'I am the Mother Superior and I am known as Mother Innocentia. With an unconvincing smile she indicated to us to follow her.

The floor was so shiny we could see our mirror image on it as we walked towards her office. Everything was dark and very cold. The only friendly thing in this place seemed to be a big stained-glass window at the end of the corridor depicting the Mother and Child. The colours were simply magnificent: blues and reds, with yellows and pinks. It stood out against the forbidding darkness of the corridor. We entered an equally dark and dismal office. Mother Innocentia sat behind an enormous dark brown highly polished desk. She pointed to two chairs for mother and me to sit on. She asked question upon question. During this interview I prayed silently that they would not accept me. This place frightened me. Mother told her I needed a good education and I needed to get out of Budapest because of the constant bombing. Unfortunately I was accepted.

We were shown to the dormitory, the refectory and the Chapel. Then the time came for us to say our goodbyes. I held my mother's hands and cried, begging her not to leave me here. She hid her tears and assured me that this place was lovely and I would like it. I would have lots of friends to play with and no need to go to air-raid shelters to hide from the bombs. She would come to visit me soon. All this meant nothing to me. I just wanted to go with my mother. By now lots of other nuns had appeared. Mother Superior showed my mother out to the front door whilst two of the Sisters pulled me towards the dormitory and my bed.

* * *   * * *   * *

The dormitory was a big room with ten beds. My little suitcase was put into a narrow wardrobe next to my bed. There were three shelves in it and a couple of coat hangers. Up until now I had not seen a single girl. I assumed they must have been in their classrooms. The nun who looked after me was Sister Clara. She seemed very nice and younger than the other sisters I had seen. She dried my tears and sat with me on the bed, held my hand and explained to me that the first few days were always very hard but in no time I would make many friends and be very happy here. Somehow I did not believe her. I could not stop crying.

A bell rang and I could hear lots of footsteps coming towards the dormitory and a number of little girls in uniforms came through the door. 'No running, walk slowly' – a voice repeated from one of the nuns. Most of the girls were about the same age as me, seven and a half almost eight. They came through the door and Sister Clara introduced me to the girls.

'This is Doriska. Look after her. She comes from Budapest and we have all to make her welcome and help her to settle. Who wants to be her special friend?' asked Sister Clara. 'Me, me, me', several girls put up their hands and wanted to be my special friend. Sister Clara chose two girls and explained they would show me what to do and if I had any questions I should come to her. She turned around and disappeared through the dormitory door.

The girls in the dormitory were very friendly, especially my two new friends, Kati and Zsuzsika. They wanted to know everything about me. I had to be very careful what I told them. As usual mother had instructed me on the story I was able to tell at this time. 'Our house in Budapest was bombed and everybody had to find a new place to live. My mother is a teacher and cannot look after me full time!' This is the story I had to stick to. Even the nuns were told the same story when they asked.

Shortly after, another bell rang and I was shown to the bathroom which contained a long row of white sinks where we washed our hands. Then in a single file we proceeded towards the refectory. The same girls from my dormitory also shared a long dining table. Everybody had to be silent. Then we had to pray before our meal. I found this to be quite strange because from where I came once the food arrived on the table we had no time to pray. We could not put the food fast enough in our mouths.

My two helpers sat on either side of me at the dining table. They were very nice, helpful and friendly girls. They whispered into my ears which was a nasty sister and which was a nice one. They warned me to be especially wary of two of the nuns who were very strict and vicious. After the meal we had to pray again to thank for the meal we had received. This I found much easier and more plausible.

Once the meal was finished we were allowed to go and play before bedtime. There was a beautiful garden with swings and slides, wooden benches and grass on which we could sit. The favourite games were hopscotch and skipping ropes. I was very good with skipping ropes. I had mastered crossing my hands in front of me whilst skipping. For a little while I forgot how sad I was. But once tucked up in bed, I felt lost, frightened and missing my mother so much, I cried myself to sleep.

* * *   * * *   * * *

Every morning, before breakfast, we had to go to mass. Nobody ever bothered to ask about my religion. I did not volunteer. I had strict instructions from my mother to deny any conversation with the word 'Jew'. I found the singing in the chapel so peaceful and beautiful. The nuns had a choir and they sang like angels; it was hard to believe that some of them who were so strict and nasty to us could have such angelic singing voices. We had normal lessons, reading, writing, arithmetic, drawing, gymnastics and catechism. I loved listening to the Sunday readings. They were like fairy tales and very beautiful. I also liked singing in the choir. These were songs I had never heard before, so very different from the songs I was used to hearing on the radio. The songs the nuns were singing did not have any rhythm at all but they sang in harmony. The church organ sounded, at times, like a thunderstorm and quite overwhelming.

On one occasion at an evening meal I could not eat what was given to me. It tasted so horrible. I just wanted to be sick. Then the strict nun appeared beside me, prodding my shoulder with her index finger. 'What is the meaning of this?' she asked in a loud croaky high-pitched voice. 'You have not touched your food.' The whole dining room stopped. You could have heard a pin drop. They all knew what was coming, except me. With her left hand she grabbed the back of my hair, pulled my head back and with her right hand picked up a spoon and tried to force the food into my tightly closed mouth. I had my mouth clenched and tried to push her hand away with both my hands. As a consequence she called another nun. This one came prepared with a big square white tea towel. She tied it behind my neck and held my arms down whilst the nasty Sister continued to force food into my tightly closed mouth. By now I was kicking and screaming and wriggling. I managed to wriggle away and ran towards the Mother Superior's office. I can remember the petrified faces of the girls at my table.

Mother Superior had not much sympathy for me. She gave me a long lecture on how grateful I should be to be fed and have a roof over my head. I was a bad little girl and must be punished for such sinful behaviour. I was marched towards my dormitory and just in front of the door I was made to kneel on a handful of dried grains of corn. This was so humiliating and painful I decided then and there to make a plan to escape from this torture chamber.

My friends came out one by one, trying to be invisible and comfort me. They were afraid to be seen because they would have had to join me, kneeling on this awfully painful dry corn. The pain was unbearable but I did not give the nuns the satisfaction of seeing me crying. I suffered in silence. I hated

51

the two nuns who had forced me to eat and then punished me. I hated them with such vengeance that somehow this anger seemed to ease the pain in my knees. My dignity had been attacked, no one had the right to force me, scream and hurt me.

After a long while the nice Sister Clara came and sat on the floor beside me and in a gentle voice told me I could get up now, the punishment was ended. She took me by the hand and we went to the bathroom where she soaked a flannel in cold water and held it on my painful knees. Then she put on some cream. I could feel she did not agree with the behaviour of the two dragons. But she did not say anything. She accompanied me to the dormitory and helped me put on my pyjamas after supervising the brushing of my teeth and washing my face. She tucked me in and said a little prayer. This night I did not cry. I did not want the two nasty nuns to think I was sorry or upset by my punishment. No, I was so angry. This was such an inhuman act to inflict on a young child. Force feeding and then having to kneel on dried corn for a time, which seemed like eternity. I would rather starve and continue running to air-raid shelters than have this treatment. I would definitely escape somehow, the sooner the better.

* * *   * * *   * * *

I began to watch very carefully every activity. I could not sleep very well. I spent hours awake planning my big escape. I could not confide in anyone because they would give away my plan. They would be punished and I would be forced to stay. These thoughts made me want to be sick. I could feel panic swelling up inside me.

One night I heard a noise outside the dormitory window so I tiptoed to the window to find out what was going on. I saw a horse and cart. A man wearing a long coat which almost touched the ground and a cap on his head, was delivering milk to the nunnery. He had a long black moustache, slightly curled up at the ends. He was a thin but strong man. I could see him carrying two large churns of milk to the kitchen He repeated the journey three times. Then he climbed into the cart and left the monastery through the big gates. It was still dark outside.

From that day on I watched this scene every morning for days and days, counting how long it took him from the cart to carry the milk to the kitchen and back. Luckily he was a man of habit. And he always stopped the cart in the same spot.

We always put our nightclothes on in the dark. This was very convenient because nobody could see that instead of my pyjamas, this time I was fully dressed under the bedcover. I pulled my cover up to my neck. I waited for a long time and made sure that there was total silence and even the nuns had retired. I had my little suitcase in my hand and my shoes tucked under one arm. I walked in my stockings out of the side door next to the kitchen. Unlocking the door I sneaked out and hid behind some bales of hay not very far from where the milkman would stop his cart.

It was pitch dark and I could hear only the sound of some dogs barking in the very far distance. I was not afraid but I could hear the pounding of my heart in my ears. I had no idea how long I would have to wait, but now I had come so far I only hoped I would not be discovered. There was no thought in my mind that I could fail. The prospect of being with my mother soon gave me more courage and determination to execute my plan.

At last in the distance I could hear the click clap click clap of the approaching horse and cart. The clanking of the milk churns against one another and the milk cart stopped at the usual exact spot. I waited until the milkman had delivered his last two churns and just as he turned to get back into his cart I dashed across and hopped into the back of the cart under the tarpaulin he had covering his milk churns. He did not see me. I lay very still. The cart was not empty. It had plenty of room for me and my suitcase. I was so lucky that the milkman did not have to deliver any milk nearby. Every time he stopped I thought I would die from the fear of being discovered.

Fortunately for me he drove into the village. By now it was becoming lighter. At the next stop I could see houses close together and I managed to slide off the cart without being seen by the milkman. He carried on. I stopped the first person I could see and asked the woman where was the railway station? I told her I was meeting my sister there. The woman smiled and commented, 'Aren't you very young to go to the railway station on your own?' I said, 'No, I have to hurry because if I am too late I would miss the train and be told off.'

The railway station was at the end of the street, which I reached in about three minutes. There I asked another young person, who was waiting on the platform, which train was going to Budapest. This schoolboy told me that it was the next train which I should be looking for. He smiled at me but did not ask me any further questions, for which I was grateful.

Soon the train, huffing and puffing, came to a halt. I kept very close to the young schoolboy to give the impression we were travelling together. The train was quite full and after a couple of whistles it chuffed off on its way. I sat down, putting the suitcase next to me.

The monotonous sound of the train engine almost put me to sleep. Then I spotted the ticket collector coming through the door. I quickly got up and leaving my case behind, passed him and went towards the carriage where the toilets were. I stayed there for quite a while. As fate would have it, just as I came out of the toilet the ticket collector was stood in front of me. I put on the best smile I could squeeze out and told him I did not have the tickets on me but my mum had them. Would he like to see them? He just patted me on my head and said don't worry. It's OK. I went back for my suitcase and moved my seat into the next carriage, sitting down next to a woman who could have been my mother. The ticket collector did not come back. After several stops the train pulled into Budapest station.

I left the train and managed to squeeze amongst the crowd through the barrier without being noticed by the ticket collectors. In front of the railway station there was a row of taxis. I approached one of the taxi drivers and told him I did not have any money on me but my mum had said she would pay the fare on arrival. I gave the taxi driver the address of the college where my mother was teaching. On arrival I asked the driver to wait whilst I collected the money for the fare from my mother. When I knocked on the door and entered the classroom where my mother was teaching and she saw me, her face did not show any surprise. She seemed to have been expecting me. I was given the money to pay the taxi driver, took it down to him, as if this was the most normal, everyday occurrence.

I waited in the canteen until my mother had finished her class. She came and sat beside me and I told her what had happened to me and asked would she have stood for this? 'No,' she said. She did not tell me off. I felt she was really proud and impressed by my actions. She did want to know how I could have escaped from such a well-guarded place. She just shook her head with a smile on her face.

MY LITTLE CHRISTMAS TREE

Keleti Pályaudvar is Budapest's main railway station. In the winter of 1943 my mother and I often spent time there. It was sheltered, warmer than walking the streets and fairly anonymous, as people were coming and going all the time.

My mother was dressed as a Red Cross Sister in white with a red cross on her headscarf. If stopped and questioned, I was a patient she was accompanying to the Children's Hospital. I usually had a bandage over my face, covering my nose, my Jewish looks. At that time we were homeless and had no permanent address. Only after dark could we go to a safe house, which changed from week to week, sometimes even daily. We travelled by bus, tram or train. Like so many other Jews under the Nazi government of Hungary, we had to keep moving. I was seven but so small and thin I looked like a child of five. We never carried suitcases as this too was an obvious give away for people on the run.

It was Christmas Eve and everything was lit up. My mother bought me a little bag of roast chestnuts. This was cheap, nourishing and kept our ice cold hands warm. The railway station was abuzz with people in a hurry to get home to celebrate. Strange, with all the sparkle and excitement, my main feelings, that evening, were tension and fear.

Suddenly the sound of police whistles ripped through the air. From every direction Nazi soldiers appeared with Alsatians and cordoned off the whole area. They were stopping everyone and demanding identification.

No one could escape the trap. My mother instantly headed towards an old woman who was selling Christmas trees. She picked the smallest tree and, gripping my hand so hard I thought it would break off, she headed hurriedly straight towards a big, fat, red-faced soldier in the cordon. In perfect German she asked him whether he could check our papers first as she was in a hurry to light the Christmas tree for me, her little daughter, before she went on duty at the hospital.

'Of course my dear Sister,' he replied. 'Do not bother about papers. We are not looking for decent people like you and this lovely daughter of yours. We are seeking out the stinking Jews; Scheis Juden. Happy Christmas Sister and God bless you and the little one.' He gave me a big smile, patted me on the head and stepped aside. We were let through the deadly cordon which was a death trap for so many poor Jewish people.

We almost ran but could not, as this would have caused suspicion. We looked at each other. I could feel my heart beat in my throat. My mother just gripped my hand even harder. I was only seven years old but I knew. This time, once more, we were saved. If only for a night! This time by that tiny, prickly Christmas tree.

Now I am over seventy years old and every Christmas I remember the little Christmas tree which saved our lives.

This is what Christmas means to me.

NIT RACING: A UNIQUE BOARD GAME

Whenever my mother went out to work she would tell me that she would be back for me soon. The time was never set but she always kept her promise and I knew that no matter what, she would always come back to me. To ask 'when?' never occurred to me, I just knew she would always care for me.

I was drawing when the door was suddenly thrown open. I had not heard even a creak on the stairs otherwise I would have known to hide under the bed or inside the wardrobe, as I had done so many times before. I knew that above all else, I must not be found. This time was different, they came out of nowhere. Framed in the doorway stood two men in grey uniform wearing polished black knee-high boots. Between them stood our kind landlady, the one who gave me sweets and told me what beautiful eyes I had. But today there were no sweets, no smiles. She looked at me with hard, angry eyes. 'This is the little Jewish girl who has been hiding in this room.' No one mentioned my mum and I was certainly not going to tell them. If they didn't know about her they couldn't find her and hurt her.

I was allowed to put my coat on and was then taken to a car that was waiting on the street. They asked me where my parents were. But I could not speak. Apart from that no one spoke to me. The journey was not very long; I don't remember having been in a car before, let alone one as plush as this one. I leant back into the soft seats and enjoyed the glamour of the ride in such a car.

We came to a stop outside a grey flat-faced building which had many floors and many square, blind, unblinking windows. The two men flanked me as we went through the massive, thick, double-height door and down a long shiny-floored corridor; turning left then right, eventually we came to a room where I was left in front of another grey-uniformed man who sat behind a desk.

He asked me so many questions and I couldn't answer any of them because I simply did not know. I was seven years old but my naturally small frame and lack of food for years meant that I probably looked much younger. By now I was very scared: How would my mother find me here? I was worried I would never see her again but I was also worried that I would be in trouble with her if she ever did find me. I must have done something wrong. Why else would the landlady have called the soldiers to take me away? I didn't know what I had done but it looked as if the punishment was going to be one I wouldn't forget.

The desk soldier escorted me up some stairs and opened a door at the end of a corridor that was identical to the one on the floor below. He left me in a big room that was full of people all sitting in little huddled groups on the floor. Here were mostly adults, about fifty, some my mother's age and some much older. I looked around and only saw one other child; a boy. He had a hunchback and his arms were very long in proportion to his body. He had fair wavy hair, blue eyes and somewhat protruding front teeth. The adults were all so nice to me, they all wanted to protect and help me.

That first night, one of the older ladies put her arms around me and huddled me up close to her. Apart from when the hunchback boy taught me to play chess, I spent most of my time with her and she held me tightly each night. I still remember how her arms felt. I wish I could remember her name.

I never learnt his name but I remember another game the hunchback boy taught me. To pass the time, we had nit races.

The rules were simple: on a piece of paper we drew as many lines as there were players. Next we all picked a nit out of our hair. Each champion nit would then be placed on the line that had its owner's initials at the end. Then the fun would start; each 'trainer' would shout encouragement to their nit to urge it on to cross the finishing line first. Each new game called for fresh nits, and there was no shortage. Every competitor had a thriving stable of racing nits at their fingertips. This was enormous fun, a welcome distraction from the fear of what was going to happen to me next. I remember hearing several of the grownups pleading with the soldiers that guarded us. They begged them to take me back and kept repeating that this was no place for such a small child. I had absolutely no idea where I was or what kind of a place this was. I knew I was afraid and I knew that my mother would come for me. She always came.

Each day, the guard would come and choose five to ten people to take away with him. Every day these few would be replaced with new scared people all with yellow stars sewn to their coats. Relatives and friends pleaded to stay together. No one knew where they were to be taken or what would happen to them. No one ever came back. This was a sorting centre from where those selected were sent to other, more permanent camps.

One evening, a man in light brown overalls, who kept looking all around him, nervously came over to me and started to talk to me very secretively. I know he was talking to me but his eyes kept looking everywhere but at me and it was obviously important that no one saw him or heard him.

He spoke very slowly and quietly. 'I have a message from your mother.' My heart jumped. 'Now listen and listen well, there must be no mistakes. You must do exactly what I tell you to do if you ever want to see your mother again. You must be very brave and do exactly what you are told. After supper, when the lights are put out, you must pretend that you need to visit the toilet, you must not tell anyone what I tell you to do, not even your friends. They could get into big trouble.'

His voice was full of fear and I had no doubt that if we were found talking it would be very bad for both of us. He went on, punctuating each new instruction with 'Do you understand?' I tried not to look at him but nodded each time he asked. 'Turn left and walk towards the toilet. Opposite the toilet there is a corridor with a door on the right. This is the room where the coal is kept. The door will be unlocked. You have to get in and hide behind the heap of coal. It is dark and cold and you will be all by yourself but you must wait. You must wait until you hear three knocks on the door. This will be the time when the dirty washing is collected. The laundry trolley will stop in front of the door. You must climb into this trolley and hide yourself in all the dirty linen. Do not forget to close the door of the coal room behind you. Get as low as you can in the basket. Don't talk. Don't move.' He paused and rubbed his forehead with his hand. 'The trolley will be pushed by someone who will take you to a place where your mother will be waiting.' I turned to look at his face but he stared steadily ahead. 'Whenever the trolley stops you must be completely still. The soldiers will poke their bayonets into the bag to catch anyone hiding. If you get stabbed, don't cry out, be brave. If they catch you, you will never see your mother again.' Now at last he looked at me. 'Good luck little girl,' he stared deeply into my eyes. 'Your mother told me you were a brave and clever little girl and you can do this.'

I felt so happy and I did exactly as I was told. The lights were out, everyone was huddled up. There were no beds so people slept on the floor under woollen blankets, all lined up and squashed together like sardines in a tin. Being close to another body keeps you warm so in the day people tended to sit up in the same places where they lay down to sleep at night. Occasionally we were escorted outside by soldiers with guns and fixed bayonets into a bare yard where we walked round and round before being herded back to the room.

When I opened the coal room door I was amazed to see the huge mountain of coal. I was completely dwarfed by it, which was a good thing because it meant that I could climb over and hide behind. Should anyone open the door, I would be completely hidden. I clambered on. Right at the back of the heap of coal I found a blanket which I wrapped around myself gratefully. It was frighteningly dark but as my eyes grew accustomed to blackness, every now and then I saw a tiny blink of comforting light come through the keyhole from the corridor beyond. My excitement faded as the hours passed and I started to wonder whether I had been forgotten. After all, I was only a little girl, why would they remember where I was? I resolved that if no one came for me I would sneak out in the morning and pretend that I had been playing hide-and-seek. Time seemed to lose its shape. For all small children waiting seems endless. In that storeroom at seven years of age, time had no middle and no end, only a vast beginning with no markers.

I was freezing cold, despite the blanket, and I worried that my teeth were chattering loudly enough for me to be heard by the soldiers. Several times I heard heavy footsteps approach the door then go past. What if the knocks never came? I remember thinking that I may die in that coal room. It is odd that the thought was not particularly frightening to me. Death was no stranger to any of us and I accepted the possibility without fear, probably because at seven I could not have imagined that it was final. I knew I might die because that's what happened to people like us in my experience. Rather than fear, the overwhelming feeling that I do remember was the longing to see my mother again.

Three short knocks! At last! I climbed out of my hiding place and opened the door to see the same man in the brown overalls who had spoken to me. He made some room amongst the washing for me then, once I was in he covered me with the grey, oily and smelly clothes and told me to make myself as small as I could. The ride was very bumpy, as the wheels were so very small. From time to time it stopped and I heard the man exchanging jokes with the guards. When the trolley was pushed down a few stairs I thought it would break in two and that I would surely be discovered. The stench in the trolley was so strong that my eyes were watering. I know now that the smell was urine and worse but at the time I couldn't imagine how clothes could smell like this. Suddenly I was flying as two men swung the trolley onto the back of a truck. The truck lurched and swerved and stopped and started for what felt like an eternity but finally it came to a stop and a new man pulled me out, patted me on the head and called me a little hero.

And there, just behind the man, was my mum. Just as she had promised, she always found me. She handed something to the driver and they hugged. He ruffled my hair again and then climbed back into his truck and drove away.

We never went back to the place where the evil landlady snitched on me. Now as an adult, older than she was, I wonder what could make a woman call for the arrest of a small girl and send her to certain death. What terrible lack was there in her heart or what bitter poison had robbed her of basic human kindness? How evil we humans can be.

Then I think of the woman who folded me in her arms at night in that awful place and I wonder at how, in such grim circumstances, we can also be so noble.

Now when I play chess with my grandchildren I remember how I learned to play chess and I wonder what happened to the blond-haired, blue-eyed boy with the hunchback.

PÉCS: THE KINDNESS AND COURAGE OF THE ENEMY

We travelled straight to the Keleti Pályaudvar, the central railway station in Budapest. Mum told me it was time to start somewhere new. The Gestapo would not rest until they found us. It was 1944 and by now Germany had occupied Hungary. She said, when the SS discovered that I had escaped from the sorting house in Budapest, they would try to track us down. They would be looking for me and they would be looking for my accomplices because it would be unlikely that a little girl could have planned and executed such an intricate escape.

'We are going to Pécs,' Mother told me. 'I was there when I was a little girl. It is much smaller than Budapest. I remember it was very clean, but it was a very long time ago when I was much younger.'

The train journey was long but as I had been reunited with my mum; it did not matter how long the journey was, neither did it matter where we were going.

My mother had many connections and on a scrap of paper she had an address in Pécs. My mother told me as little as possible, the less I knew the better and as usual she made a game out of each situation to ease the severity of our circumstances. My reading was not too good as I had only been to school occasionally because we never stayed long enough in one place for a school to accept me. It was too dangerous. They would ask too many questions which my mother could not answer. She was afraid we would be found out and it be discovered we were Jewish. As a consequence my mother taught me how to read and write.

Life seemed less dangerous in Pécs, no bombs and only occasional explosions. We lived in a lovely little place of our own. My mother seemed to know lots of people who she met and with whom she talked. She had quite a lively social life. She was working in a school, teaching German. We both felt safe and settled. My mother even had time to read me bedtime stories and bedtime became my favourite time of the day.

However, early one afternoon there was a loud, unexpected knock on the door. Both of us froze. We could not think who it could be. My mother opened the door, and there stood two very tall German soldiers, dressed in black uniforms, with long leather coats and black boots up to their knees. Even their caps were black. They both had rifles and in the collar of their jackets there were two very close initials: the letters 'SS'.

'You have to come with us immediately.' These were German-speaking soldiers. They searched everywhere, opened drawers and rummaged through them, opened cupboards, looked under the beds, aimlessly searching. I did not know what it was they wanted to find.

We were ordered to walk in front, with the two SS soldiers behind us. They kept on shouting, *'schneller, schneller'* (faster, faster). My little legs could hardly keep up. My grey, ribbed knee-high socks kept sliding down to my ankles as the elastic was too loose to keep them in place. I kept on hobbling on one foot and trying to pull the socks up. But the soldiers would not let me slow down.

People stopped on the streets, looking at us, wondering what was going on. No one dared to ask. Little did we know that only the previous day six thousand Jews had been deported out of Pécs to the gas chambers. You could see the fear and the pity in their eyes. Some must have been thanking their God it was not them who were being marched down the street by the SS.

I noticed that on the way, my mother had put some scrambled-up pieces of paper into her mouth and chewed and swallowed them. This she did very secretly and made sure the soldiers did not notice. I too wanted to help and chew some papers. We had never played this game before. I was really disappointed that she played this all by herself. But I felt I should not draw attention to what mummy was doing. I had never seen her eating paper before. She must have had a really good reason for doing this.

We stopped at a building, the entrance guarded by two soldiers in grey uniforms. As we got to the big arched door they clicked their heels and saluted the SS soldiers. We were led up a few stairs through a shiny polished corridor to a room where a grey uniformed soldier sat behind an enormous, wooden, carved desk. He stood as we entered. He seemed to have been waiting for us.

The two soldiers in black saluted the soldier in the grey uniform. He had many medals on his chest and many thin black stripes on his epaulettes. The men in black yanked their right arm suddenly up in the air with their palms open, and in unison they loudly said, 'Heil Hitler!' at the same time clicking their heels. The soldier in the grey uniform and the medals did not raise his arm; he never even gave them a glance, but coolly gesticulated with his right hand that they were dismissed.

Now I looked around this office. There was a door leading to the next room. This door was ajar and I noticed that this door was not like any other I had ever seen. It had a quilt stuck to the inside of the door. The soldier in the grey uniform told my mother to enter into the room with the padded door. In the middle of that room there were two chairs and a spotlight shining down at one of them. He told my mother to go in and sit.

67

The man left the inner door ajar so that I could still see my mother sitting motionless on the chair with the glaring spotlight shining straight into her face. Her expression told me she was very frightened. I had never seen her look like that before. I was very panic-stricken. It was as if every drop of blood was draining out of my body. I just wanted to go and hug my mum.

He told me to sit on the window seat in his office and wait. He spoke in a very quiet and clear voice. He sat down at his desk. The silence was so uncomfortable. He had a big pile of papers in front of him. He was reading through this very intensely.

I sat quietly for a while where I was told to sit but then I don't know what possessed me. I left the window seat and walked up to the desk behind which the man with the soft voice was seated. I stood there and heard words coming out of my mouth involuntarily. In perfect German, I asked if he had any children. He kept his eyes fixed on the papers he was reading, but he stopped turning the pages. He did not move. Very slowly he raised his head and looked straight into my eyes. He had the most beautiful pale blue eyes. He took his time before he answered. 'Yes I do, two little girls. They must be just about the same age as you.' He showed me a photograph in a frame of two little, blonde, smiling girls.

They must have been twins. I handed the picture back and told him how lucky he was to have two such pretty daughters. Then I looked him straight in the eyes and asked him: 'Are you going to hurt my mummy? Please let her go, don't hurt her. I don't have anyone else, just my mummy. Why are we here?'

He turned his head away from me. He did not say anything. He did not move. We were both motionless. Then suddenly he hit the desk with both hands. '*Scheise* (shit) I cannot do this any longer!' He got up and went into the inner room where my mother was sitting under the light, with his right hand he beckoned her to come into his office. Then he took out his wallet, in which I could see some more pictures of his two daughters, he took out all the paper money it held. 'We Germans are not all evil pigs. We follow orders. Here, take this,' and he pushed the money into my mother's hands. 'Don't go back to your home. Go straight to the railway station. Take the first train out of Pécs. It does not matter where it goes. Just take your little daughter, who by the way is your guardian angel and a very brave little girl. Don't look back. Don't pick up your belongings. Just go as you are. Not all of us Germans agree with what is happening, and we are not all heartless.'

He repeated his instructions. Then he accompanied us out of the building to the front gate. Luckily the railway station was almost directly opposite the Gestapo headquarters. We did not have to wait long. We got onto the first train that was leaving Pécs. It took us back to Budapest.

Mother was very quiet and so was I. While it was not obvious to me what it had all been about, I was very afraid for my mother. This game had been different from our usual games. This game was one we had never played before, and I hoped we would never play it again. Our most popular game was hide-and-seek, which could be funny sometimes, but this game was far too scary.

Mother told me that this amazingly brave man had risked his life to save ours. We never found out what had happened to him. If it were not for the compassion of this German officer, my mother would have been tortured, even killed. She might never have come out alive or undamaged from this padded room. I often think of and thank this German officer who gave us our lives back. This experience taught me that not all Germans were bad.

Years later, whilst discussing this episode with my mother, she said, she thought she had been picked up, not because we were Jewish, but because they thought she was a communist spy!

HIDING IN THE OPERATING THEATRE

My mother was on night duty in a hospital and I went with her. I could sleep on stretchers which were laid in the corridor next to the operating theatre, in a nice warm dark hidden corner. My mother would make it comfortable for me. I had a pillow and a cover but I had always to keep my clothes on to be ready if we had to run. This was a very quiet place. Suddenly I could hear my mother running towards me. 'Wake up,' she whispered in my ear, 'we must hurry.' She took me by my hand and we ran into the theatre. She opened a cupboard door and I had to hide in there. It was so small I could not stand. I had to sit with my legs crossed. She said, 'Listen, you must do exactly as I tell you. You must not come out, no matter what happens, until I come for you. I will shut the door but leave a small gap for you so that you can breathe. You might hear some people scream, but don't worry, they are here for us to help them.'

Before I was properly settled, the big doors opened. All I could see were people's feet and wheels which must have belonged to a trolley. Everybody seemed to be running. I could not see, from where I was hidden, who was on the trolley. The noise was louder and louder, the trolley and the feet stopped not far from where I was. I was so frightened. I had both of my hands over my mouth. The noise never stopped. Now the screaming was louder and louder. Maybe they were cutting her to pieces. Then I recognised my mother's feet in the circle among the rest of other people's feet.

I knew that my mother would not cut anybody to pieces or agree to it so I was a little bit reassured. I could see water splashing all over the floor mixed with blood and then more blood. By now the screaming was so loud that I was sure she was dying. Suddenly there was dead silence and I could hear a baby cry and the screaming woman suddenly laughed with happiness.

If this is how it sounds when having a baby, I thought, I did not want one, thank you very much. As quickly as the feet came in, with the same speed they left again. Somebody came to clean up the mess. My hands were still on my mouth when they switched the light off. Shortly after this my mother came for me and explained that I had just witnessed how a baby was born. She wanted to know how much I could see and she gave a sigh of relief when I told her all I could see were feet and more feet and lots of blood and water, but I could hear the screams and then the baby cry. I wish I could have seen it all, but my mother assured me that she was very happy that I did not see anything.

It was the end of my mother's night shift. We were on the way home when we had to turn and go to the hospital shelter because the bombing was starting again, carpet bombing. This was the biggest and longest bombing that I could remember. The bombs shook the whole building, patients were evacuated, and there was total chaos. I had both of my hands over my ears to lessen the deafening noise.

Explosions, one after another, damaged the building because suddenly there was a hole in the wall and people were running through it from the next door building. They were followed by a mass of white feathers and then more feathers. It looked like the building adjacent to the hospital was a feather warehouse. The nurses and doctors rushed to the aid of the injured people in the factory. There was an unbelievable sight; no horror film could equal it. People were choked by the exploding feathers which were imbedded in people's nostrils, their mouths, their ears and all over their hair. Everywhere was completely covered.

There must have been at least twenty such people. Some had died with their faces distorted with fear.

As my mother was in a nurse's uniform she too was expected to help, but when her colleagues saw her with me, they told her she should go home. This was not a sight for a little child and there were no more survivors anyway. As we turned towards the front door a woman with a girl, more or less the same age as me, stopped my mother. She grabbed her by her hand and pleaded with her: 'Please have mercy on my child, can you give us your papers? We are Jewish and we are sure to be killed. As your daughter is the same age as mine the papers will not raise any suspicion,' she cried. She begged my mother, who knew exactly how the poor woman felt, as they were in the same predicament as us.

She could not tell her that our papers were false and that we were Jewish too and also on the run. There were people watching for my mother's reaction, which made things even harder for her: She grabbed my hand without answering the woman, turned around and we both ran out of the hospital.

There was really nothing that she could say. If she had tried to explain or find an excuse, who knows how the woman would have reacted. Out of vengeance she could have reported us and then what? In situations like this one cannot trust to confide in anyone.

Without turning back we managed to get out of the bombed hospital. We completely lost our orientation. As a result of the carpet bombing there were no houses left around. We did not know whether to go left, right or straight ahead. It was impossible to know which way to go.

Eventually we found our bearings but neither mother nor I spoke much on our way home.

The horrendous images of those feathered corpses stayed with me for a long time. I could not get them out of my mind. Luckily, memories fade, but it takes a long long time.

THE LITTLE WHITE NUN

Christmas time 1943 in Budapest was bitterly cold. Mother and I were roaming the freezing streets of Buda, which is opposite Pest, separated by the Danube River.

In Hungary, even during the war when there was very little food and not much reason for joy or happiness, people would still celebrate Christmas. Of course, everybody was frightened, depressed and hungry. The people's clothes were shabby. The clothes mirrored their hopeless grey faces. But it was still Christmas, and that meant there was a buzz in the air and a lot more hustle and bustle than usual as people tried hard to make their lives more festive.

That Christmas Eve we had nowhere to stay, but my mother had been given the address of a place that we were told was a safe house. The house belonged to a vicar who had five children. Full of hope we searched for the house. He could not possibly turn away a young woman with a seven-year-old girl, not on Christmas Eve.

We got on the last tram that crossed the bridge from Pest to Buda, and then we had to walk for a very long time before we found the address. We searched for the house in the dark but it was very difficult to find as there were no streetlights. At last, there it was! A long pebbled footpath led up to a big wooden, carved front door. My mum lifted the thick iron doorknocker and knocked firmly. The door opened, just barely ajar, and the vicar peered out at us. Through the opening I could see a ceiling-high Christmas tree, shimmering with glitter and Christmas decorations. It was beautiful. I had never seen such a wonderful Christmas tree. Five little children about my age

74

were singing, laughing and dancing around this magnificent vision. The smell of food hit my nose and I felt my eyes close and my mouth begin to water. I don't remember ever having experienced such a tantalising smell. This made me realise how hungry I really was.

I hoped that at any moment I would be dancing and playing with the children, and could share some of their food. The exquisite smells wafted through the front door towards us. The nice warm air inside the house floated over me and felt like an embrace, it was so different to the freezing air where the two of us were standing.

The vicar pulled the door towards him even tighter so it was nearly closed. Only one half of his body was visible, the other half was firmly tucked behind the big wooden carved door.

'Sorry,' he growled in a very deep voice. 'You must be mistaken. You have been given the wrong address. You cannot possibly come in.'

'But my little daughter is only seven years old. We have nowhere to go and it is freezing. We are hungry. At least let us go to your cellar. Just don't let us freeze, it is Christmas Eve,' my mother pleaded.

She begged him to have a bit of compassion. He was a man of the church and even had his dog collar on. He should have understood, after all he had five children of his own. He slammed the door in our faces.

Seldom did I see my mother cry but this time she was sobbing bitterly. Everything seemed so sad and hopeless. It was me who tried to cheer her up. I tried to convince her we still had each other, and that this was the most important thing. I repeated the same words that she used to say to me when situations seemed hopeless. Our relationship was not only mother and daughter but also war comrades. Although I was only five years old when the war started I had to become an equal partner in our fight for survival, and I had to pull my weight.

Usually my mother had a contingency plan. If one plan did not work out she had another one up her sleeve. But this time it was not so. It seemed the end of the road. We had nowhere to go. Perhaps she was more upset because it was a man of religion who had turned us away, or perhaps it was because it was Christmas Eve. This was beyond her comprehension, just unbelievable.

We walked aimlessly on the completely deserted streets. We did not know which direction would be the best to take. The ice and the snow were glistening on the road. We could see how our breath turned into steam as if we had been smoking. It was so bitterly cold that we could not feel any sensation in our toes or fingers. The air burned our cheeks. The tears on our faces turned into icicles. We had to walk very slowly and carefully to make sure we did not slip, as the road was thick black ice.

It seemed as if we had been walking forever when at last we stopped in front of a big house with arched iron gates. Above the big door there was a small bell that sounded very nice when my mother pulled the chain to which it was attached. She had to ring many times but nobody seemed to want to open the door. 'This looks like a nunnery,' she said. She put her arm upon my shoulder and squeezed out a little smile. She nodded reassuringly. 'It will be all right, you'll see,' she said.

She rang the bell again. The building looked very dark and forbidding. Eventually, after a long wait, the big door opened with a squeak and a groan, and a very small figure in a nun's attire appeared. She looked very young. She wore clothes that were a different colour from any nun that I had seen before. Her clothes were all white, so was her headdress, all pure white.

Only the rosary and the large cross that hung down from her belt were dark.

'We have nowhere to go my little daughter and I,' my mother began, 'it is Christmas Eve. We are cold and hungry. Please can you let us in?' My mother's voice sounded very sad; pleading and tired.

There was a long silence before the nun answered and when she did, her voice was soft. She told us the building was no longer a nunnery but had been turned into a military hospital. The entire lower floor had been turned into operating theatres for high-ranking officers. The nuns were a nursing order and were looking after the injured soldiers. She whispered, 'You see it would be impossible to let you in. There is nowhere you could hide, but I cannot turn you away either.' She put her hand in front of her mouth and looked very frightened. For a moment she was hesitant, then she turned to my mother and asked her, 'Would you mind if I hide you in the loft? That is the only place where no one ever goes.'

'Just let us in,' Mother said eagerly.

Luckily, everybody was occupied with the wounded soldiers. As we followed the little nun through the endless dark corridors in the distance we could hear singing: '*Stille nacht, heilige nacht …* '

The three of us walked through dark corridors, and climbed seemingly never-ending winding steps. Eventually, we came to a locked door at the end of a corridor at the very top of the building. The little nun stopped and unlocked it. She had lots of keys on her enormous key ring. She must have been the official key-keeper.

The loft was huge. There were a few small, blacked-out windows in the roof, but some tiles were missing, so we could see the stars.

There were lots of discarded furniture and boxes scattered around. The little nun and my mother chose the corner where we would settle, then the nun told us she would be back as soon as she could, and she left us. Suddenly it was very quiet, dark and cold. After a while she returned, bringing us blankets and pillows. The dark did not seem so fierce anymore. Our eyes got used to the surroundings and the missing roof tiles gave us light. The stars were flickering and somehow it gave a festive feeling.

Although it was freezing cold, it was a lot warmer than being out on the street. At least the wind was not blowing. Here we were sheltered and we had blankets.

The little nun left again and when she returned she brought us bread and chicken legs, hidden in her apron. She even brought us a few biscuits. Now this was a real feast. We were warm, had a good meal, and we huddled close together, my mum and I, ready to sleep. When the nun left us again we felt warm and safe.

We were just about to fall asleep when suddenly the silence was broken and all hell was let loose. The roaring sound of the bombers growled and groaned, becoming louder and louder. The sirens were shrieking, and then one bomb after another pummelled the building. Everything shook and the sky roared. Amazingly, the little nun reappeared. She was out of breath and must have been running up all those stairs. She knelt down next to us, putting her little arms around both of us. She was crying. 'I cannot possibly stay downstairs safely in the air-raid shelter, knowing that the two of you are here in the loft, which is the most vulnerable part of the building. God forgive me,' she whispered. She clasped her little hands together, clutching her rosary, and looked up towards the sky.

'God, help us?' She kept on repeating this as if she was

waiting for an answer from up above, and tears were rolling down her cheeks. All this time the bombs were pounding the building as if it was specially targeted. I feel sure now that it was. The little nun sobbed and told us that she couldn't live with her conscience knowing we were up here. She had come to move us to a safer place.

Each time a bomb hit the building it shook violently. The earth was trembling, the walls were shaking. Bright red flames were licking the walls. There were lots of sparks, like fireworks. The black smoke was blinding, our eyes were burning with searingly painful tears. Then, suddenly, there was dead silence. We could not hear anything for a while. We went completely deaf. Luckily, this did not last too long.

The entire time we were holding onto each other tightly, not wanting to let go of each other. Then we heard the sounds of many fire engines that had arrived. They must have surrounded the whole building. The bombs and explosions were relentless. The thick black smoke was just like in Belgrade only two years before, when the war first started and we had escaped from a burning house. This had the same noise, same smoke, same fire, and same fear.

We hurried to the door that would lead us to the inner corridor. As the little nun opened it we saw there was nothing beyond the door! No staircase, no corridor, no building, just an enormous empty nothingness. The rest of the building seemed to have disappeared, sliced off like a piece of cheese. Only the three of us were standing amidst the fire and clouds of smoke, as if we were cut off from the rest of the world, marooned on the only remaining part of the collapsed building. There was no way that we could get down. We returned to the loft. We could hear the fire engines and the voices of the firemen. It was not dark anymore, the flames lit up everything.

Most of the roof had disappeared too. Hoping to get the attention of the firemen we all shouted and screamed, 'Help! Help!' We were petrified that nobody would hear us through the chaos. The little nun used her white apron like a flag of surrender, waving it through the roof. Miraculously a long ladder poked up through a hole in the floor and three firemen appeared, ready to carry each of us down.

The ladder was very long, wobbly and scary. I did not dare to open my eyes and look down, but when I did just for a second my head started to spin and I wanted to be sick. So I quickly shut my eyes as tight as I possibly could and held on to my rescuer until I was safely on the ground. There were hundreds of people there. Everybody seemed to be talking at the same time. People were running around in all directions. There were nuns, firemen, civilians, wounded soldiers, some on trolleys, others in wheelchairs, but the majority of the military patients had been buried under the rubble.

Only a handful of the injured soldiers had come out alive. The bomb must have hit the house diagonally. It had sliced the building in a most peculiar way. As if by some miracle the three of us were saved high up in the attic, just hanging there whilst the rest of the building was destroyed. The bomb must have hit the operating theatres and the surrounding rooms where the majority of the soldiers were situated. Hardly anyone came out alive. If it was not for the compassion of the little nun coming to rescue us she could have been one of the victims in the 'safe' air-raid shelter. Coming to rescue us saved her life too.

Luckily for us there was utter chaos. Nobody had time to ask questions. The little nun gave us a big hug. My mother and I were invisible. We vanished as soon as we could. We just disappeared. We ran as fast and far as physically possible.

Looking back from a safe distance, most of the houses

around the nunnery were razed to the ground. It was simply unrecognisable. My mother and I looked at each other and wondered what had happened to the mean vicar's house.

For us this was a truly lucky Christmas. We had escaped death yet again.

THE RUSSIANS

In 1944–1945 the bombing of Budapest was getting worse and worse. It was too dangerous to leave our air-raid shelter. It was safer simply to stay hidden. The family came together; we made our home downstairs in the air-raid shelter. We had a little corner in which we had a single steel bed with a mattress on it. This was shared between grandmother, Hedi, my mother, Zorica and me. We had our blankets and pillows and made it as comfortable as possible. During the day we would be sitting on the bed and during the night we took up our sardine positions.

We spent the last eight months of the war in this cellar, until it ended. As there was constant carpet bombing, it was unsafe to go outside. On one side wall of the cellar facing the courtyard there were long narrow windows with bars on them. By this time the Germans had occupied Hungary. We could see their black boots marching up and down in front of these windows. Actually I don't even think they realised we were hiding down there in the cellar.

At night there was a small group of people who sneaked out to pilfer food out of the bombed shops. From each of the ten families there would be one person chosen who was the fittest and quickest. From our family this was Hedi. My mother at this time had just come out of hospital with pneumonia. She was very weak and fighting for her life. It was very exciting when the raiding party returned with various bits of food. Our party was not the only one who practised this. Most of Budapest was out raiding, stealing whatever they could get their hands on. There was total chaos.

One night there was no food to be had because the shops were all empty but they brought back with them jumpers, fur coats and shoes. These were all shared out amongst us. Although on one hand it was disappointing not to have had any food brought back it was quite fun to have all these various pieces of clothing given out. It was a pretty hopeless situation but we never gave up.

Late one evening when we were all ready to huddle up and go to sleep we heard a knocking on the middle of the wall next to our bed. The knocking became stronger and by now everybody was listening to this sound. Eventually one brick was removed, then the other and in a very short time there was an opening large enough to let through a grown man. This man was dressed practically in rags. This man's face was different to the other men I had seen before. He had a round face, darker skin and slit eyes.

Before we realised what was happening they were pushing through, dozens and dozens of similar looking men who were coming through this small opening pushing and shoving each other. They had long rifles on their backs. In no time the cellar was overcrowded with them.

There were so many of them that it was impossible to defend ourselves. They attacked and raped every woman in the cellar except my mother, grandmother and my aunt who hid under the bed. They did not touch us children. Zorica and I were sitting on the bed absolutely petrified. We were crying and hid our heads under the pillow not to hear the screams. Those men who tried to protect the women were hit with the rifle butts so hard that they fell unconscious and were bleeding. It was not just one person raping one. There were many of them raping the same woman. If they had known my mother, grandmother and aunt were under the bed, they surely would have raped them, too.

Shortly after this, other soldiers came in who looked different to the first lot. They wore proper uniforms and pulled the first lot off the women and threatened to shoot them if they continued. These were the Russian soldiers, but the first lot, I learned later, were Mongolian soldiers.

As he came through the opening, a very young Russian soldier spotted Zorica and me sitting on the bed petrified, crying and hugging each other. This young soldier was only a boy. He sat on the bed and tried to comfort us. He took a special liking to Zorica who was a very pretty little girl with curly hair. She was only five years old. He sat her on his lap and stroked and kissed her hair. Tears came out of his eyes. He took a picture out of his wallet and showed us a little girl. He pointed at it saying this was his little sister.

He gave us chocolates and he sat there with us to protect us. Eventually the noise and the screams settled down. The Mongolian soldiers set about attacking the opposite brick wall to create an entrance to the cellar next door. In our air-raid shelter cellar there was not a single soul who was not traumatised. Everybody was crying and shaking from this horrendous barbaric episode.

Later on we learned that Budapest was built on catacombs leading from one building to another underground and that is how the Russians had captured Budapest from underground without the Germans realising what was happening. The Russians took them by surprise. When we next looked out of the little windows to the street we could see the black boots dangling 10 cm off the ground instead of walking past.

The three ladies re-appeared from under the bed and looked much older than when they took refuge there. Mother and Hedi had more grey hair than my grandmother. They must have used some leftover flour to disguise the colour of their hair. My mother even grew a hunchback. She looked very different from the mother I knew. They had disguised themselves to appear old and uninteresting to the marauding soldiers. As my mother spoke Yugoslavian, which was very similar to Russian, she volunteered her services as an interpreter, which was accepted.

When she felt a bit more secure she removed her hunchback, which consisted of her crunched up jumper pushed under her blouse. She brushed off her grey hair and she started to resemble the mother I knew.

Aunt Hedi and my grandmother were very worried about the young boy soldier making such a big fuss of Zorica. But it was soon made clear to them that she reminded him of his little sister. They brought us lots of food. However the injured women were still crying and bleeding and extremely traumatised. It was a very frightening situation.

The Mongolians disappeared to the next door cellar and so did most of the Russian soldiers. There was a constant flow of soldiers from one opening to the other. There was an endless convoy. The flow of soldiers never seemed to stop.

And there he was – another Russian soldier. This one had on a big rucksack and he was obviously searching, as if he was looking to find someone. Suddenly my mother and grandmother and Hedi started screaming and crying and jumped on this soldier. Miki Miki!!! And the soldier cried and hugged the three ladies and they all cried but this time out of happiness. We children had no idea what this was all about. We were most surprised to witness such an unexpected event. Here was my mother's brother, my grandmother's son, Hedi's husband, Zorica's daddy, my uncle Miki.

Needless to say the rest of the onlookers stood around gaping with their mouths open, wondering what on earth was happening. Once they realised that this Russian soldier was speaking Hungarian their surprise was even greater.

Fortunately the Russian soldiers had distributed plenty of food to the others. Otherwise they might have lynched my uncle and stolen the stash he saved for us if and when he found us. Miki was not stupid and did not show what was in his rucksack to anyone else. He just revealed it to us. He had salami, bread, bacon, chocolates, everything you could dream of. We cried, we laughed, we hugged, and we kissed. None of us could believe this miracle. Miki told us the long, unbelievable story of how he had escaped from the labour camp and joined the partisans, then the Russian soldiers and volunteered to liberate Hungary. He went to Buda to Auntie Gitta's house hoping to find us all there only to be told by the next-door neighbours that part of the family was taken to a concentration camp and the other part with the young children were hiding in Pest. Somehow he found the district where we were supposed to have gone. Miracles do happen.

The Germans were forced out of Hungary and the Russians liberated us; Hungary accepted them with open arms.

People went back to their homes. Having spent over eight months in the cellars just seeing the sky again was a wonderful feeling. We tried to get back home to Yugoslavia again as soon as possible but there were no regular trains. The Germans did not give up easily and tried to retake Hungary. The shooting and bombing started again. Whilst before, it was the Russians who were bombing Budapest to get rid of the Germans now it was the Germans who were bombing to get rid of the Russians. To us, the poor victims, it did not really matter whose bombs they were. They did not carry a visiting card on them so that we should know where they came from. All we knew was that they were killing us and destroying more houses. The bombing started again with a vengeance. We escaped to the border on an open train which usually carried coal. This open carriage was cramped with people: there was hardly any room to move.

There was snow all around. It was freezing cold. This was a steam driven train and the black steam from the engine was choking us. The train came to a sudden halt and a low-flying plane emptied its machine gun onto the train. There was so much blood everywhere and the people could not stop screaming. It was very surprising that there was only one death in this open carriage.

At the next little village the train stopped. The train driver refused to go any further because it was unsafe. The villagers stood at the platform with their baskets filled up to the brim with food, bread, fried chicken and sausages. They were just throwing them onto the train to the starved people, who were just devouring every morsel that came their way. Often their eyes were bigger than their stomach because when you have been starved and had no food for such a long time, your stomach shrinks and you are unable to keep big portions of food down. Such generosity from these village people was unbelievably kind, especially when one is reminded that the same race had previously been capable of carrying out such inhuman behaviour, torture and mass murder.

My family was always very inventive but the following experience out-did all the rest. There were no more trains going over the border and we were only 20 km away from the Yugoslav border. Miki, Hedi and Zorica had gone on a previous train back to Novi Sad, so there were only my mother, grandmother and I left. Another young man attached himself to our family. He too wanted to go back to Yugoslavia. Somehow my mother acquired a horse, a big laundry basket and a pair of skis. With a help of a few men from the village they constructed a contraption that would take us over the border back to Yugoslavia. They somehow attached the basket to the skis. The horse was in front of this improvised sleigh. The basket was high enough when we sat on the very bottom of it you could hardly notice we were inside. We put some blankets into the large laundry basket and it just fitted three adults and me. My mother had the reigns to the horse and off we went. She had each leather reign twisted onto her hands and wrists round and round so she would have had a good control of the horse.

My mother sat in the basket so her feet could push against the front of it. We sat around her. We had plenty of blankets given to us by the kind people from the village. These we had wrapped around our heads and bodies. It was a very open landscape and my mother drove as if possessed by demons. We reached about half of our journey when suddenly there were gunshots aiming at us. Luckily they were far enough away and their aim was not very good, so we were not hit. We tried to find a piece of white cloth that one of us could hold and the only thing that resembled a white flag was our young companion's shirt. He had no choice or option but to take off his shirt and hold it in a way that would look like a white flag. He had the choice of freezing or being shot.

Fortunately for him, before we set off on our hazardous journey, he was given an overcoat from one of the generous villagers. When we reached the Yugoslav border icicles were hanging off our hair and noses. The reigns froze onto my mother's hands; consequently the reigns had to be cut off with a knife. Her hands were stiff blue and white and it was a miracle she had not lost both of them. Somebody up there must have loved her.

The reception at the border was great. We must have looked like ghosts. The fear, the hunger, the cold, above all the surprise that we had made it. I cannot remember what happened to the horse. It could be that my mother gave it to somebody in exchange for something else which we needed more than a horse. Maybe a new shirt for the young man? He disappeared as soon as we crossed the border.

BACK TO NOVI SAD

Coming back home to Novi Sad where I was born, who could have ever imagined what we would have had to endure since we escaped the bombing in 1941? The Russian army liberated us from the German occupation and the Nazi regime. By this time I was weighing three to four stone, I was a living skeleton. My hair had fallen out and my skin was like fish scales as a result of malnutrition. I had pleurisy and pneumonia. This was the result of having spent the last eight months hidden in a cellar in the ruins in one of the back streets of Budapest, not daring to go out into the fresh air from fear of being picked up by the SS.

When we arrived in Novi Sad we returned to the house where my father grew up hoping that we would find some surviving member of the family, only to find that the whole family had been wiped out. My grandfather, Dr Sigmund Handler, a renowned solicitor, had lived here with his second wife Rosenstein Babuzi who was twenty years younger than him. They had three sons: Josi, Dodi and Walter, twelve, fourteen and sixteen years of age.

When the Germans invaded, from talking with neighbours, my mother learned what had befallen the family. When the German soldiers came to the door Babuzi opened it and they shot her point-blank. They captured my grandfather and his three sons and they took them down to the tree-lined shores of the Danube. It was winter time and the Danube was frozen solid. My grandfather was ordered to cut three openings in the ice with a pick axe provided by the Nazi soldiers. Then they tied him to a tree in full view of the three holes that he had been forced to cut.

He had to watch how his three sons were, at gunpoint, one by one, forced to drop through the icy hole into the freezing waters of the Danube beneath. My grandfather had to watch his sons scream and beg to be allowed to stay alive and he had to watch how they froze to death. Their screams were at first loud, then slowly very slowly their screams became quieter and when they stopped, so did the young lives of his sons. He could do nothing as his hands were tied behind his back at the back of the tree. He too begged for mercy, pleaded for his sons' lives. These devils knew no mercy. This horrendous experience made him lose his mind. After this they transported him to a prison and kept him as a hostage. Whatever did they hope to find out from my grandfather?

The Germans questioned him, tortured him but he knew nothing. His only crime was to be rich, intelligent and a Jew. He was highly respected. Some years later, my mother took me into a kind of sanatorium somewhere in Hungary. This is where he was taken after they interrogated and tortured him. He was just sitting and staring into nothing. There were numerous other people with the same blank expression, as if life itself had been beaten out of them. My mother and I sat on the grass beside his wheelchair, for a while we said nothing, we just sat there quietly.

'This is your granddaughter, Papa, your eldest son Desko's little girl.'

My father was the oldest son from my grandfather's first marriage. Suddenly he turned his head very slowly towards me. I could see his gold-rimmed glasses, his bald head and two very sad watering eyes. For a few minutes he looked at me and I could see tears rolling down his grey-coloured cheeks. His expression never changed, nor did he say a word. I was not sure whether he understood or knew who I really was. Mother and I talked to him and hoped that we would get some kind of an answer or reaction but he just sat there motionless without any expression like a man who was in a different world. After a while we left. Neither of us knew what to say to each other, we both cried. Did I cry because I lost him or did I cry because I never knew him, though my mother did? What had they done to this amazing and talented man?

I never saw or heard about him again.

* * *   * * *   * * *

The house in Novi Sad was very elegant and beautiful in the most expensive part of the town. The house was full of squatters. As my mother was considered to be a war hero she requisitioned the house back in no time. As I was the only living relative I had the right to the house. The house had been completely emptied. There was nothing, not even a single chair, left. The neighbours had looted and stolen all the contents. My mother was a very feisty and determined lady. She was allocated two armed soldiers from the Yugoslav army. Accompanied by the two armed Partisans she went from door to door and retrieved the furniture, the cutlery, crockery and carpets. She even found the Steinway grand piano which a 'kind' neighbour had saved for us. It was amazing how suddenly there were so many good Samaritans in the street. They all portrayed themselves as great do-gooders to have looked after the treasures for us until we returned. Did they really think that we believed their story?

I was very proud of my mother; she was very impressive, she showed no mercy. In no time at all, the villa was almost restored to its former glory. Daily we hoped that somebody from the family would turn up. Sadly nobody ever did. It looked as though I was the only survivor from my father's side of the family. Living in such a big and elegant villa was like living in a dream.

After spending years living in one room or in the corner of an air-raid shelter, suddenly to live in such a big house was an overwhelming change. So many big rooms, parquet flooring, the bathroom attached to the large bedroom. This my grandmother Oma and I shared. I was afraid of the dark and could not bear sleeping alone in a bed.

* * *   * * *   * * *

The food situation was not all that much better than in Hungary, except now we were entitled to food coupons. We had the opportunity to use them to get food from the nearby shops if they had any. My grandmother looked after me full time as my mother worked in Belgrade. Yet again she was the only breadwinner in our family. Belgrade was about two and a half hours from Novi Sad by train.

The news spread very quickly that the granddaughter of Dr Handler had returned from Hungary and was very ill, nigh on death's door. Many people came to call. Some came out of curiosity, some out of pity. At times people would leave on the doorstep an egg or a cup of sugar, various bits of food which were more than welcome.

I could not walk very well, I was very weak. I spent most of my time lying in a deck chair wrapped up in lots of blankets; only part of my face was exposed to the air. It was supposed to be good for me to breath in the fresh air. It was meant to cure me. Fresh air was good for my lungs. According to the lung specialist I had six months to live, at the most. I had overheard this conversation and instead of breaking down and crying, I had decided that, if this was my fate, I was not going to spend it in a deck chair, wrapped up in blankets. It was fascinating looking at the sky and I was able to create whole stories out of the formation of the clouds.

Only six months: these words kept on repeating in my mind. There were better ways to spend the short time that was left for me. Now the Steinway has been returned, I will spend it playing the piano. I has never played the piano before; to tell the truth I had never even seen one. To my amazement and surprise I was able to create a song with only one finger, but it was still only a faint resemblance of a tune.

I practised endlessly. Nobody was more surprised than I to suddenly feel so much pleasure and enjoyment out of the tunes that I created. After my one-finger system, eventually the rest of my fingers joined that single finger. This started my musical career. My left hand picked up chords which were in harmony with my right hand. One day to my greatest amazement when I finished playing the piano, I heard people clapping outside the window. I looked and saw half a dozen people standing there. I had an audience! This of course encouraged me to practise more and more to improve my dexterity. The tunes got bolder and louder. I improvised, I composed. I felt like a real virtuoso and after each of those amazing outbursts on the piano, I would tiptoe to the window and try to peep through the curtain and wonder whether my audience had come back or whether they had deserted me. I had to make sure that my repertoire was varied. Every now and then I would sing. I accompanied myself, of course.

Grandma was my greatest admirer. Whatever I did was outstanding and genius in her eyes; this of course was very good for me as the smallest praise would go a long way at this time of my life. Eventually my mother employed a spinster with an old wrinkled face, little piggy eyes, strict and boring.

She was supposed to teach me how to play the piano, English and basic reading and writing. During the war I could not go to school. It was too dangerous as a Jew. I really disliked this poor woman. When I knew she was coming to give me a lesson, I would hide in the apple tree in the back garden. My grandmother would come out and call my name knowing full well that I was hiding in the apple tree. She apologised to the piano teacher but she had no idea where I was and said how sorry she was that the teacher had a wasted journey. She solemnly promised that it would not happen again. Grandma was my best friend. In her eyes I could do no wrong.

To everybody's great surprise, the dreaded six months passed and I did not die. I am glad that I made the decision and got out of the deck chair and escaped the blankets. I decided to follow my dream and become a singer. The applause outside the window reminded me of the times when they called me 'the little angel' of the air-raid shelters. I was a lot prettier then. The malnutrition caused my sickly looks. Now when I ventured out of the house children and their parents would look at me with horror calling me, 'skeleton, walking death'.

The abusive language had changed from Hungarian to Serbian. Not a nice position to be in. Kids would throw stones at me and hurl anti-Semitic abuse. By now of course I knew I was Jewish. I still could not understand why I deserved this kind of treatment. I did not like going out. Forever I had to turn my head checking whether there was anybody following me. When I got back home I spent a long time looking at myself in the mirror. I did not find myself all that horrible looking but I suppose I was used to seeing myself. I wore various scarves on my head to hide not having any hair.

One day my mother came back from work with a beautiful curly wig. This must have cost her a lot of money but this was the best gift I could have ever wished for. We often managed to put different coloured ribbons into my new hair. This was an amazing boost to my self-confidence. I still looked like a skeleton but now I was a skeleton with hair, which was a lot more presentable from my point of view. This new appearance gave me enough confidence to start school at the age of nine and a half.

The school was a thirty-minute walk from our house through the park. There were sixty-five children in my class from the age of seven to fourteen. During the war the schools were all closed and most children had no opportunity to attend school. I had to start at the lowest class to learn basic reading, writing and arithmetic. Whilst I had learned how to read Hungarian during the war, now I had to learn to read and write in Serbian. Some of the older children were orphans and as the eldest in the family they had had to provide for the younger siblings, none of whom could read or write either.

The children in the school gave me a very hard time. I was singled out in the playground. In the break time they circled around me, I was in the middle. They just stared at me as if I descended from the Moon or some kind of a different planet. With a tape measure they even measured the circumference of my head comparing it with the size of their own.

Eventually the headmaster held an assembly and explained to the rest of the children what I had gone through and that I was a victim of persecution. He told them why I was so thin. I had been hiding in a cellar for months and had very little food. Instead of teasing me and making fun of me they should help me get better. His speech made a big difference to me and their behaviour towards me changed for the better.

Patriotism was the strongest subject in the school. We all became Little Pioneers learning how to march singing patriotic songs in harmony. We were taught how to adore Marshall Tito, whose pictures were everywhere, on the walls, even in our school report booklet. I was very proud to be a little communist. I enjoyed the marching and the singing most of all. There were lots of folk songs which were mainly about Comrade Tito, praising him for all the wonderful things he had done for us and all of Yugoslavia.

The national dance in Yugoslavia was called *kolo*. This was often spontaneously performed on the street accompanied by people singing or playing an instrument, mostly a squeeze box. Whenever there was an occasion people would burst out singing, harmonising. The Slav people are very musical. People sing on trains, others just join in.

Food was still very scarce after the war. Now that I had survived, my grandmother's main aim was to provide as much food as possible for me to recover. Her grasp of the Serbian language was very poor and very funny. Luckily for her many people spoke Hungarian or German in this part of Yugoslavia. In order to subsidise food she managed to buy a goat. Heaven knows how and where she got this goat from. We called her Sári. She had pale-coloured long fur. She was a nanny goat. She had great big pale-green bulging eyes, and long eye lashes any woman would desire.

As we lived in a residential area no domestic animals were allowed to be kept in the garden. Therefore Sári moved in with us and lived in the reception room amongst the gold rococo-style furniture. We had to cover the parquet floor with straw. We did not come from a farming background. We got very worried as we did not know why the goat was bleating non-stop until a friend of the family pointed out that the poor goat had to be milked as she was in pain. Grandmother had to learn how to milk the goat. This gave her the idea – to start her black-market business.

She started selling diluted goat's milk to the neighbours. It had to be diluted with water as goat milk is so strong it would be undrinkable in its pure state. Grandmother got carried away sometimes and put so much water in the milk that instead of being yellow it turned into a whitish pale blue colour and tasted a lot nicer than in its original form. She would trade a jug of milk for eggs, sugar, flour or potatoes. Milking Sári was a problem to my grandmother as touching the teats with her bare hands would make her feel sick. So she wore a pair of long leather evening gloves when milking Sári.

Sári was also pooing a lot, but strangely her poos were like little raisins and did not smell bad at all. These were very easy to pick up wearing a different pair of gloves. So Grandma had the poo gloves and milking gloves. The poo was used to put around the vegetables. Grandma had turned the beautiful rose garden into a vegetable patch. Her comment was: 'One cannot eat the flowers'. Given that we had to clean Sári's deposits I was very grateful that Grandma had bought home a goat and not an elephant.

We began to enjoy life, there was no bombing, we did not have to live underground, and we had our own home. Visibly I was getting better each day. However we could not understand why Sári was getting fatter and fatter, surprised because she was not overfed. Food was very hard to find, especially for a goat.

One morning to our biggest surprise there were four beautiful little baby goats. They were so tiny they could hardly stand up. They were the same pale brown colour as their mom. She was such a wonderful tender, caring mother. She would lick the little goats clean and then just lie there and let the little goats feed on her milk. They never stopped. The little goats were beautiful but Grandma was not too enthralled. Her business suffered greatly.

Unknown to myself I changed all that. I dressed the four little goats up in doll's clothes which my grandmother had made to please me. They were so beautiful and warm and I wanted to give them my love and warmth and I hugged, cuddled and kissed them. I had never had any toys or opportunity to play with anything. This was such a wonderful experience for me. It was very cold and they loved to be covered with the feathered duvet. I took them to bed with me. We all fell asleep happily. But the little goats must have fallen into such a deep sleep because they never woke up.

I could not stop crying. I tried to revive them with Grandma's help. We did not dare to show the little goats to Sári as she would have been so upset. We could not even call a vet because it was illegal to keep domestic animals, other than cats or dogs, in the residential area. I could detect in my grandma's face a small smile. She was not half as upset as I was. I had the feeling that she was even quite glad. She did comfort me and eventually we buried the little goats in the garden and decorated their grave with the flowers I picked. In hindsight I was not convinced that they did not end up on our plate. Knowing my grandmother, she would have humoured me and given the baby goats a beautiful funeral. But nothing would have stopped her sneaking out at night and recovering them for the Sunday meal.

Business was back to normal. Nobody snitched on us as it was not in their interest. The black market in goat's milk provided us with food that was much needed for me to get back on my feet.

As time passed, a high-ranking officer requisitioned the big garden room which was the best room in the house. We could not complain; it was out of respect for my mother that we did not have someone living with us earlier; we had to get rid of the goat as his room was Sári's living quarter. The major was a very handsome, tall young man who had his own valet. The valet regularly cleaned his black shiny boots and jumped to his every wish and command. He was also the major's driver; he drove him home in the evening and would pick him up as regularly as clockwork every morning.

The major often bought various bits of food for us. I was not allowed to go anywhere near him. One afternoon the door from the major's room was ajar, Grandma spotted that he was lying on the beautiful cream bedcover with his boots on. She jumped as if she was bitten by a wild dog. She opened the door a little bit more and at the top of her voice shrieked like a mad woman at the major, in her broken Serbian with Hungarian accent: 'How dare you lie with those dirty boots on this beautiful bed? Did your mother not teach you manners? Would you dare to lie with your boots on the bed in your mother's house?' The major jumped off the bed, took his boots off and apologised frantically.

Little did my grandma know that this high-ranking officer could have shot her on the spot or taken her away. He could have done anything, but luckily he must have had a good upbringing as he did the right thing. From that day on, he tiptoed around the house, left the boots outside and his valet was instructed to clean the floors even in our part of the house. We were very fortunate. He was the best protection we could have wished for. There was an invisible bond between the major and Grandma. They respected each other. She even shared our meals with him.

GRANDMOTHER AND MUSIC

Living with my grandmother in Novi Sad in this beautiful house was a great adventure. Every day different amazing things happened to us. Grandma had not done much cooking in her life except the occasional scraps in Budapest, but now she developed quite extensive menus. She was very inventive and she could create a meal out of scraps.

The next door neighbour kept chickens in the back garden. Like us with our goat she also had to do it on the quiet, because nobody was allowed to have farm animals in a residential area. This was, of course, a farce, as during and after the war people had to improvise and find ways and means to feed the family. Grandmother tried to buy a chicken but the next-door neighbour would not hear of it. She could not strike a deal with her milk either, so this was a bit of a tricky situation as grandma was completely obsessed with feeding me and keeping me alive. One day I noticed her at the back of the garden near the fence where the neighbour's chickens were. I saw how she loosened one of the fence planks. She put down a trail of bread-crumbs from the chicken run all the way to our old-fashioned cellars. These consisted of two slanting doors which had to be opened on both sides with steps going down to where the coal was kept, the wine and all the necessities that a big house like ours used to store before the war.

She patiently sat hidden behind the kitchen window and waited. Of course the breadcrumbs went all the way down the stairs into the cellar. As soon as a chicken appeared on the horizon, happily following the tasty breadcrumbs, she tiptoed and hid behind the cellar door. As soon as the chicken disappeared down the steps she quickly shut the door as if nothing had happened. We had the best meal I can remember.

* * *   * * *   * * *

My mother came back to Novi Sad and started a ballet school. One day she told my grandmother and me that she would bring a friend home and he would have lunch with us. She did not tell us too much about him except that he was a very nice educated man and that he was a German. When she mentioned the word German both my grandmother and I stopped breathing for a second. I felt as if somebody had stabbed me with a knife.

A few days later Werner came for lunch. He had fair hair, pale blue eyes, was very slim and of medium height. I felt very uncomfortable and so did my grandmother having to sit at the same table with a German. Neither of us could understand nor believe that my mother could do such a thing. Maybe she had gone mad. He ate and ate non-stop. He was obviously as hungry as we were. I was told that he used to be a teacher in Germany and that he was not a professional soldier. He had no choice but to join the army because if he had refused they could have put him into prison. He did play the piano, far far better than me. I was really impressed with that.

I was so disappointed with my mother, I hated the situation and I could not understand or forgive her for bringing a German into our house. Inviting him to our table, what on earth possessed her? Had she forgotten what the Germans have done to us? She tried to convince me that not all Germans were the same, and that not all Germans were bad. She reminded me about the German officer who saved our lives in Pécs, risking his own life for us! Werner is a good-hearted kind man. I was

101

not really interested in her explanations. This was unforgivable. The memories were still too fresh in my mind; and I was too young to be able to rationalise and I was far from wanting to understand. I hated my mother.

I know my grandmother felt the same, both of us walked out without saying goodbye. We both just felt unable to sit there, in a civilised manner, entertaining the enemy, as if nothing had ever happened. We did not hear mother and Werner leave. We went for a walk in the park. When I saw my mother next I could not bear her hugging me. Her touch made my skin crawl. What she had done was unforgivable. Could this be the same woman who I adored – who was my hero? My love for her filled my whole being and yet the shock of her bringing home a German seemed to have destroyed all that with one swoop.

Not long after this she informed us that the only way to get out from behind the Iron Curtain would be to marry a foreigner in order to attain a foreign passport. She was planning that eventually she and Werner would get married. Then we could start a new life in a place where one could be free. Coming back from Hungary to a communist country such as Yugoslavia, she said, was like jumping out of the frying pan into the fire.

But I was proud to be a communist at the age of ten. I loved being a little Pioneer. Communism was being equal, not poor, and not rich, we were all the same. What was wrong with that?

* * *   * * *   * * *

Through my musical talent I received a state scholarship to one of the top music academies in the country. There were only about 400 children who were sufficiently outstanding to be granted this privilege and I was one of them – the youngest one. This music school was in Montenegro Cetinje. An old army barracks had been transformed into this boarding music school. We went to the local school for lessons in reading, writing, maths, history and geography but the rest of the time was dedicated to music. We had our own choir, our own orchestra. Four pupils were allocated a room with a piano and we would take turns practising. We each practised on the average two or three hours a day. Different instruments had different studios to practise in. We studied music theory and conducting. It was fascinating and we got the best musical education that anybody could hope for.

Unfortunately, my mother got a job as a dance teacher in the same college. This made my life unbearable. At the end of the term we each had an exam and had to perform a special piece of music. Reading music was my weakest point. While I knew I had to learn how to read music, at times I felt I was much too slow. The pieces that I could read were too boring and uninteresting. I wanted to play more advanced pieces of music than my knowledge of reading music allowed me. I only had to hear a piece of music once or twice and I could repeat it. I learned many fabulous piano pieces, needed no encouragement for practising. This is where I came alive: playing the piano and singing, music was my life.

My mother was the only person in whom I had confided that I could hardly read music. Even my music tutor had not realised it. I was convinced that my big secret was safe with my mother.

It was my turn to play for my Grading. The grand piano was positioned in the middle of the room and the various teachers sat in a semi-circle. I had chosen a piece from Chopin. I played with such passion and I was really good. I played as if my life depended on it. Suddenly in the middle of my performance my mother got up and stopped me and said: 'Would you please play this, and she turned the page and pointed with her index finger to page three, row five, here; she pointed at a note, turned and went back to her seat. I stopped playing; you could not hear a sound out of anyone. I just looked at my mother and so did everybody else in the room. I could feel the warm tears running down my cheeks.

I got up, turned around and ran out of the examination room and I refused to play the piano for many years to come. My mother explained to me later that she did me a favour because if anybody else found out that I could not read music it would have backfired on her. As a member of the staff she could not allow me to pass the exam because it would be dishonest of her not to divulge this knowledge. I did not deserve to pass as I did not know how to read music.

How she could betray my secret? Did I mean so little to her to embarrass me in front of all the teachers and the students? I just wanted to die.

Yet again my amazing mother had managed to destroy my world.

EMIGRATING TO ISRAEL

It was 1948 ad my mother and I had to wait for a long time to get our papers to emigrate to Israel. As Yugoslavia was at that time a Communist country, travelling to another country other than another Communist country was very difficult. We moved to Opatia which was not far from Trieste. This is from where the ships sailed to Israel. It used to be called Abazia when it was part of Italy. It is a very old port. It had the most beautiful old buildings. When it was Italian the hotels were luxurious and the town was bustling with holiday-makers and tourists. Now many buildings were damaged by the bombs but still one could see the past history reaching out from every corner. This was once one of the major ports in this part of the world.

We rented rooms from a Jewish lady who had a fourteen-year-old disabled daughter. I was twelve at the time. We struck up an instant friendship. We were made very comfortable. The landlady's husband had been killed in the gas chamber. Werner was left behind in Cetinje waiting for us to send him a visa from Israel once we were there. Werner was not Jewish, therefore not eligible for immigration into Israel, especially not as an ex-German prisoner of war. He and my mother had got married. Our lodgings were in a very elegant apartment in the posh part of Opatia.

Our emigration documents to Israel at long last arrived after more than eight months.

* * *   * * *   * * *

Radnik was the ship that was to take us to Israel. Standing on the quay just about to board this huge ship I felt so very tiny.

105

This ship was as long as a street and it was as high as a six-storey building. It had endless little round windows covering both sides of the ship.

Mother and I walked up the gang-plank to board the ship and so did hundreds of others. So many people: this was another exodus. Once we were on board, mothers and children were given cabins which were overcrowded. The rest of the passengers claimed benches or seats wherever they could. Many of them had no choice but to sleep in the corridors or on deck.

And here we were, all sailing towards a new continent, towards a new life and towards a new beginning. This ship was like a floating village. There were not enough toilets and people would have to use buckets and throw their contents overboard into the sea. Once underway, people started to puke, left, right and centre. Even over each other if they could not make it to the railings in time. The stench was unbearable. If you were not seasick yourself then, for sure, the stench of the vomit would instantly turn your stomach. After a day or two there were less people who were seasick. This must have been because the seas were calmer or they were getting used to the movement of the ship.

The cabin which was allocated to mother and me was so full we could hardly breathe or move. Yet again my mother's inventiveness came in very handy. To this day I have not found out what my mother said to the captain. But within two days, both of us were transferred into a very nice cabin, which was a sick bay, well away from the rest of the passengers and very comfortable. She must have invented some contagious illness but she was treated with great respect and everybody kept away from us.

The journey was very exciting. While in the docks, the ship looked colossal in size but here in the middle of the ocean it felt

106

like a tiny little rowing boat being tossed from side to side and floating helplessly, exposed to the mercy of the elements. At night the stars were so close that you could almost touch them. Every now and then you could hear a group of people singing in perfect harmony. This was particularly lovely at night-time. The joy of going home, to the *Aretz* (homeland) was such a joyful journey. Back to our roots to the Jewish Land, the Promised Land!

Once the sun had gone down there was a breeze in the air, which was very comforting and enjoyable in contrast to the day when it burned mercilessly on our skin. All you wanted to do was to find a corner with a bit of shade. Even the air you breathed would burn your nostrils and your eyes. The nearer we got to the Port of Haifa the hotter it became. Because the ship was so overcrowded, it was quite slow. Eventually, the ship came to a standstill. We waited for hours and hours to get permission to sail into the port but for some reason we were denied passage.

The ship had to turn back a sufficient distance so as not to block the passage for other ships which wanted to sail through. We were denied entrance by the British five times, by which time the ship was running out of food and water. Nobody was allowed to have a shower. Grownups and children got diarrhoea; the combination of heat, not enough food, shortage of water, thus all contributed to a potential epidemic; we could have all perished.

This episode was in the newspapers and only by intervention from other countries, who took pity on the hundreds of children, were we eventually granted passage on humanitarian grounds. At long last the *Radnik* docked in Haifa.

What excitement in the air. There were hundreds of people waiting at the dock to welcome the arrival of relatives or friends. Some of them had been waiting there for months. Many of them slept on the dockside and waited for each ship to arrive, hoping that someone from their family or friends would be amongst the new arrivals. Hundreds of thousands simply had had no opportunity to communicate with their nearest and dearest. They did not know if they had perished in the concentration camps. They did not know who was dead or who was still alive.

There had been families on the quay here from the day that they arrived in Israel who would not move because they just could not give up hope.

We were lucky because Miki, my mother's brother, was waiting for us. He had emigrated six months before us. Everybody who came off the ship was given lots of oranges. This was the first orange I had ever tasted. There was chaos of tears and laughter, of hope and despair. Many disappointed sad faces had to turn away after the last passenger had disembarked.

People were approached and quizzed: 'Have you heard of my son Shlomo Berkovitch?' Another asked, 'Have you heard of my father Ariel Rosenberg?' The questions were endless. Surprisingly some people did get answers, but not always the ones they hoped for. It is hard to be the bearer of bad news. But in this case it was often inevitable.

The new arrivals, called *'olim chadashim'*, were taken to an enormous campsite. There were endless tents on the white sand. There were all shapes and sizes. And depending from which country you came, you were directed into a specific area. None of the new arrivals spoke Hebrew, so being together with people who spoke your language was helpful. I was amazed to see people from different ethnic origins such as Africa, China, America, France, Yemen, and yet they all shared one thing: being Jewish. We all had to stay in this camp until such time as we were allocated houses in different parts of Israel.

* *   * *   * *

Those of us who had relatives in Israel were processed within seven to ten days and could join their families. But the others had to wait longer. We shared a large tent with ten families. They had all been on the same boat from Yugoslavia. I can remember the excitement of looking around and seeing so many different people. How could they really be all Jewish? I had the urge to go up to people and tap them on the shoulder and ask: 'Are you Jewish too?' I later learned that lots of people had the same feeling. We did not have many belongings, but it was a new start, a new beginning, new expectations of life.

* *   * *   * *

The authorities encouraged us to stay in the area we were allocated, as in such a vast place, where there must have been thousands of immigrants, it would have been very easy to get lost. Since they came from all over the world, many of them could not understand each other; as I said, most of them could not speak Hebrew.

I had to go to the toilet and was pointed towards the smallest tent. Inside, there was a chemical toilet and some cut paper that had been strung from the ceiling. I was just about to use this paper, when I burst into tears – there were holy letters on the paper. There was no way I could commit such a sacrilege as to wipe my bottom with it! Horrified, uncomfortable and in floods of tears, I rushed to my mother. She looked terribly worried because she thought that something horrible must have happened. I sobbed as I explained to her that I had found letters from the Holy Bible in the tent, and I could not cleanse my bottom with them. Outside the tent people heard my sobs and witnessed my despair. They then explained that it was actually newspaper written in Hebrew, using the same letters as those used in prayer books. As I had only seen Hebrew letters in religious books, there was no way I could have known that this was just newspaper.

Sand storms would blow up out of the blue, coming from nowhere, unexpected and cruel. The sand would be whipped up by an unknown force which would pound against the flapping tents. If you were caught unprepared, your face would feel as if hundreds of little needles were piercing through it. Your eyes would burn and hurt and your nostrils would feel as if somebody was blowing scorching sand up them. You had to protect yourself with a handkerchief or a scarf or whatever was handy. This was referred to as *ham sim* (sand storm).

As rapidly as it arrived it would disappear in the same mysterious way. Sometimes it would last for days, but then people would be prepared and stay put.

* * *   * * *   * * *

Once our papers were in order, we were allowed to go with my uncle Miki to his bungalow *'shikun'*. So we left for Gedera, where he lived. The bus journey was incredible. All bus drivers in Israel wore gold-rimmed dark sunglasses. The scenery was like nothing I had ever seen before, sand, sand and more sand. The road went on endlessly and from both sides all you could see were a few palm trees, with every now and then a little white building. But mostly sand. On the bus everybody was talking to everybody. Endless questions: where did they come from, where did they spend the war, how did the Holocaust affect them, how many people had they lost? It was a wonderful warm feeling of unity and belonging. Everybody had an amazing tale to tell.

Gedera is a very small settlement. It lies at the foot of the Negev Desert, which is the last stop for motorists.

Here is where Miki lived in a small prefabricated house which had two bedrooms, a dining/sitting room, a small kitchen and a shower room. There were about ten of these little shikuns, close together, just off the main *kwish* (highway). We all stayed with Miki and Hedi until we found somewhere else to live. Just imagine in such a small house, there was my grandmother, Miki, Hedi his wife, and Zorica who by now was seven years old, her little brother Alex who was now two years old, and my mother and I. Seven of us squeezed into this tiny house but we were very happy to be alive. We would not have felt more comfortable and happy if we lived in a palace.

What luxury to be able to buy food. There were plenty of all sorts of delicacies, fruits I had never seen or tasted before. I think we had chicken every day and there was no shortage of eggs. On the other side of the road, there were vegetable fields. Behind Miki's house were the *pardes*, the orange groves where we could pick oranges freely, as many as we wanted. On one occasion when we, my cousins and I, played hide and seek in the orange grove we discovered lots of eggs under an orange tree. We filled our pockets and we took home as many as we could. We found a basket in the house and returned with it to the place where we found the eggs and we filled the basket with more eggs up to the rim.

Auntie Hedi and my grandmother wanted to know from where we had found this vast quantity of eggs, and they insisted that we show them the place.

It turned out that there must have been a few chickens which had escaped the *lull* (a chicken farm). But it was impossible to know from which farm they had escaped as there were about half a dozen in the neighbourhood. Thus we were on to a good thing and had free eggs for a very long time. I am sure we were not the only ones who discovered this God-given present.

Not far from Miki's house, about 15 minutes' walk, amongst pine and palm trees, was a little settlement, which was a former sanatorium, which had been for people with lung disease. It was owned by a Doctor Ben Gefen. By now there were no more patients but various small scattered buildings which he rented out. My grandmother moved to a one-bedroom little flat, whereas my mother and I rented a small building. It had a corrugated iron roof and consisted of two open-plan rooms. One of them had a corner with a shower in it. Mother rented this, without knowing it had previously been the place where they washed dead people before they were buried. The existence of water being connected to the place was what attracted my mother to this little shack. Mother made it very comfortable. She whitewashed all the interior walls and she fixed some net curtains to the walls. In order for me to practise the piano, she somehow acquired a baby grand, which took up some three quarters of the room space; therefore we used the top of the piano as a dining table. I strongly believe she did this because she had a bad conscience for the way she had treated me in Cetinje during my concert.

* * *   * * *   * * *

I started in the local school and as I could not speak, write or read in Hebrew I had to attend the first class where the average child's age was seven years old. There were also a few more children of my age in the same predicament as me. So it was not too bad. In the break time I mixed with the children of my own age, but until such time when I could understand and follow the curriculum I had to stay with the young ones. There was no stigma attached to this. There were quite a few newcomers who arrived in the country and could not speak Hebrew and therefore were not able to follow the lessons in the classes where they should have been by rights.

As soon as my Hebrew was better I joined the class of my own age. Hebrew is a difficult language but when you are a child it is very easy to learn a new language. I can say that in easily under a year I spoke fluent Hebrew. I enjoyed going to school and made lots of friends. The youngsters in Israel had a very good social life. This was the first time I went to a party. In the evening we built a fire in the playground and would throw whole unpeeled potatoes into the fire. We sat around in a circle, ate the baked potatoes, drank Coca-Cola, sang songs and danced the horah. This was a '*Kumsitz*'.

* * *   * * *   * * *

My mother slept with a shotgun under her bed. Most nights the Arabs would come from the Negev side and steal whatever they could lay their hands on: chicken, lamb, donkeys, bicycles – it was very frightening. Our little corrugated iron building was on the far border of the little settlement. Possibly it was very easy to break into. Many times we could see a shadow tiptoeing in front of the door and my mother stood there behind the door ready to shoot anybody who would come through the door uninvited. There was no time for questioning or politeness as your own life was in danger.

At night two people from the village, armed with rifles, would patrol the streets. They took turns, night after night, to ensure the safety of the village.

* * *   * * *   * * *

A few months later my stepfather Werner followed us to Israel. His first job was very exciting. He was a surveyor and got the uneasy and dangerous job of surveying the border between Israel and Jordan. As he was a Christian, I suppose he was trusted more by both sides, the Arabs and the Jews.

* * *   * * *   * * *

By now we knew the majority of the local people. I had a very nice group of friends. They were supportive. This was the first time in my life that I felt I belonged. To my great surprise I was quite good at sport, running, long jump, basketball and netball. In the break we would play catch. It was a mixed school and I noticed when boys were chasing girls they tried to ping the back of their bra.

However when they tried to ping my bra they were disappointed and so was I because I did not have a bra yet. As a matter of fact there was nothing to put into the bra.

A couple of the girls took me aside and educated me about the facts of life. If I wanted to be popular with the boys I would need to wear a bra and perhaps fill it up with a bit of cotton wool. This would gain me respect. I convinced my mother how important it was for me to have a bra. Strangely enough my mother just smiled and next day we took the bus to Rechovot, which was the nearest town and had many shops.

The hunt for the bra was very exciting but also embarrassing for me. The sales lady in the underwear shop was very laid back and not embarrassed at all. I obviously needed the very smallest size that existed. It was a pale blue organza with tiny little pink roses. It was the most beautiful and cherished garment I had ever possessed. The main part of the bra was the fastening at the back that slightly protruded and was easily visible through my T-shirt. The sales lady wanted to put it into a little bag but I wanted to wear it straight away. I wore this bra with great pride on my way home. I am sure people turned their heads and admired my feminine figure. I walked very tall.

I could hardly wait to play catch next day in the playground. As I had hoped the back of my bra would be pinged, sure enough it happened.

I felt like a fully-fledged woman just like the rest of the girls – who were unfortunately far better developed than I.

* * *   * * *   * * *

My friends decided to have a little conference about me and six of our group wanted to have a serious talk to me. They explained that as I am now an Israeli I needed an Israeli name. I completely agreed with them since I could not stand my own name. It was Theodora. I just did not feel my given name had anything to do with my persona. The girls threw all sorts of strange names at me, names I had never heard before. Then they came up with the name Dorit. I loved the sound of it instantly. I felt it suited me like a glove. I became that person Dorit straight away. I loved the way it rolled off the tongue and I liked being Dorit. I would not change it ever.

THE CONVENT SCHOOL IN JERUSALEM

Our idyllic way of life in Gedera came to an abrupt halt. Mother decided that Gedera was too small and our lives were going nowhere. She had plans. Not that she ever spoke about them either to Werner or to me. Some things never changed. My mother had an idea and we had to follow. This time it was Jerusalem. At that time my mother had just converted to Christianity, the religion that had given so much support when we were being persecuted in Hungary. However, her conversion to Christianity was never discussed and I was unaware of it.

She had arranged our lodgings in a German convent that was run by nuns who took in selected paying guests. They had turned the dormitories into comfortable hotel-like dwellings. I had my own room. Mother and Werner were in another. We had a bathroom to share and a nice big sitting room.

This building must have been built before Israel became independent. The walls were very thick which protected the occupants from the unbearable heat from outside. It was a much regimented life. Breakfast at eight o'clock, lunch at one o'clock, and dinner at seven o'clock. These meals were served on long wooden refectory tables. We sat on long wooden benches. On average between ten and twelve people shared a table. There must have been about thirty families living there plus the resident nuns and the priests. The complex was surrounded by high stone walls. The gardens were the pride and joy of the nuns. There were palm trees, exotic shrubs, sprinklers kept everything green. There were little wooden benches scattered all around. This was a perfect place where one could sit, read or just relax.

To my greatest disappointment I was enrolled into the French Convent School, 'Notre Dame De Zion'. All the teaching stuff were nuns. Yet again, I had to start at the beginning in the first class as I did not speak any French. The embarrassment and humiliation I was forced to go through, yet again, was incredibly demoralising for me. I was again the oldest one in the class. After six months my French was adequate, not perfect, but sufficient for me to attend the class in which I belonged. After the easy atmosphere that I enjoyed in the Israeli school in Gedera, this highly strict and dictatorial regime was very hard for me to accept. This complete change was very unsettling and confusing for me. Waking up in the morning to the ringing of church bells telling one it is time to have the Morning Prayer before breakfast became an everyday routine.

One of the residents was Pater Benedict Scholz, an Abbot of the Benedictine order. He was very tall, had bushy eyebrows and a dark beard. He had this dark brown, almost black habit of the Benedictine Order which had an attached hood. He took it upon himself to teach me about Christianity. I enjoyed the beautiful stories. Every week we had a lesson for an hour. I questioned him a lot and we argued as I did not accept anything on its face value. I was very glad he never became angry.

At eight thirty every morning I got onto the bus which dropped me a five-minute walk away from my school. I never looked forward to the days I took French as the teacher was this very bitter, angry nun. She had this most irritating and unfair punishment that she would dish out when anybody did something that was wrong. She took her ruler and smacked your outstretched fingers. This was very painful and I rebelled against it pointing out to her that I did not join the school to be beaten. I could feel this was going to be one of those days.

We had a French poetry lesson. Our homework consisted of

learning a poem and then reciting it. This term Jessica, a little American girl, joined us. She was very shy and could never stand up for herself. She stood up to recite and there was silence. She did not know the poem. Sister Barbara said Jessica must do two hours detention. Then she approached her with the ruler and she was just about to punish her when I spoke. 'Sister Barbara, Jessica was ill for a week, so she could not have known what the homework was. It is unfair that you should punish her for something that she was not responsible for.'

The silence in the class became so obvious. It seemed as though everybody stopped breathing. All eyes were fixed on me. 'How dare you challenge me?' snarled the Sister. She went back to her desk and commanded me to kneel in front of her and beg her for forgiveness. I refused to do so and told her this is not the right behaviour of a nun who should be humble and that she was not God therefore she could not demand another human being to kneel in front of her. The class started to roar with laughter upon which Sister Barbara screamed at the class: 'For this behaviour you will all stay in after school for an hour.' With this she picked up her ruler and was just about to attack me with it. I swiftly turned and walked out of the door.

I was in a hurry to make sure she would not catch up with me. I must have slammed the classroom door behind me. The glazed panels broke and the glass crashed to the floor. I hurried as fast as I could towards the Mother Superior's office. Sister Barbara was in hot pursuit. Without knocking I entered Mother Superior's office. She was a very dignified and calm, no-nonsense lady. No sooner had I entered than Sister Barbara burst in waving her ruler and shouting. Mother Superior got up and with a very calm voice looked at Sister Barbara and said: 'What do you think you are doing?' We both started to talk at the same time. Mother Superior interrupted us. 'This is not the behaviour that I expect from anybody in this school.' She turned very slowly and sent me out of the room to hear Sister Barbara's story first. Ten minutes later it was my turn to enter the office. She looked at me very calmly. 'I understand that you behaved very disrespectfully to one of your superiors.' She paused. I said, 'She commanded me to kneel in front of her and to apologise for my behaviour. I did tell Mother Superior that I refused to kneel in front of Sister Barbara and as she was not God and that as a nun she should practice humility.' Mother Superior turned away looking out of the window trying to hide her smile from me. I could see her shoulders going up and down as she tried to control her amusement. She asked me to go back to the class and come back in an hour by which time she would have made a decision.

The girls in the class were sitting just as they were when I left them. I told them that I had a feeling that I might be expelled. But I would always stand up for people who are being unfairly treated. 'I am going to stay with Jessica for her detention. Who is going to join us?' Everybody put their hands up. Not only did our class stay in but this news spread to the whole school like wild fire. The whole school, in excess of two hundred girls, decided to have a sit-down strike out of sympathy and solidarity with me, Jessica and our classmates. This action caused a major traffic jam. The big chauffeur-driven limousines from the various consulates that were picking up the girls from school had to park outside, so the whole street came to a standstill. Even the traffic police had to be called in.

Mother Superior informed me that I would be excluded for ten days. I could not help myself and asked the Mother Superior whether they would also exclude Sister Barbara too, for ten days. This remark did not go down very well.

* * *   * * *   * * *

I hoped to attend the high school in Jerusalem. Here I had a friend who I met at the bus station in the mornings. She too had emigrated from Yugoslavia. We were the same age but she was much more grown up than I. Gilda was the first girlfriend that I had in Israel. Every day after school we would meet up. I noticed her next door neighbour. He was sixteen, tall, with wavy hair, very beautiful brown eyes with long eyelashes, and he smiled a lot. His name was Elijahu. His family had emigrated from Bulgaria. My afternoon visits to Gilda became more and more exciting knowing that Elijahu would be there. Luckily Gilda had a boyfriend; otherwise I do not think I would have stood a chance because she was so much more attractive than I. She was blond and had tweezed eyebrows and her bra was filled out much more than mine.

Elijahu started to walk me home. In the beginning we could not stop talking. Eventually we held hands. This was very exciting. We had to be very careful that nobody would notice this. From the time we started holding hands strangely we did not talk. The highlight of our romance was going to the cinema, sitting in the front row for four hours, watching *Gone With The Wind*, holding hands and getting a stiff neck. This was heaven. My whole life had a different meaning. I had not experienced such happiness ever before.

As Werner had just received his diploma as a civil engineer, he got a job in Turkey with an Anglo-American company. So, I was told that in a month's time we were going to Istanbul where he was starting his new job. I did not want to go. I did not want to leave Israel. But above all I did not want to leave Elijahu. We had endless arguments. I begged my mother to leave me and let me stay. I was quite happy to be Jewish and live in the land where I could be Jewish. I had friends and this was where I would like to spend the rest of my life. As soon as I found out what my mother's plans were, I ran to Gilda and then to Elijahu. I just did not know what to do. Elijahu's parents said that I could stay with them until I finished school and they would look after me, whether the romance between their son and me continued or not. But my mother would not listen or entertain anybody else's opinion. From that moment on until we left Israel, I could hardly eat. I cried most of the time. I just wanted to die.

THE FLIGHT – DEPORTED FROM TURKEY

The Turkish policemen came one Friday afternoon, knocking at our door, with deportation papers and the instruction to deport me to the nearest border of Turkey. This could have been Syria, Iraq or Bulgaria, to name but a few. None of those places would have been safe for a fifteen-year-old single European girl to be left unaccompanied. Besides, none of those countries would have given me a visa either. Was I expected to disappear into the ether, or become a time-traveller? A very frightening predicament to be in through no fault of my own. My mother showed the policemen her old Yugoslav passport and my status on it, but he insisted that over the age of fifteen I needed to produce a passport in my own name. Even one of the policemen realised what a hopeless situation this was.

This policeman was a corpulent man, with a dark moustache and a gold front tooth. He was extremely sympathetic and helpful. He told us he had a daughter the same age as me, and if he was in the same situation he really would not know what to do either. He suggested to my mother that she should immediately contact the German Embassy. As she was a German citizen she should seek their help. The Germans were very popular and well loved by the Turks. He in return would pretend not to have found us at home as it was the weekend. He would then come back on Tuesday or Wednesday and by then hopefully my mother could make some arrangements with the German Embassy.

Being deported from Turkey as a fifteen-year-old girl was a terrifying experience. It happened because I had no passport of my own. As a fourteen-year-old when we moved there, I was included on my mother's German passport; I was 'and daughter'. Apparently up to the age of fifteen one is a child. At fifteen one is not a child anymore, and one needs to have one's own passport. All of this was news to us.

My mother had a German passport as she had married Werner, a German citizen, two years earlier. I was born in Yugoslavia, now a Communist country. At fifteen I was fully entitled to apply and obtain a Yugoslav passport. However, I would promptly have been repatriated to Yugoslavia where I had no one, no relatives. Those that had not fled had all been killed by the Nazis during the Second World War. Even to get a Yugoslav passport would be impossible in the short time available. In any case I was not thrilled at the prospect of having my own Yugoslav passport. A passport from any Iron Curtain country was not an advantage; they would not let you travel abroad as they were afraid you would not return.

It had been suggested that Werner would adopt me. If this had been possible, he would have adopted me long before I turned fifteen.

But at that time to adopt a child there had to be twenty-five years of difference between the age of the child and the adopting parent. Werner was four years Mother's junior; thus he was only seventeen years older than me and therefore he did not qualify.

My mother went to the German Embassy and managed to obtain a 'Laissez-Passer' for me. This consisted of a sheet of white paper with my passport photo glued to the top right-hand corner. 'To whom it may concern', was the title of this letter. This was to certify that I, Theodora Handler, was the fifteen-year-old daughter of Mr and Mrs Albes and that I was travelling to Munich to continue my schooling and would be met by my grandfather on arrival at the airport. On the bottom was a signature and a big stamp: Deutsches General Konsulat Istanbul and a signature from the Konsul himself. This looked a very impressive piece of paper.

Mother scraped sufficient money together, I don't know where from, probably she sold some jewellery or borrowed from someone. She had enough money to buy me an airplane ticket to Munich. It was not permitted to take any money out of Turkey except the sum that you brought in, which was noted on the last page of your passport.

As I had to have some cash on me, my mother unpicked the stitches on my dolls neck and folded several notes and hid them inside the doll's head. She then carefully replaced the stitches, so that no one could tell the difference. I was given strict instructions not to undo the stitches until I arrived at my grandparents' house. Then, and only then, was I to unpick the stitches, take the money out, ask the grandparents to help me change the money into German currency and give them the money. I was to keep a little money for myself in case I needed anything so that I did not have to ask. I was petrified to be found out. I packed my doll into the suitcase. It would look extremely odd for a fifteen-year-old girl to hold her doll in her arms.

The flights were not direct in those days; we had to stop for refuelling in Rome and stay overnight. The airport bus was waiting to take the passengers to the hotel before continuing the flight to Munich next morning. As we landed at the exit door the immigration police checked everybody's passport. When it came to me I produced my piece of paper but it did not seem sufficient for the immigration people. After the officer read my document suddenly there was lots of toing and froing. There was a big uproar and suddenly there were two or three more officials appearing. Where is the child? What did you do with it? He pointed at my special paper and kept on hitting it, this document clearly says 'and child'. I replied, saying, 'I am the child'. He read out loud, 'The document clearly states Mrs Albes and daughter.'

'I am the daughter'. This was all I needed; to be accused of disposing of a child. What did you have in mind, I asked, do you think I flushed a child down the chemical loo? You can check the plane. I wondered what else could go wrong.

Finally they worked it out that I must have been telling the truth. However, they refused to let me off through the immigration desk. This caused a great argument between the captain of the plane and the immigration police. Under no circumstances was the Captain or any of the crew going to stay with me the whole night on board. Nor did they expect a fifteen-year-old girl to be left on her own throughout the night. It would be unsafe and inhuman. It was an unbelievable situation. Finally the Captain had to sign a document in which he had to guarantee he would take full responsibility for me, and guarantee that I would be on the plane next morning with the rest of the passengers on the flight to Munich. The Captain, to me, looked like a film star. He had an aura of commanding authority.

After a long delay we boarded the bus. The rest of the passengers were not very happy. They could not understand what the delay was about. We arrived at this very luxurious hotel in Rome. I had never seen such luxury in my life: with marble floors, lots of mirrors, tropical plants, crystal chandeliers, and lots of people in colourful ornate uniforms bustling importantly around. These must have been the bellboys and porters.

The guests were very elegant. All this pomp was new to me. My eyes practically popped out of my head. I did not know where to look first. As it was evening they had obviously dressed for the occasion: with furs, jewellery, long skirts, tops embroidered with sequins, and high heels. The men wore dark suits and white shirts. What was most noticeable to me, people were smiling and laughing out loud.

After the meal in this luxurious restaurant, most people went into the bar downstairs where there was music and dancing. I was invited to join the aircrew. They were so nice to me; obviously they felt very sorry for me. I was too frightened. I thanked them for their kindness and went up to my room. Part of me wished I would have accepted the invitation but my fear was greater than the temptation. My own room had a big double bed, its own bathroom, lots of towels with the hotel's initials, and little bottles filled with all sorts of luxury items for ladies, such as bath oils, perfumes and shampoos. Again, this was new to me because I had never ever seen anything like it before. I had a hot bubble bath, I felt very grown up. I emptied all the pretty little bottles into the running water. The foam was overflowing out of the bath.

At breakfast in the hotel I could feel the searching eyes of the Captain. He gave me a little nod and a smile. I bet he was relieved to see me and that I had not disappeared. I wonder what would have happened if I had not shown up at breakfast. What if I had not woken up in time?

The same reception awaited me at Munich airport. The immigration authorities refused to let me leave the plane and insisted that I should stay and be returned to Istanbul on the same flight. How could they send me back if they were the ones who threw me out in the first place? Did this mean I was to spend the rest of my life on the plane travelling between Munich and Istanbul? They insisted that I did not have a visa and I explained to them I did not have a visa for Turkey either and that the document was from the German Embassy. I should be allowed to stay in Germany as I am more German than Turkish. I explained that my grandfather would be picking me up to take me to Augsburg. I think they must have taken pity on me eventually. They must have realised the situation was impossible. They put me in a little waiting room which I was not allowed to leave.

Having waited and waited, which seemed forever, through a window that was facing the airport's main building I could see, in the distance, a small figure approaching. I could not believe my eyes. This little person looked like an elf out of a fairy tale. He wore knee-high Lederhosen, grey socks up to his knees, a short little loden green jacket and a hat with something that looked like an upside down shaving brush – this was called a Gamsbart.

He was wearing a traditional Bavarian outfit. He had very bushy eyebrows, sparkling dark brown eyes, a shiny red nose and a great warm smile. He headed straight for the office where I was held. In all my dreams I could not have imagined that this was Werner's dad, my step grandfather. He was a very short man in stature, but when he opened his mouth he commanded respect. He was a no-nonsense person. An immigration officer with a loud voice approached my grandfather and started to lay down the law. My grandfather, whose height barely reached the shoulders of the loud, arrogant immigration officer, pushed him aside, ignoring his tirade, shook my hand, introduced himself, patted me on my back and said: 'Everything will be OK. Don't worry; we'll have this nonsense sorted out in no time.' His German was very strange. It did not sound like the German I was used to. I learned soon, this was a Bavarian accent.

I loved this man straight away. He was the same size as me and I was not even 5 feet tall. I was completely mesmerised. His clothes, his hat, a grown-up man in short Lederhosen. He really looked comical, but I felt safe with him. This very man is going to be my father if he adopts me – that means my stepfather would become my brother and my mother, his wife, would become my sister-in-law. This would mean I am going to be my own .... What? It resolved itself. In total I was to spend the best part of a year with my step grandparents in Augsburg before I was reunited with my mother.

But they were very good, kind people. Opa was a very famous oboe player. He was a member of the symphony orchestra. The story goes that during the war, at a rehearsal, the Nazis came and commanded that every Jew should get up and get out, because they were not allowed to play in the orchestra.

Out of solidarity, Opa got up as well and walked out with the rest of the Jewish members of the orchestra. He was very open about his disagreement with this kind of treatment. He was promptly put in jail for a while.

BACK TO ISTANBUL – MY DOUBLE LIFE

I had spent almost a year in Augsburg with my stepfather's parents, who were both in their mid-eighties, and were the nicest people I could have wanted to have as grandparents! But I started missing my mother very much. I was sixteen and having missed months of my schooling it was very important for me to return to Istanbul and finish my exams. The situation had not changed; I still had no passport and wouldn't have been able to get a visa. The only way I would be able to return was on an artist's visa. Luckily, my mother's inventiveness had not left her and yet again she came up with a marvellous plan. She was commissioned by the Istanbul Theatre to put a show together. She came to Augsburg and started advertising for singers and dancers to join her dance troupe. We were so happy to see each other, and the prospect of being together again after so many months apart was heaven.

The candidates for auditions were endless. Everybody wanted the opportunity to travel. It sounded so glamorous to have a job in the Middle East. I had to go through the full audition just like everybody else. At last my years of studying ballet paid off. My mother selected eight dancers plus a male and a female singer. The only way I could go back to Istanbul was as one of the dancers in the ballet. As such I would be granted an artist's visa and be able to continue my schooling.

Although I was very petite I was a versatile performer. Was this luck or Mother being clever? There was another dancer of similar size to me so we could partner each other. We had daily rehearsals. My mother was in her element because choreography and dancing were her forte. She was a brilliant choreographer, very imaginative. We managed to create eight routines.

The big day came. We were all to meet at eight o'clock in the railway station to catch the train to Istanbul. The tickets were ordered, the suitcases packed and my mother asked me to go and pick up the twelve tickets that were waiting in the travel agency. Everything was paid for. All I had to do was to collect the tickets. Everything went according to plan. As agreed, I phoned my mother from the first telephone box that was available and told her I was in possession of the tickets in my smart red wallet. Then I took the next bus home.

When I got home to my greatest horror there was no red wallet! We panicked. Straight away we telephoned the travel agency, thinking I had left the tickets there, but they could not find them. We immediately took a taxi to the telephone box from which I had phoned, thinking I might have left them there. Alas, there was no red wallet. Then we went to the police station and reported the loss of twelve tickets to Istanbul.

Time was ticking away and by this time I was suicidal. It was already seven o'clock. In an hour we were meeting all the people, ready to board the train for the lifetime adventure. The situation was completely hopeless.

When we got home from the police station, empty handed, I broke down. I couldn't see a way out of this hopeless situation. Without my mother noticing I locked myself in the kitchen, turned the gas oven on, knelt down, and put my head into the oven. I just could not face all those people at the station who had worked so hard and were looking forward the start of their new lives. And I had let them down. This thought was simply unbearable.

I can remember hearing the hissing sound of the gas coming through, then nothing. The next thing I remember was two paramedics who tried to put some kind of a mask over my face resuscitating me. I could not have breathed in too much gas because after I was sick I recovered quite quickly and did not have to be taken to the hospital. After a lot of persuasion from my mother I agreed to join the waiting company at eight o'clock. I was mortified about how the rest of the troupe would react to me.

At eight o'clock mother and I joined the waiting company as planned. Not only were the dancers and the singers there, but their friends and families. The press was there too, and even a small 'oompah' band to see us off. My mother had to announce the mishap. They could all see my tearful eyes which were all red and swollen. I must have been a very sorry sight. The train was already in the station. I was expecting everybody to be very angry with me but to my greatest surprise the girls were wonderful. They hugged me and reassured me that it could have happened to anybody.

Then one of the relatives had this brilliant idea: have a whip round. Everybody put their hands in their pockets, friends, relatives, dancers, and even some bystanders contributed. This was unbelievable. We managed to scrounge enough money to buy new tickets for all of us and with a slight delay of departure we were able to board the train for Istanbul.

* * *   * * *   * * *

We filled two compartments on the train to Istanbul. Not often had the passengers seen such a glamorous group of girls. This was a journey of adventure and great promise, from Germany to Italy, then Greece and on to Turkey. The train was an international melting pot and it was very exciting to hear people speaking in so many different languages, their voices singing;

rising and falling to the beat of many tongues. The journey took two days.

In Istanbul, the rehearsals started at ten o'clock in the morning. Surprisingly it was a good-sized theatre with a resident band which consisted of twelve musicians. The show was a mixture of Turkish artists: singers, belly dancers, comedians, acrobats and clowns. We were the resident dance troupe and main attraction: 'The German Ballet'.

The big opening night had arrived. I sat in front of a large mirror in the communal dressing room. Each little space had a chair, a dressing table, and a big mirror framed by light bulbs. The other girls were busying themselves unpacking their enormous make-up kits, but I just sat there, looking around me, feeling panic-stricken and realising that I did not possess a single item of make-up. I had never even worn lipstick before. I was nearly in tears, just sitting there. One of the girls noticed, came to me, and asked me what was wrong. I explained to her that I did not know what to do. The girls around me laughed in a friendly way, surprised. Then one of the girls simply took over my face. In no time at all two or three of the girls were covering my face in all sorts of creams and colours. Rouge on my cheeks, eyelashes, eye shadow and lipstick.

When I opened my eyes to see what they had done to me I could not believe what I saw. I looked like somebody else. I looked glamorous, and nothing at all like I usually looked like. Oh my! Was this really me? Even the other girls were speechless. My transformation was unbelievable. I looked like a real grown-up.

* * *   * * *   * * *

It took us some time to get used to the Turkish style of music but the girls were all exceptionally good dancers. We were very successful. We had an amazing can-can routine. We tap danced. We had solos and performed extracts from classical ballets. Our two vocalists sang German Lieder. Lotte was a tall, blonde, soprano. The male singer was a baritone. It has to be said that neither of them showed any talent but both were very vain. He wore thick glasses off stage but when performing he refused to wear them. Contact lenses had yet to be invented so we had to guide him to the middle of the curtain and tell him that the microphone was two, three or however many steps ahead of him. He was as blind as a bat.

* * *   * * *   * * *

I had always been stage struck and I loved every part of performing. One day I arrived early for rehearsals. I let myself into the empty theatre. Just one spotlight was shining onto the lonely microphone in the middle of the empty stage. This was for me like the moment I had been waiting for all my life. The mic drew me like a magnet.

I tapped it, I touched it. 'One, two, three. Testing, testing'. Yes, it was live. My voice sounded so different through the loudspeakers. I started to sing, but soon noticed that I was too close to the microphone. I quickly pulled back and continued to sing. Hearing my voice through the loudspeakers was truly unbelievable.

Then I heard someone applauding. This startled me. I saw a man approaching the stage, still clapping. I was frightened. I thought I had done something terribly wrong, using the microphone without permission. Straight away I apologised to the man who had not stopped applauding.

'How wonderful your voice is,' said the man, in a beautiful voice. 'What is your name?'

'Dorit.' I replied. 'I am one of the dancers.' I knew who he was. He had welcomed us on the day we arrived. He was the owner and director of the theatre.

'Well, Dorit, how would you like to have a solo spot? You can start rehearsals today after you finish your dance rehearsal. I will inform the band leader.'

I was so astonished that I didn't even thank him. I climbed off the stage. I had to run after him. I grabbed his hand, shook it, and thanked him over and over again. The impact of his offer had just hit me. I could feel tears trickling down my cheeks.

'No, my dear, I should thank you,' he said. 'Such a voice, such a talent. I will inform the printers to add your name to the programmes.'

There was so much to learn. I had to choose my songs carefully but I loved every moment. To be paid for singing was amazing. The reactions of my peers were mixed. Some were green with envy but others were very supportive. Even, Lotte, our resident blonde singer, to my greatest surprise, did not scratch my eyes out. But instead gave me a big hug and congratulated me for getting a solo spot.

* * *   * * *   * * *

Life was full of surprises. None more than finding an invitation from the police for every member of the troupe to attend the station. When we arrived at the police station we were ushered to a room full of young women, sitting and waiting. Everybody seemed to be very chatty and friendly towards each other. When the nine of us dancers entered the room, the other girls smiled and made space for us on the benches, so that we could all sit down. One by one the girls were called in. We had absolutely no idea what it was all about because the police woman could not speak German and the girls could not speak Turkish. When my name was called I was very frightened and worried because I had no idea what to expect. I sat down at the desk and a police woman took my details: name, date of birth, etc. When she was finished she pointed to the next room where a female in a nurse's uniform was waiting for me. Lucky for me I spoke Turkish. She asked me to take my pants off and sit on the examination bed. As she was talking she was putting on some rubber gloves. I refused to take my pants off and asked what this was all about. She explained to me that all artists and prostitutes had to be examined to make sure that they did not carry any venereal disease. Each week the girls had to come to be examined. They each had a little official booklet which was stamped to declare that they were clean. 'This does not apply to me,' I protested. 'I have no intention of having sex with anybody; I cannot possibly have a venereal disease as I am still a virgin.' She looked at me and gave a sarcastic remark accompanied by a smile. 'Oh, yes? All the girls tell me they are virgins.' There was no use protesting. I had to let her examine me, which resulted in my screaming and her pulling her finger out of my body with a most sheepish expression on her face. 'I am sorry,' she said, 'but you really are a virgin.' With this she went to her desk and stamped my new little booklet to certify that I was clean and added the word, 'virgin'.

* * *　　* * *　　* * *

I led a strange double life in Istanbul. During the day I was a schoolgirl in a light grey sleeveless tunic, white shirt, blue tie, navy knee-high socks, black shoes and with my hair in plaits. In the evening I was the exotic Dorita Lahabana. Once all the paint came off it was disappointing. All that glamour was gone.

135

My whole persona seemed to change once I took my make-up off. How amazing it is to be able to create a completely different image with a bit of make-up and some know-how. Looking at my reflection in the mirror I was back to being a school girl again.

One day in school, at break time, my French teacher approached me. He was a young Parisian, very good looking and most of my class had a crush on him. 'I need to ask you something,' he said, 'but we have to keep it between ourselves. Last night I went to the theatre and I saw your older sister dancing and singing. I think she has a beautiful voice. I have fallen in love with her. I know I shouldn't ask but do you think she would agree to meet if you asked her for me?' He looked me straight in the eye. 'You look a lot alike. Do you sing too?' (If only he knew the truth!) He continued, pleading, 'I would really appreciate it if you could do this for me. Merci Merci! And please, it has to be our little secret.'

My knees were shaking and I must have blushed. I assured him I would pass the message on and I was sure that my 'sister' would be very flattered. We left it at that. She never contacted him of course and he never brought it up again, but that did not stop my stomach turning every time I faced him in a French lesson. I was terrified of anyone finding out I was a dancer by night. I would have been kicked out of the strict Catholic convent school without being allowed to finish my baccalaureate, and then this whole charade would have been for nothing.

* * *   * * *   * * *

There was a lot of romance in the air between the German ballet dancers and the Turkish members of the cast. The Turkish boys were like bees drawn to honey. The girls were beautiful and glamorous with legs up to their armpits; most of them were blonde and very curvaceous.

One of the dancers got herself into deep trouble. She became pregnant, which was absolutely unacceptable. They had to find a place where she could have an abortion, which in those days was almost impossible. It was very costly, illegal and life threatening, not to mention that if my mother had found out it would mean a return ticket to Germany, without question. We all had to cover for the girl and took it in turns to look after her.

For a while we thought we were losing her. She had a very high fever and she would not stop bleeding. The logical thing would have been to call an ambulance and take her to hospital, but we could not do this because inevitably the police would have been involved and we could have all been arrested and put into jail. We had to tell my mother that Inge had food poisoning and we closed ranks. It was a horrible situation to be in. But she pulled through and a week later she was dancing as usual.

MY LIFE AS A DANCER IN THE MIDDLE EAST

As soon as we stepped out of the train in Ankara I could sense the excitement of this vibrant city. Even the word 'Ankara' has an exotic ring to it. There were ten of us, including my mother who was the choreographer and the principal of our dance troupe. We were known as the German Ballet Company. In front of the railway station there was a long line of taxis waiting for passengers. The taxis had black and white checked stripes around the cars. With our luggage crammed into the boot or on the roof, we managed to squeeze into three taxis.

The hotel was very elegant with lots of mirrors and chandeliers. There was a red carpet that led from the cars, up the stairs, right to the entrance. A very impressive tall moustachioed man stood at the entrance of the hotel oozing an air of confidence and command. He was dressed in a black gold-braided jacket with large epaulettes and gold stripes down each side of his black trousers. He had numerous medals on the left side of his jacket, and wore a black top hat. To me he resembled a circus director. The only thing missing was a whip in his hand to direct the horses in the arena. I could see how important he felt.

Men, on the whole, seemed to feel that they were a gift sent from heaven and every woman's dreams, especially the Middle Eastern men. Even the bellhops had an air about them, as if expecting our knees to tremble each time they passed by.

The lift landed on the very top floor of the hotel. As usual we had to share rooms. We had already chosen our partners. Soon after unpacking we were due for rehearsals. We were all very anxious to get to the club for it had the reputation of being one of the most elegant clubs in Turkey.

We could not believe our eyes. What a luxurious, beautiful and elegant place it was. The entrance, as well as the rest of the club, was decorated in art deco style. There were fully-grown palm trees in huge, symmetrically placed jardinières, crystal chandeliers, no end of ceiling-to-floor bevelled mirrors. Red velvet sofas and chairs were scattered around the highly polished white marble floors. Just being in the club made us feel important, elegant and special.

The twelve-piece band was already there when we arrived. There was no raised stage as the huge marble dance floor was used as a stage during the floor show, and for dancing after the show. The band was situated at the back. We had a couple of hours to rehearse our routines and to make sure that the band played the right tune to the right dance. This was sometimes problematic because European music was completely different from the Turkish music, both in rhythm and melody. This sometimes caused serious problems. Some bands were more versatile than others. This time we were lucky as the band was well accustomed to accompanying and playing European music for the international artists who performed at this club. Also it was fortunate that most of them could read music.

The dressing rooms were quite squalid but adequate. We were all prepared for our big night. This was our first performance in a night club, as up until now we had worked in the theatre in Istanbul. The audience here was only a few metres away from us, whilst in the theatre there was a safe distance between the public and ourselves. Wisely the management provided six security men at strategic locations. We found out later that this was because often an overzealous male would be overcome by the urge to grope one of the dancers. This would cause chaos. Some would return to their seats with only a slight warning and we could continue as if nothing had happened, but there were times when it took the security men to remove an over-keen fan from the dance floor.

We were a great success as our members consisted of trained ballet dancers, and our repertoire was very modern and varied. Our can-can was the most successful number. Our costumes were stunning, decorated with plumes, sequins and glitter. The girls were beautiful and curvaceous. Even though at sixteen I was less curvaceous, males in the audience could not take their eyes off us. There was so much beauty, so much talent. It was only in recent years that European dancers had been allowed to come to the Middle East to perform.

I retained my solo spot as a singer. Since Istanbul I had learned more songs. I was even brave enough to sing a Turkish song. To the great amazement of the audience, and me, it was really successful.

After our performance we changed into our party clothes. We were then ushered to our tables from where we could watch the rest of the show. We enjoyed being a part of this elegant atmosphere, people-watching and soaking in this whole new world which was like something that one imagined, never believing one could be a part of the pomp, the glamour, and the glitz. It was all almost unreal until a waiter appeared and asked Gerda and Inge, two of our German dancers, to go and join a group of gentlemen at their table. We were all shocked and surprised. The girls protested and told the waiter they did not know the gentlemen. They thanked them for the invitation but refused to join them at their table. After a short while the manager came to our table. He was very agitated and surprised that the girls had had the audacity to refuse the invitation. He pointed out that to entertain, drink and dance with the customers was part of the contract! The money that we would earn would be a percentage of whatever alcohol we consumed with the customers, which would be a substantial amount, but if we refused this would be a breach of contract and we would all get the sack immediately. As my mother was the principal of the ballet company she had a big argument with the manager and pointed out that this was not written in our contract. We were well-respected and well-known dancers in Turkey, and we were not prostitutes who would drink and entertain the customers. His answer was loud and clear, and by this time he was furious. Eventually we came to an arrangement.

We found out that the majority of the other dancers in the Middle East were not always trained dancers. They only used the title in order to pursue their 'other' activities. As a sixteen-year-old innocent girl being amongst prostitutes was a bit of a culture shock. I had never even heard the word 'prostitute' before, nor did I know the full meaning or use of this title, but I was soon enlightened.

Secretly I hoped I would be invited just like the other glamorous girls. I was skinny and only sixteen and a half, and I was afraid to be left out as a wallflower. How wrong I was! In no time (with another girl), I was invited to join a group of gentlemen at a table. This was the first time in my life that I'd sat at a table with a strange man, or indeed had an alcoholic drink.

I had no idea what to expect. To my greatest surprise the conversation was uncomplicated and turned out to be very interesting. The usual questions, 'What is your name?' 'Where do you come from?' 'Why did you come to Turkey?' 'What made you become a dancer?' and so on. If I am honest I really enjoyed it. I was complimented on my beautiful voice. There were comments like 'How unbelievable and surprising to have such a Big Voice coming out of such a tiny girl'.

The first man who asked me to the table was a well-mannered, well-dressed middle-aged gentleman and perfectly behaved at all times. He was also an excellent dancer. To be held in this manner by a complete stranger was a very frightening, yet exciting experience. I had never been held in this way by any man before. I wasn't sure whether I was terrified or whether I enjoyed it. All I can remember was that all of my body was shaking. He and his friend ordered a bottle of champagne for us to drink. The bubbles went up my nose and I instantly had hiccups, which caused much laughter as everybody found this hilarious. After the first two glasses I felt a bit giddy and light-headed. The gentleman realised this and ordered a glass of cold tea for me. This looked like whisky in the glass. He was a very kind man because in order to save me from becoming drunk he paid whisky prices for the glass of lemon tea. My first experience as a dancer/hostess was a pleasant one to remember.

* * *   * * *   * * *

Going out in the evening to a night club, having a meal, drinks, and watching the floor show, was the usual entertainment in the Middle East. The wives or girlfriends would accompany their men on special occasions. This place had a casino attached to the night club. Visiting the casino for the first time was the highlight of all my experiences so far. The shows were very high class in most of the places at which we worked. The artists came from all over the world. There were magicians, acrobats, fire eaters, sword swallowers, clowns, musicians, animal acts and singers. The acts of famous Turkish or Arab belly dancers or Turkish singers were particularly popular. Belly dancing was most fascinating. We all practised. I wished I had a bit of a belly, as without one it is not possible to get the right amount of wobble. These acts were called 'Ala Turka'. The house band was also amazing. It took a while to get used to listening to Turkish music especially if you had grown up with western tunes, harmony and rhythm.

I had non-stop requests to join men at their tables. Usually there were groups of two, three or maybe four men in the party, so depending on the number of gentlemen at the table the same number of girls were invited to join them. Sometimes single men came to watch the cabaret. There was not much other choice for recreation at night. As it happened, I enjoyed talking with and meeting people, but I made it a rule that as soon as I sat down with the gentlemen who invited me, I would point out that I was very happy to talk, dance and drink with the gentlemen but I was not going to sleep with them as I was still a virgin and I intended to stay one until I got married. I also pointed out that just because I am in show business it does not make me a prostitute, as this seemed to be the opinion of most of the men who came to the club. I did not want to lead them on, and if they wished me to stay with the knowledge of my conditions then that was fine; if not they could choose another girl.

However, many girls did sleep with the customers and made lots of money – far more money from sleeping with the punters than they were paid for dancing. We did make a good percentage from the drinks we consumed with the customers, almost double the amount of what we got paid as dancers. Champagne was the most lucrative drink to have, of course. If a waiter liked you and you encouraged your customer to give him a nice tip, he would look after you by giving the bottle of champagne a good shake before opening it. So with a bit of luck much of the champagne would have spilled from the bottle when opened and we would have less alcohol to drink.

I learned all sorts of tricks from the other girls. As I was the youngest of the troupe they all looked out for me, especially the resident prostitutes and hostesses. One of the first pieces of advice I received was to eat a spoonful of mayonnaise before I started to drink. This would line my stomach and I would not be so likely to get drunk. I was instructed to never drink any alcohol through a straw because this method would make the alcohol go straight to my head. I was also warned never to leave my drink unattended in case it would be spiked.

If you felt that the alcohol was taking effect on you, you would dash for the toilet and put your index finger down your throat to make yourself sick, then rinse your mouth out, drink black coffee or drink plenty of water. If you were sitting with other girls and one of you was dancing, the other girl left at the table would take the opportunity and empty your glass of alcohol into the nearby flower pot, the one containing the palm tree. You would return the favour. This made it possible to consume more bottles of champagne.

There were times when dancing became a wrestling match. Some men just acted as if they had more than two hands. Once they bought you a drink they thought they had the right to maul you. They would hold you so close that you could hardly breathe. The more experienced girls were very happy to give me advice and believe me there was plenty to learn. Not everybody was horrible. Some men danced beautifully, made good conversation and were well educated.

* * *   * * *   * * *

Once I established my situation I had a great time. Often I was asked the cliché: 'How come a nice girl like you is working in a place such as this?' I had to explain many, many times that I was stateless and that the only way I could finish my education and travel was on an artist's visa.

I was constantly surprised that any man would ask for my company. After all, the rest of the girls were glamorous and had feminine bodies. I was very slim; I did not have much on the top. However I did have long dark hair and green eyes. I was bright, a good dancer and singer and I had lots to talk about. The fact that I spoke fluent Turkish was part of my attraction. I was often mistaken for a native Turkish girl. Often I was even booked in advance for the next evening by the same gentlemen even though I made it clear that I was not available for sex. To my great surprise almost everybody accepted my rules and this even added to their respect of me.

* * *   * * *   * * *

There were three different ballet troupes working at the same time. The French ballet had ten girls, all tall, the same height and all platinum blondes. The second ballet was Spanish. They were very noisy, lots of castanets and stamping! Our ballet was a mixed lot: There were three German girls, one French girl, two Greek girls, two Turkish belly dancers, and me.

As it happened the French ballet dancers were staying in the same hotel as us, even on the same floor. They had the most beautiful clothes: silver fox stoles, lamé dresses and amazing jewellery. We were a bit envious of them. However, one evening we just happened to arrive back at the hotel at same time, about five o'clock in the morning; the French ballet and us. To our great amazement they were queuing, one by one, peeling off their expensive garments, the fur stoles and the jewellery and handing them all to the ballet master.

He was standing there, in the corridor, in front of their rooms, as one by one they handed their clothes to him until they had nothing on but their panties and bras. This meant that the poor girls did not even own the clothes they were wearing. It looked as though they could not go out or leave if they wanted to. They had no clothes of their own. These were the same girls who looked a million dollars at the club. They outshone and out drank our girls. I saw some of the girls in the club toilets lying drunk in their own vomit. The stench made my eyes water but this was an everyday occurrence. I got quite used to the stench, but never got used to feeling sorry and pitying the girls who let themselves go. Their boss lady would come and force black coffee down their throats, trying to sober them up so that they could go back and drink some more with the customers.

One of the French girls came knocking on our door in the early hours of one morning. All she had on was her skimpy little see-through nightie. Without her make-up she looked like a little girl. She cried and begged us to let her join our ballet. She told us how the couple engaged them in Paris. They signed a contract which stated that they could wear the beautiful clothes, work in a night club and dance. They had no idea that the clothes would be taken from them after each show by the bosses. The couple also took a percentage of what the girls were paid for drinking with the customers. The girls did not know where their passports were kept, which were confiscated on arrival. This poor girl's story was heart-breaking. If I hadn't heard it first-hand and seen what had happened previously I would not have believed that it was true. These girls were treated like slaves.

My mother took great pity on this particular French girl, and went straight to the French consulate in Ankara. She told them what she had seen and heard, and soon after the officials from the French embassy arrived with many Turkish policemen, and arrested the evil couple. They were fined and deported to France. Some of the girls also went back home to France, a few stayed in Ankara working as hostesses in the clubs.

ADANA

We had an exclusive contract with an artist agency for the Middle East. They were responsible for all of our bookings, wages and the venues we performed at. Our next engagement was in Adana, over four hundred kilometres (two hundred and fifty miles) away in the south of Turkey. Again, we had no idea what to expect. Our suitcases were loaded up in several taxis, and off we went on another adventure. I felt a bit sorry about leaving Ankara. There were so many places that I would have liked to have seen.

Once we'd left Ankara and its outskirts it suddenly became very bleak and uninhabited. From fairly well-surfaced roads we found ourselves driving along unmade, bumpy and very dusty trails. The further we drove the worse the roads became. The cars had to keep a big distance from each other to avoid the dirt and the sand that came off the wheels onto the windscreens. This road seemed to be endless. After a while the dotted buildings completely disappeared, and all we could see on either side of the road were cotton plantations. We could see girls in groups picking the cotton. When they saw the cars they would all wave, and we would wave back to them. There was hardly any traffic, the occasional bus laden with people. There were people riding donkeys. The poor donkeys looked so small between the thighs of their big fat riders. The men's feet were practically touching the ground. I felt it should have been the other way around! There were usually three or four donkeys following each other's dust trail.

The heat was unbearable. Every now and then the driver would stop at a remote little shack with a corrugated iron roof improvising as a roadside café. They would serve Turkish coffee which you could have 'sweet', 'medium' or without sugar. You could have hot tea, which was surprisingly thirst quenching, but we all went for the cold coke or iced lemonade.

Behind the 'café' was a very small wooden shack which contained a simple hole in the ground. This was the Turkish toilet.

We finally reached Adana. This place was a complete contrast to Istanbul or Ankara. The tallest building seemed to be the minaret of the mosque. There were no red carpets or porters awaiting our arrival, only a short, fat, bald-headed man who came out to greet us with a big grin from ear to ear, rubbing his hands together all the time as he was speaking to us, and bobbing his head up and down in a very subservient manner. He shook my mother's hand, introducing himself as the proprietor of this establishment, actually the only hotel in town.

There was no air conditioning, but each room had an enormous fan in the middle of the ceiling which was spinning round and round, circulating the air. In each bedroom we had smaller fans which would make the horrendous heat a bit more bearable. The rooms were clean but very basic. After our lengthy, bumpy, uncomfortable journey we could not wait to get to our rooms to have a rest. How we all wished we were not required to work that night!

Not only did we have to unpack our personal belongings, but we also had to unpack our costumes and iron them.

We did this every time we reached a new destination. The can-can dresses were the most difficult to iron. All those frills! I had to iron two extra dresses as I had my solo spots.

The 'theatre' where we were to perform, 'The Cabaret', was a godforsaken dump. Wooden tables covered by white tablecloths, and wooden chairs on parquet floors. This resembled a church hall more than a nightclub. The manager's office doubled as our dressing room. The so-called band consisted of six members. Only the piano player could read music, the rest of the group followed him as well as they could. Our music did not sound anything like the music they were expecting to hear, but the show must go on. Luckily I could play the piano, so I rehearsed with the musicians. They tried their very best but they could not get the sound quite right. After three hours of rehearsing in the unforgiving heat we were ready to go back to our hotel and sleep.

Our ballet was a great attraction, especially because it consisted of mostly tall, blonde, glamorous German dancers. In that part of the world we were a unique vision.

We had to drastically change our usual dance routine because of the heat otherwise we would have collapsed on stage. My solo singing performance was added. This gave the other girls a chance to luxuriate in ice cubes behind the curtains. It gave me the opportunity to practise and gain confidence to become the singer I aimed to eventually become. My repertoire was as limited as my costumes. I had a pale blue taffeta, strapless, short, cocktail dress which was embellished with a thick black velvet sash around my waist and an oversized big black bow at the back. I was singing a French chanson, 'Domino', and I finished with 'Istanbul Was Constantinople'. In between I added a Turkish song which I had learned, 'Usküdara Gideriken'. This drew a standing ovation and I became an instant showstopper. They were so impressed that I could sing and speak Turkish.

One evening an extremely overweight customer sat at the table nearest to the dance floor. He suddenly jumped up from his seat. His short fat little legs could hardly move fast enough to get to Trudi and grab her arm. Shouting at the top of his voice, 'This one is mine! I'll give you five hundred lira, six hundred if I have to!' He must have been one of the wealthiest cotton tycoons in the area. He took it for granted that we were for sale. The whole nightclub was in shock. The waiters, the manager and the bouncers, all came to rescue Trudi but this man could not be dissuaded to let go of the girl. It took six men to eventually free her and explain that this was not an auction to sell women. They were not to be touched, only to look at, enjoy the show.

Trudi was my best friend. We first met at the auditions for the Middle East tour.

While she was only six months older than me she was a fully developed young woman. She was also an excellent dancer. Looking at her I must admit my feeling of instant liking was accompanied by envy. I wanted to be her friend. This girl, Trudi, was five feet six inches tall, blonde, with a perfect profile, a great smile, and she had amazing boobs. She had a tiny waist and long, long legs. She moved graciously and her dancing technique was second to none. I was five feet tall, not much to show, and my profile was not something that I hoped people would notice. I did have lovely long black hair but my classical dancing came nowhere near Trudi's wonderful style. I suppose because of our differences we were drawn to each other and became inseparable. We complemented each other and also protected and stood up for each other when needed. To have a best friend who will look out for you is reassuring and vital, especially travelling in those circumstances and in such godforsaken places.

Trudi had a solo act as an Indonesian temple dancer. She was transformed into a gold statue with the help of gold make-up all over her body and face, including her bra and panties. On her head she would wear a very impressive pagoda-shaped headdress which was decorated with what appeared to be precious stones – in reality coloured glass. She would sit in the lotus position in the middle of the stage and graciously perform, almost in slow motion, an Indonesian temple dance. Everybody was completely mesmerised. After the show half the audience wanted to buy her. We almost had a riot on our hands. Perhaps they didn't realise that the gold was going to be washed off. As soon as Trudi was off stage we all had to help to remove the gold colouring from her skin as soon as possible. If it was left on her body for longer than the recommended time she could have suffocated. Her nickname was 'The Golden Girl'.

The whole company was worried about the behaviour of the men in the audience. More than worried. We were petrified. Maybe they were planning to sell us off? After all, we were far away in the middle of nowhere, in Adana. How long would it take until our friends and families would miss us? How would they even discover where we were? After this experience we had a police escort from the hotel to the night club and back again every night. We didn't dare to go out unless there were three or four of us together.

My mother had a serious talk with the agent, telling him if he ever pulled a stunt like this one again, signing us up to perform in a place like this, we would cancel our contract with him and sue him for putting us in danger. We all gave a sigh of relief when our contract ended. We hoped for better things at our next destination, Iskenderun.

ISKENDERUN

The journey from Adana to Iskenderun was by train, and was far more comfortable and interesting than our previous journey. We had a chance to look at the scenery while the train was weaving through picturesque countryside. The contrast was fascinating. One moment it was bleak and grey, with no vegetation in sight, the next moment there was lush greenery, palm trees, and here and there a dotted collection of dwellings. In the distance one could see camels laden with colourful bundles hanging on either side of the saddle, following a trail known only to the riders. Here and there I could see the sad little donkeys, which somehow always seemed to be weighed down by heavier loads than any other of the pack animals, like horses or mules.

On arrival I liked what I saw. Iskenderun was like a picture postcard. It was a coastal town, surrounded by mountains and green vegetation. There were even horse-drawn carriages, with the horses trotting along cobbled streets. I fell in love with this town.

The nightclub's main feature was a long, long bar which stretched from one side the whole length of the entire club, to the other. White leather bar stools were standing like soldiers guarding the precious bar. There were endless rows of bottles filled with different-coloured liqueurs. Three men and three girls worked behind the bar. A jukebox was blaring loud American songs. This club did not have the atmosphere of a Turkish nightclub because most of the guests were American sailors in their white uniforms.

The house band was amazing. They played all the latest pop songs, lots of blues, Turkish-style jazz. The occasional sailor would join them for a jam session. These boys could dance, and this is how I learned how to jive and jitterbug.

The American Navy anchored their ships and submarines here. The sailors would take their shore leave in Iskenderun. Each ship stayed for a different length of time, some one week, some two or three weeks. The sailors who had been at sea for over a year did not come ashore for sightseeing. Some were like hungry wolves, like children let loose in a sweet shop. There were some individual sailors who would have a few drinks and dances with the resident hostesses or prostitutes, but some were so eager that as soon as they came through the nightclub doors, they would zoom straight towards their target. They would negotiate the price and the length of time they would get for their money. The revolving door of the club never stopped. When the proprietor of the club knew a new ship had arrived he would call on the ladies 'in waiting'. The club owner preferred the resident prostitutes. He did not welcome or tolerate outside 'poachers'.

The floor shows were fun, as unlike the other clubs our audiences were young sailors. They enjoyed the show. This was the first time I had come across men who wore M.P. on their steel helmets, armbands with bold black initials: M.P. – military police. They also carried a big, thick wooden truncheon. These individuals were usually big, and would always walk in pairs. The Americans were very hot-headed, and the smallest thing would flare up into a fully-fledged fight. Then their friends would join in the brawl, often two M.P.'s were not enough to break up the trouble. The club had its own bouncers but often reinforcements were needed. These seemed to appear from nowhere, very fast. Once the brawlers were separated they would be taken to the waiting military van probably back to their own ship to calm down. At times fights would flare up more than once per night. It was far more dangerous when an American and a Turkish man started to fight. Knives would suddenly appear. Then both the American M.P.s and the Turkish police had to get involved. We were instructed to stay well away, out of sight, preferably locked inside our dressing rooms, and not to return until we were given the all-clear.

This club was regularly raided by the plain-clothed drug squad. The resident prostitutes also had a resident pimp. Having a respectable pimp seemed to be very much needed in such a place. He protected his girls from the often misbehaving customers and made sure the girls got their money, and would not get beaten up or abused. He was nice to us, too, especially to me. Hassan was very curious to learn about my story. Again, my perfect understanding of Turkish really impressed him. The fact that I was so young and innocent reminded him of his younger sister. Therefore he felt especially responsible for my safety. Any men, Turkish, American or otherwise, who made me an indecent proposition would find Hassan there, in a flash, to come to my rescue.

One evening, a young sailor came up to me. He looked younger than eighteen years of age.

'Hello ma'am.' He grinned and looked very embarrassed and sheepish. He must have had lots to drink as his words came out slurred. 'How much for a short time?' he whispered in my ear.

As I had never heard this question before I had no idea what he meant. Luckily for me Hassan was standing just a few steps away. 'Hey Hassan, can you please tell me how much I charge for a short time?'

Hassan's face turned as red as a tomato, almost resembling a grimace. He leapt at the young sailor, grabbed him by the throat. His nose was almost touching the poor petrified sailor's nose. 'This girl is not for sale! She is not here to give you or anyone else a short or long time! Get someone else!' I stood there shaking. I had no idea why Hassan was so furious. The poor young sailor ran out of the club with tears in his eyes. When Hassan did explain to me what the question meant, I found this very funny and burst out laughing. This incident went around the club like wildfire; in fact it was the joke of the week.

My singing was much appreciated in this club. The American sailors taught me many new songs and I had many requests for special songs and I loved every moment of it. I enjoyed dancing, especially with the younger boys nearer my age. The slow dances sometimes confused me, being so close to a man's body, swaying in perfect harmony to the rhythm of the beat. Being engulfed in strong arms, feeling the passionate breath of my partner on the nape of my neck was a new experience for me. I felt emotions and excitement flowing through my whole body. Sometimes I wished the dance would never end. My feelings confused me. I could feel a tingle running through my body. I felt I was growing up. I realised this and became worried. How easy it would be to give in to my feelings and what then?

* * *   * * *   * * *

Romance was in the air! Carmen was an exotic belly dancer who had attached herself to our ballet in Adana. Carmen was beautiful, with blue-black, wavy shoulder-length hair, black eyes, perfect features and pearl-white teeth. She was of a Mediterranean origin, but never revealed her background. She could not join in with our dance routines as the only dance she was capable of was her belly dance, so she had a solo spot.

A very handsome, tall, exotic looking American sailor walked into the club one evening. He took one look at Carmen and fell in love instantly. The feeling was mutual. The sailor originated from Hawaii. He was the son of a chief, or this is how he introduced himself to us. We, of course, thought: here we go again, another son of a chief, perhaps the son of a king. We had heard it all before. To our surprise his commanding officer told us that his story was true. Within two days of his shore leave he had proposed to Carmen. We had a lavish engagement party in the club. The engagement ring boasted a big, glittering diamond. The engagement party was a pompous occasion. We were all invited including his peers and commanding officers. His ship stayed in the harbour for four weeks. To our great delight and surprise the promised ticket to Hawaii arrived for Carmen. Our Carmen had hit the jackpot! This was every girl's dream; to be saved from the struggle, the drinks, the prostitution, and to be carried away to America, the land of promise. How wonderful.

Many months later after we had left Iskenderun we received the most beautiful dream-like wedding photos. They looked so happy, the perfect couple. Dreams do come true!

* * *   * * *   * * *

Before our contract came to an end I went shopping to the centre of the gold and jewellery market, which was famous for miles around. I did not have a bank account in those days. It was unheard of for a woman, especially one of my young age, to have one. Carrying cash around was very unsafe. So I spent all of my savings and purchased 22ct gold bangles, a ruby ring, and big, gold hoop earrings. I knew I could turn these items into cash if and when I needed it. I was told and advised by my 'advisors' that the best and most important thing I should buy was gold.

* * *   * * *   * * *

We were all very sad that our contract was nearing an end, and we would have to leave Iskenderun. Two weeks before the end of our contract a big German circus arrived in town. This was the greatest attraction, and people would travel for miles to see one of the shows. In those days they still had live animals performing. As the members of circus staff were mostly from Germany the girls were very excited to meet people from their own country. Instant friendships were formed. One of our best dancers attached herself to the handsome bear tamer and left the ballet instantantly. Another dancer fell for the circus electrician. She too left us. Lily joined the circus as she was an accomplished acrobat. Dancing had been her second choice. Understandably, the German circus was a far safer place to be than touring the night clubs.

ATHENS

The flight from Istanbul to Athens was so quick it seemed to end before it had started. Our contract was for a very high-class international cabaret just off Omonoia Square, the centre of Athens. There were at least eight or nine major avenues and streets branching off the square, which were crammed with the most expensive and fashionable shops imaginable. The accommodation we were staying in was more of a guest house than a hotel, and a lot cheaper than the usual hotels. We had cooking facilities and were allowed to use the communal kitchen. This made us feel at home straight away. While it was nice to eat at restaurants, we saved a lot of money this way.

As soon as we could we went out to explore the shops. We were lucky that the guest house was within walking distance from the club, and the shops were within walking distance, too. For us this was a shopper's paradise. Before we'd even earned enough money we already knew what we wanted to buy with our first wages.

Athens was a gourmet's paradise with endless restaurants, tavernas and coffee bars. It had the feel of the capital city that it was. At night the streets were lit up everywhere; the city never seemed to go to sleep. People would be laughing and singing in the streets.

We did not stand out amongst the rest of the population as we had done in Turkey. Here the women and girls wore make-up, had modern haircuts, and they were dressed in the latest fashionable clothing, so we blended in. Couples would walk arm-in-arm and could show their feelings for each other without being stopped, or made to feel that they were behaving improperly. In Greece to drink alcohol in public places was not forbidden. The work in the club didn't seem so hard because we could hardly wait for the next day to explore Athens with its shops. It had so much to offer.

* * *　　* * *　　* * *

By now my solo singing had become an important attraction in our ballet. I was a very quick learner and in no time I included a few Greek songs which often received standing ovations.

Our routine was the same as it had been in the other night clubs we'd toured in the Middle East. No matter how good or famous the act was, as a female you were expected to double up as a 'hostess'. By now we had got over the shock and embarrassment of having to drink and dance with the customers. As a matter of fact we were quite used to it and proficient by now. We had learned the tricks of the trade and made lots of money out of it.

It was fascinating to watch how fun-loving the Greek people were. When the band played one of the Greek folk songs men and women would get up onto the dance floor and perform their own special routines. Sometimes this would be a very complicated and skilful performance. Some men would engage in a balancing act, having a full glass of ouzo on top of their heads whilst dancing, bobbing up and down managing not to spill a drop out of the glass. Some would wave white handkerchiefs around whilst bouncing up and down on one leg, whirling round and round like a dervish. This would often be accompanied by a group of men encircling the dancer whilst clapping their hands and shrieking noises of appreciation. This style of dancing was usually performed at weddings and parties, exclusively by men. It was nice to see people being so uninhibited and being able to let themselves go with the music. When it was the ladies' turn they would all link together. One girl would lead and the rest would follow, copying her steps. I joined in with this dancing as often as possible, which was most enjoyable. I felt Greek.

* * *   * * *   * * *

When I first arrived in Athens I spoke no Greek at all, but within a few months I was fluent. Here in Athens I did not feel that my looks were standing out. I looked just like any other young woman. I had shoulder-length, wavy dark-brown hair, green eyes, and my nose seemed to be just like most of the Greek people's. This made me feel comfortable and relaxed. Throughout most of my youth I had to put up with jibes and rude comments about my long nose, not to mention the secret sniggers that constantly accompanied my presence. In Israel my nose did not seem to have a special impact, because many other people had been well blessed with a prominent nose.

I celebrated my seventeenth birthday in Athens. I had a cake with seventeen candles. My friends from the ballet came to celebrate with me, along with Franz, the young German mechanic with the wavy blonde hair and pale blue eyes, who worked for a German car company. I had met him when sightseeing with my friends from the ballet at the Acropolis. He was a keen photographer and was taking endless pictures of the ruins. He approached me and asked if I would stand in front of one of the columns because he would like to have a souvenir – a photograph of a real Greek girl.

Franz introduced himself, told me he came from Germany but had a contract in Athens. I was really pleased to meet a nice young man, and to his surprise I spoke German. We discovered we had lots in common. One of his favourite hobbies was ballroom dancing. For me, this was a big change. To meet a young man outside the seedy world of pimps and weirdoes who got their kicks from squeezing and fondling the dancers on the dance floor. He joined us for the afternoon, and we continued sightseeing. Before we parted Franz asked me if I would like to meet the next day to have coffee with him. I met him the next day he took me to a five o'clock tea dance. I did not know such things existed. Franz was a wonderful dancer, and he was very pleased that I was so talented. He, of course, had no idea at that time what I did for a living.

As our friendship and attraction developed I had to tell him the truth about my real reasons for being in Athens, and my profession. Franz was shocked, but once I explained about my situation, being stateless and without a passport being forced to travel on an artist's visa, he wanted to marry me to save me from the life I had to lead. He told my mother that he was earning enough money and could keep me, take care of me and offer me a good life. He said he would be quite happy to wait until I was 'of age'. He promised to buy me a mink coat of my choice in whatever colour I desired. The rest of the girls from the ballet were very jealous. At that time mink was very popular in Greece.

Franz was my first marriage proposal and I was very excited and flattered, but I had to thank him and explain that I was not quite ready yet.

PIRAEUS

Piraeus was the major harbour in Greece. American warships would dock there for the sailors to enjoy prolonged shore leave. The streets were crowded with the blinding white of sailors' uniforms and the numerous M.P.'s, walking in pairs and usually bigger than the average sailor. The M.P.'s were kept very busy because time after time fights would flare up for no apparent reason whatsoever.

In our wildest dreams we couldn't have imagined what a complete dump the next nightclub would be. Unknown to us the American Bar was situated in the heart of the red-light district.

The words, American Bar, were displayed in red neon lights over the door. As we entered we noticed that on the right hand side the bar started, and continued all the way to the end of the club. There must have been seating for thirty or forty people. On the left side there were rows of benches. The band was situated at the back of the long club on a small raised stage, with the space in front of it designated for the floor show. Near the front entrance there was an enormous juke box, dominating the club. This was kept on all of the time, blaring, full blast. You could hardly hear yourself talk. The name American Bar was an apt name as 90 per cent of the clientele were American sailors on shore leave. It was a very similar set-up to the nightclub in Iskenderun, except this was an open, undisguised knocking-shop.

Our dressing rooms were situated on the other side of a thin wall, behind the orchestra. This was very convenient. The band consisted of seven musicians, and a handsome male singer. He was extremely conceited. I suppose this went with the job. When I rehearsed my songs for the show he seemed to be extremely put out. He might have seen me as competition, but after the first few songs his attitude towards me completely changed. He came up to me, gave me a big hug, kissed me on my cheeks, and told me that I was a great singer and he had become my fan. As it happens, Kostas had a beautiful singing voice himself. He taught me many Greek songs. Sometimes we even sang a duet.

The audience was very noisy and rowdy during our performances. The waiters and the bouncers had a constant battle with the drunken sailors who tried to approach the stage to touch us, the dancers. Sometimes the sailors even tried to join in with our dance routines. We often cut performances short as it was pointless to prolong the dancing on such a battlefield.

Niko was the resident pimp at the American Bar. He had a dark moustache, piercing dark eyes, bushy eyebrows and receding hair. He had a no-nonsense look about him. He was slim and fit, and always dressed in a very smart suit. He took his business very seriously. He carried a flick-knife. I frequently witnessed Niko's dexterity when using it, which was on a nightly basis. Fights broke out without warning, usually between American sailors, and the M.P.s would have to get involved. However, when the Greeks and the Americans fought, knives were almost always involved. If a fight flared up inside the club, Niko would join the bouncers to get the fighters onto the streets, where the fight would continue.

Every male seemed to be very handy with a flick-knife. It seemed Piraeus was a flick-knife jungle. I was given a flick-knife by Niko, who insisted I carry one in my handbag for protection, and he also taught me how to use it just in case...

* * *   * * *   * * *

163

Our show consisted of our usual routine, our can-can, and then the banana dance which was a samba. I wore a costume that made me look like a skinny version of Carmen Miranda. This was an extremely popular number because our costumes consisted of silk fruits that dangled from our waists and several other parts of our bodies. The fruits swayed in all directions in rhythm to the sound of the bongo drums.

One of the attractions in the floor show was performed by Ninochka. She had a pigeon act. Ninochka was in her early thirties. Her costume consisted of a G-string made out of white marabou feathers and a teeny-weeny bra. On her head there was a marabou feather creation resembling a bird's nest which was attached firmly to her platinum blonde hair. She wore a pair of twelve-inch silver stiletto sandals on her feet. She just appeared on to the middle of the dance floor accompanied by some exotic music. She stood there with both of her arms outstretched, her wide smile beaming from one side to the other. Her ruby-red lipstick, and her thick long black false eyelashes, gave the impression that she was wearing a mask. This was such a contrast to all of her white marabou costume feathers. She looked like a Greek marble goddess, a perfect body, so white it was hard to distinguish between the white feathers and her skin.

The men in the audience waited with baited breath in anticipation of what was to come. The suspense was unbearable! She just stood there, motionless. Then, suddenly, two snow-white doves flew out of the nest fixed on her head. Each dove flew onto an outstretched arm, and then with a flick of her wrist the two doves changed from one arm to the other. This was repeated a few times. Then Ninochka turned elegantly and slowly around and around, and the birds flapped their wings until she came to a standstill. The slightest movement from Ninochka brought great applause from the audience. Then the birds flew around the room before returning to their nest on top of Ninochka's head; she bowed gracefully and the applause was amazing.

There were occasions when the birds did not do as they should, or as they were trained. Instead of the normal routine, flying back to their nest, they decided to have some fun and flew round and round, dropping poop all over the heads of both the musicians and guests. This caused chaos. Some people thought it was funny, others not so. From the waiters to the audience members and musicians, everybody tried to capture the birds, which seemed to be petrified from all the noise in the club. Ninochka would stand there, still, graceful, like a marble statue, by now her smile was frozen, but she waited patiently, not being distracted by the chaos until the two birds returned as if nothing had happened. The next act had to wait for the situation to calm down as the victims were desperately trying to clean off the bird deposits.

Soon Ninochka became very friendly with our girls. When it came to the end of our contract she joined our ballet. She had to learn a few routines; in order to fit in she just had to learn. She was not a talented dancer, but she did find a niche in our troupe. It was far safer to travel with a group of people than as a solo performer. She drank like a fish. She was showered with the most expensive presents from 'her men', and she had plenty of them.

* * *   * * *   * * *

The star of the show in the American Bar was the jukebox which played the latest songs from the Hit Parade. The sailors and the ladies of the night fed the hungry jukebox endlessly. This was where dancing for your decency and sometimes your life took place. The sweaty groping hands found every part of our bodies, often similar to a wrestling match. We would try to enjoy the dancing but it was quite impossible because along with the groping we had to endure heavy breathing. At times the men almost choked with their own heavy breathing, but worst of all was the fact that it seemed the men enjoyed demonstrating their excitement and their intentions. We were supposed to be impressed but some of us were repulsed, disgusted and offended. They rubbed themselves up against our thighs, bragging with their erections during slow dances. They believed they had the right to do this and to be proud of their arousal, which was easily felt behind the thin white trousers of a sailor's uniform. In my innocence I was not sure if such obvious arousal of a man should be taken as a compliment or as an insult!

This is one of the reasons I enjoyed jiving. I loved the rhythm of rock and roll, but above all I did not have to endure the groping procedure as this kind of dance was not suited for it. When a slow dance started I would often hide where I hoped I would not be discovered.

The American Bar had resident prostitutes like most of the other nightclubs. They came in all shapes, sizes, ages and nationalities. The customers had a truly international choice of prostitutes. By now it had become obvious to us that dancing was the last thing expected of us. The fact that we were all excellent dancers came as a big surprise both to the management and to the staff. Through this we gained respect and admiration. We all realised that our style did not fit in at all and we had signed our contract under completely false pretences. There was no way that the contract could be negated. Somebody would have received broken knee caps or even worse.

Piraeus had many seedy hotels along the quayside where rooms were hired out by the hour. It seemed to be a 'knocking

My mother, Zita Magda, in her improvised Red Cross Sister uniform – a perfect disguise that saved our lives many times.

Me at the age of six. This is when the landlady reported me to the Nyilas soldiers and I was taken to the pre-concentration camp sorting house.

My only crime was to be born Jewish.

Me at the age of seven. This is when we were captured in Pécs, where I pleaded for my mother's life with the German interrogator.

This is the *Radnik* – the ship that took the Jewish immigrants from Yugoslavia to Israel. This is the sad story of where the ship was not permitted to enter the harbour of Haifa, and where we floated for six days, not knowing what would become of us. The ship was full of children, and due to the lack of water and heat, most of us caught dysentery. We were only allowed into Haifa on humanitarian grounds.

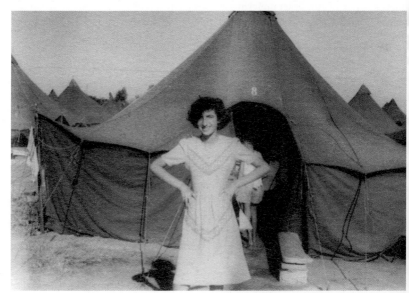

This is me, an '*Oleh Chadash*' (new immigrant), in front of the tent in Haifa on arrival to Israel, waiting to be re-housed. I was full of hope and expectations, having arrived at the land of promise and freedom.

Part of my double life – me as a dancer by night.

The other part of my double life – me as a schoolgirl during the day.

My first job in Hamburg in the jazz club 'Gallery Twenty-Four'. This is where I was discovered.

Checking to make sure that my plastic surgery had not reverted.

Here I am in the TV show, *The Seventh Man*.

Three weeks before my Desi was born. The gown was designed by me, trying to disguise the fact that any minute there would be two of us.

Me as a new mum with Desi. This is the time when I was arrested by the police in Hamburg for my mother's company debts.

Now I had become 'Dorit Wolff'.

My star photo and autograph card – this was the image of 'Dorit Oliver'.

Me, present day.

shop' paradise. Luckily for me, at the time I honestly did not know what was happening all around me.

The height of fashion at that time in 1953 was to own a mink coat. Those who could not afford to buy a coat made from a full-sized mink pelt could purchase and become the proud owner of a 'patchwork' mink coat. These were very cleverly put together from many small pieces of mink. At less than 10 per cent of the cost this was a very inexpensive price. I saved up for my dream fashion item and managed to buy my first 'patchwork' mink coat before I was eighteen years old! It made me feel like a million dollars. For all intents and purposes it was still a mink coat. The rest of the girls all invested in their own irresistible must-have fur coat. I was especially proud because I had bought it with my own money, which I had saved, instead of having had to 'perform' for it like many of the other girls.

Stella, the resident boss prostitute, took me under her wing to everybody else's great surprise. She had the reputation of disliking every other female who came through the door of the club, especially any female who could potentially encroach on her status as the 'queen'. On many occasions she jumped to my rescue when a sailor had approached me to seek my 'services'.

One night Stella took me by the hand and led me to the furthest table in a dark corner of the club. Her fingers had long, dark-red manicured fingernails. She gazed into my eyes with her own piercing and almost black eyes, which usually appeared cold and frightening. This time her look was full of kindness and caring. She told me about herself:

'I have been married. I was only fifteen. My parents arranged a marriage with one of my distant cousins. He was twenty years older than me. His first wife died and left him with three young children. His daughter was only two years younger than me. This is the 'done thing' in the villages. I had no idea what was going to happen to me. The wedding was a big celebration. Everybody was there, the whole village. There was dancing, music and lots of food. Everyone was merry except me. I felt as if it was going to be my funeral. The whole experience came as a big shock to me.

'My husband was no stranger to me as I had often seen him at family gatherings. He was the second cousin of my father. He and his family lived in the same village as my parents. Stavros was a farmer and a sheep herd. He had a big herd of sheep and goats and spent most of his time out in the fields with his animals. He must have learned how to have sex from his goats! He used to jump on me just like the goats did on each other. He demanded sex whenever I was near him.

'I was an innocent, slender, young fifteen-year-old girl. He was a thirty-five-year-old big bull of a man. Sex with him was very painful and I was very scared of him. He was not choosy about where he would stick his "thing". Any hole would do. Oral sex was his favourite. I almost choked on his semen. Many times when I had my period he forced me to have anal sex. I had no right to refuse his demands. If I tried he would shout at me and beat me. After two years of this unbearable torture I ran away. I could not go back to my parents because I had dishonoured my family which, of course, would not do in those days. The only friend I had who I could trust was my younger sister.

'I ran away to the only place I would be welcome – a whorehouse in a big city where I could stay with no questions asked. They gave me refuge and kept my identity secret. I was not the only runaway. I was not beaten. Yes, I did have to have sex but I got paid for it. People look down on prostitutes. The married women, the so-called "respectable" women, do the same things as I do. They are being humiliated too, beaten if they dare to refuse. Married women get regularly raped by their husbands. A woman has no rights where I come from, especially when it comes to sex.

'I have chosen to become a prostitute. Now I can choose who I want to be fucked by, and if the client wants to have a blow job or any other trick he has to pay extra. When I was married I was beaten if I tried to refuse. I had no money to call my own. I had nothing, not even dignity.

'So you see my girl? In my opinion there are only three types of women: stupid whores, who do the same for free, and clever whores like me who make lots of money! Then there are those who do it out of love. These are dishonest whores because they do it for nothing. These are amateur whores. Nobody has married them and nobody is paying for them, so they are very stupid, and if they think they get respect? No chance. Men respect what they pay for. At least they know what they are getting for their money with a prostitute.

'I have my regulars. They confide in me, cry on my shoulders, tell me secrets they cannot tell their wives, trust me with their hidden cash, and in return I make sure I'm discreet and stay clean. I satisfy their needs so they always come back to me and I like it this way.

'I do tricks here in the club, but on my own terms. I am in charge of the rest of the prostitutes and I dictate who stays and who goes. You see Nicos, there? I don't work for him – he works for me. He is my pimp but I do not give him my money. I pay him for the protection he provides. I won't let anybody ever be in charge of me.

'I have a car, a big, beautiful house and a live-in servant. I also have a fourteen-year-old daughter who attends the best convent school money can buy. Angela is her name. She is beautiful and clever. She thinks I am her auntie. It would be very embarrassing for her if she found out her mum was a prostitute, but this way we are very close and we love each other. She has the best of everything and I am teaching her that she has the right to say NO. Angela has the freedom and choice to marry whoever she wants to. I will make sure she will have enough money of her own that nobody can touch and a good education, which is most important to have. I had neither.'

Then Stella turned her attention to my situation, emphasising every word to ensure it sank in.

'You are a bright girl and have such a beautiful voice. You are talented, I can tell. I have heard and seen them all in this shit hole, my dear. You are too good to spend time with the likes of me. I am telling you all this because I have been watching you ever since you started here. You are different, Dorit! Don't ruin your life. Don't sell yourself too cheap. Don't look so shocked, my love. Everything can be bought. Everything and everyone has a price, make sure you sell what you have to offer to the highest bidder.'

A long silence followed. It was quite a revelation and an eye-opener for me but I took in every work that Stella had said to me and her wisdom stayed with me for a very long time. She became a dear friend to me while I worked in the hell-hole in Piraeus. She protected me from the gropers like a lioness defending her young.

Shortly before I left Piraeus Stella invited me for a meal at her impressive house and it was truly elegant. It was located in a very good neighbourhood and her garden was full of the most beautiful selection of flowers. None of her neighbours knew who she was or what her job was. Stella dressed completely differently from the person she was at night. She wore no make-up and her raven-black, wild, shoulder-length hair was neatly tied in a bun at the back of her head. She wore a highly fashionable black suit with a white silk blouse. Stella was the perfect hostess.

MARRYING TIM

The anticipation for the new adventure that awaited us was greater than usual. Cyprus was a very desirable and exotic island. Everybody wanted to go there. We accepted a contract to perform at an exquisite nightclub in Nicosia. None of us were sad to leave Piraeus as the experience of the American Bar was not something any of us would like to suffer again.

The moment we set foot on our plane it felt as though we'd stepped in to a new world. The stewardesses welcomed us with their pretty smiles and for a change in English. We could read all of the notices because we could understand written English better than Greek or Turkish.

We did not know what to expect but we were sure it would not be worse than the last few venues we had endured. We were looking forward to a new adventure, to learning about other people's cultures, to seeing the beauty of a different country and trying to soak up the local knowledge. Sadly we soon discovered that whilst the language and architecture could be different, once the punters entered the night clubs somehow the majority of them turned into the same unpleasant, groping predators. It seemed that in their eyes any female was flesh that could be bought. I'm glad to say that there were a few exceptions, but they were few and far between.

Nicosia airport was much smaller and far less busy than those in Athens, Istanbul and Ankara. The entire atmosphere seemed to represent the tranquillity of this beautiful, ancient island. Even the porters were laid back and very obliging. The taxi journey into Nicosia was not a disappointment. There was not much traffic.

171

On arrival at our guest house, which had been designated for artists, we found the rooms to be clean, friendly and very inviting. Our routine was always the same: choosing a bed, unpacking, ironing, and meeting at the night club for rehearsals.

The Roxy Bar was the night spot of Nicosia, and it was a pleasant surprise. The members of the five-piece band all read music and sounded as a band should. It was a pleasure to listen to them play, particularly the trumpet and saxophone players. My, did they swing when they played the jazz numbers.

After we had rehearsed our various dance routines it was my turn to rehearse with the band. We just clicked. They loved my singing and I felt confident that my performances were going to be great. My rehearsals lasted much longer than usual because we ended up having a proper jam session. It instantly became a mutual admiration society between me and the band.

Not only did I sing my solo spots, but when our floor show ended I would be encouraged by the band to join them long into the early hours of the morning, To my great delight and excitement the requests for my singing were constant and I learned, and learned, and learned. It was the perfect foundation to my future career because I was like blotting paper, soaking up the songs and their words. It was here I came to realise I could perform as a singer in my own right. I collected such a varied repertoire that from then on I was billed as a solo singer, separate to the rest of the troupe. I chose to sing under the name 'Dorita Ramon'. This name suited me because I sang a lot of Latin and jazz.

The British influence was everywhere. British soldiers were stationed in Cyprus. Many English people had bought houses and settled there. For all intents and purposes Cyprus was like a miniature England. Little did I know this 'paradise' was to come to a bloody end.

* * *   * * *   * * *

Our next stop was Famagusta. White sandy beaches as far as our eyes could see. Elegant hotels built on to the beaches, breath-taking villas scattered around, endless tavernas, little English tea rooms serving typically English tea with scones, clotted cream and jam. This was where I tasted my first toasted teacake. You could not get more British than that!

Famagusta was a holiday resort. If I was not dancing every night in the cabaret I would have felt as if I was on a permanent holiday. We blended in perfectly with the rest of the holiday-makers as we spent most of our time in our bikinis on the beach. We lounged on deck chairs, drank endless daiquiris and just enjoyed being alive. I could have happily spent the rest of my life there.

My mum and dad rented a bungalow right on the beach. The rest of the girls rented a large house to share. Not living in hotels or guesthouses gave us the feeling that we were leading a normal, everyday life. We all appreciated this.

The night club in Famagusta was also practically on the beach. It felt wonderful being appreciated as a singer. One memorable night I sang one of my favourite songs, 'Oh, mein Papa!' All the lights were turned off except for a spotlight shining on me. A young man stood up and played the solo trumpet part of the song, walking towards me as he played. The sound of his trumpet was outstanding, better than any of the trumpet players who had accompanied me in this song before. He must have been well known because even as he stood up the audience started applauding. We were given a standing ovation. Years later I discovered that this talented trumpet player was Kenny Ball, the future famous jazz musician.

* * *   * * *   * * *

The clientele in the night club was a mixture of English air force and army men who were either stationed in Cyprus, or had come for a short break, and local Cypriots. Although we did not meet this is where I first set eyes on Tim, my future husband, a signalman in the British Air Force on a week's leave.

I loved walking on the beach and listening to the waves that rolled on to the shore. As I sat there, suddenly the feeling of what might happen to me in the future overwhelmed me. I did not want to spend the rest of my life in sleazy, smoky nightclubs where I was exposed every night to lecherous advances. I was a smart, intelligent, educated and talented eighteen-year-old. It had become more and more apparent to me as I met people during the day, outside the nightclub, that I was almost embarrassed to admit that I was a showgirl in a nightclub. This work, of course, was frowned upon. The native girls and boys did not mix and party together except for weddings, birthdays and other social gatherings. Cyprus was a very strictly segregated society where boys kept to boys and girls kept to girls. They were only permitted to talk to each other in public if chaperoned. This was expected from the 'nice' girls. The more friends I made in Famagusta, the more I kept my night-time activities to myself.

One afternoon the bell rang in our home. It was a lady and a gentleman in their mid-forties who wanted to talk to my mother and father. The lady was dressed all in black and had a very pretty face. The gentleman had a suit on. They both looked at me from top to toe, grinning at me for no reason while I was calling my mum and dad. None of us had any idea what this was all about. My mother politely invited them inside and offered them Turkish coffee. They had brought a very large box of mixed baclava with them as a gift.

My dad could not speak or understand a word of Greek, whilst my mother had picked up a few words here and there. For a while we all sat around the table sipping our Turkish coffee. The couple looked at me, smiling and nodding their heads, and my mum and dad sat there waiting to find out the reason the two strangers had come to visit us, with a gift. This visit must have been important for them. The man wore a three-piece suit. He had a gold watch hanging form his waistcoat on a gold Albert chain, which was secured to one of the buttons. The lady was very bejewelled, with big gold hoop earrings, diamond and gold rings on her fingers and numerous gold bangles on her arms. The suspense was unbearable. Then the silence was broken when they started talking about their son, Andreas, and what a fine, kind, intelligent, well-educated, hard-working boy he was. They explained how he would take over the family business. They had a rubber plantation somewhere in Africa, which of course would belong to Andreas when his dad retired. This meant he would have a big house and a good enough income to support a family. They pointed at me simultaneously with grins on their faces, indicating the right person for Andreas would be me. It sounded like a well-rehearsed speech. A big silence followed. The visitors were both rubbing their hands and smiling in expectation, waiting for my mum and dad to jump up with joy because of such a fantastic offer. Instead my mum and dad jumped out of their chairs as if struck by lightning.

My dad was the most quiet, composed man I have ever known, yet his face turned red and his voice was louder than I had ever heard it before.

'How dare you come here and insult my little girl! She is going to marry somebody that she knows and falls in love with!'

175

He put his arm around me in a very protective manner. He practically threw the couple out and told them that as nice as Andreas sounds I was not for sale. In my dad's defence this was the first time that he had ever been approached in this way.

After that we had numerous similar approaches. This matchmaking tradition was called 'cenekesio'. Mostly these meetings went quite smoothly, but on occasion the parents of the potential groom became very insulted and angry because they could not accept the rejection.

Often my parents would have it aggressively pointed out to them that because I was eighteen and not yet engaged I might be left on the shelf as an old maid. All I wanted was to go to university and study. The prospect of becoming somebody's wife did not appeal to me even a little bit, especially because I would have liked to marry somebody I loved. Nobody I met in the night clubs where I worked had even remotely fitted the bill.

The urge to go to university had been growing, getting stronger and stronger each day. The only thing that had held me back was being stateless and not having a passport. After all, not having a passport was the very reason that I became a dancer, to enable me to travel. If I stopped being part of the troupe I would no longer be able to travel because I would lose my artist's visa. If I stayed for five years in Cyprus I would automatically be nationalised, thus becoming a British citizen. By that time I would have been twenty-three, a bit late to enrol in university. My only option was to get married to a British citizen, a marriage of convenience. However, if I was found out this would mean we could both be punished and face imprisonment. It seemed a hopeless situation to be in.

Every time I felt sad or upset I went to the same place on the beach where I felt I could cry without people witnessing my pain. Tim must have crept up to me silently because without hearing or noticing him he was suddenly beside me on the sand. He just sat there, looked at me, offered me his white handkerchief to dry my tears. In a very quiet, warm voice he asked, 'What can I do for you? How can I help? You seem so upset.'

I accepted his handkerchief, wiped my tears, blew my nose and without even thinking I looked him straight in the eyes and heard myself say, 'If you really want to help me then marry me.'

I don't know which of us had the bigger shock. Tim hearing me say those words, or me hearing my own voice saying those to somebody that I'd only had a glimpse of in the club the night before. The silence had to be broken and the young man needed an explanation. He asked, 'And how would this help you?' I explained the hopeless situation with my passport conundrum to him. I also explained to him that I had been accepted to universities in both Zurich and Munich. There was something very charming and likable about this young man. Perhaps it was his shyness, which was so different from the men I usually met in the nightclubs.

Tim was very easy to talk to. He was a very good listener. I found him attractive. He was tall, slim, fair-haired, with big brown eyes with long eyelashes and a perfect set of teeth.

We walked barefoot on the white sandy beach for miles. We hardly noticed when the sun set and it was time for us to part. I had to go home and get ready for that night's floor show. Tim asked me for a date the next day and I accepted. One of the attractions about Tim was that although he first noticed me in the night club he still treated me with utter respect when we got into conversation on the beach.

Tim had a friend called Austin who hired a car for the day and drove the three of us around the island visiting different villages, monasteries and churches. We had a wonderful time together on that day and met up every day to spend more time together. I had never before had the time, opportunity or urge, to spend that much time with a person of the opposite sex. We held hands, which felt very romantic, and one evening he even kissed me when saying goodbye.

On the last day of his leave, before he headed back to his job in the air force, Tim proposed to me. He told me he understood it would be a very difficult decision for me to make after only knowing each other for such a short time. He said he was in love with me and would be happy to marry me in order for me to get a British passport. Then I could go to university and leave the night club life behind. He wouldn't mind waiting for me, waiting until I got to know him better and hopefully I would fall in love with him as well. Then we could fulfil our marriage vows.

Tim kept his promise. Within ten days I had received a letter from the British Air Force officials. A British padre came to visit my parents and me, asking us all sorts of questions, wanting to find out the sincerity of my relationship with Tim. There were pages and pages of questions. He was reassured by both my parents and me. He saw I came from a good family and was a nice girl, quite suitable to marry a nice English boy.

Papers were then sent to the British High Commissioner who had to make a decision about whether our marriage would be permitted and accepted.

Tim and I wrote letters to each other every day. It is surprising how much of an insight one can get through letters. The letters between us developed into romantic love letters. When I think of them now, after all these years, Tim must have had a lot of laughter when reading my letters, as neither my grammar nor my spelling resembled English, as I know it now.

My mum and Werner dearly wanted to settle in Cyprus and

so did I. Once the contract we had in Famagusta came to an end we all decided to accept the final contract in Limassol. We had been touring for the last three years. Most of the girls wanted to go home. A few of them had saved some money, accumulated lots of clothes, shoes, and of course a patchwork mink coat. All of us had had a once-in-a-lifetime experience in different countries and nightclubs. We decided that Limassol would be our last engagement before we went our separate ways.

My mum and Werner were looking for a nice bungalow for us settle in to and to make it our new home. Werner got a job as an engineer working on the new Akrotiri Military Airport.

Within two months of satisfying the criteria for marriage Tim and I were married on the 13th March, 1955. I was just nineteen years old. Tim was given weekend leave for our wedding and our honeymoon. On our wedding day I wore a three-quarter-length white taffeta dress with long sleeves, and a little veil caressing my long, dark hair. I carried a big bouquet of white lilies. It was a church wedding.

Our honeymoon in Kyrenia, one of the most romantic, beautiful places in Cyprus, had to come to an abrupt end because Tim received a telegram from England telling him his father had died suddenly. He had to go back to England for the funeral. The air force gave him compassionate leave to attend. My marriage so far had lasted two days and three nights.

I was very proud of myself as I had fulfilled my promise to myself that I would marry as a virgin. I wish I could say that entering 'womanhood' was a wonderful experience, but sadly it wasn't. As fate would have it I became pregnant after the first time in my life that I had sex. This gave me no option other than to follow Tim to England and to put my ambition and hopes to go to university on hold.

STICKING OUT LIKE A
SORE THUMB – ENGLAND

As it was the end of Tim's commission he did not return to his job. Three months later I followed him to England from Cyprus to fulfil my duty as a wife and a future mother. Tim met me at St. Pancras station in London; we stayed for the first night, before continuing our journey. We took a train to a tiny village near Uttoxeter in Staffordshire. The village consisted of two pubs, a doctor's surgery, a post office, a 'Co-op', (where many items were sold) and an ironmonger. To my great disappointment the greengrocer did not sell green peppers and he'd never even heard of them. Mind you, this was the fifties.

I stirred up quite a commotion in this small, sleepy village. It was noticeable by the twitching lace curtains when I walked down the road with my mother-in-law. I admit I did not look like the average English girl. I wore my hair with a long plait on one side of my shoulder wore fashionable clothes, which had been prepared for me by a tailor in Cyprus for my trousseau. I wore stiletto heels, which were most unsuitable for the cobblestone streets.

In order to show me how welcome I was Tim had installed an inside bathroom and toilet. I had so many suitcases that I never managed to unpack all of my clothes. They wouldn't have fitted into the small wardrobe in the bedroom.

I must have been a great disappointment to Tim's mother, as my skills at peeling a potato did not meet her expectations. Neither was my housework or my general 'helping' good enough. It was quite obvious that Tim did not marry me for my domesticity.

Tim's elder brother Archie, who had now taken over the running of the family business building firm, would come in every day at ten-thirty in the morning, sit in the same chair as always and unfold a big newspaper, and have a mug of tea with milk and one sugar. He would read this whilst slurping tea noisily from the mug that awaited him daily. Both Tim and his mother joined in this ritual. I sat in the chair that was designated for me, being completely ignored by all three. They had an invisible bond. They repeated the same routine every day, never saying a word to each other and never trying to involve me in a conversation. I felt invisible. The only word that was uttered when Archie had finished his tea and just as he reached the door as he left, without even glancing at his mother or anybody else, was, 'Ta!', and he disappeared.

Once Tim's mother realised how useless I was she very politely refused to let me help with any household chores. Tim would put on his white overalls and leave every morning for work. I stayed in my bedroom most of the time, reading, as it was pointless to join Tim's mother. She had made it completely clear that I was not welcome, that she was very disappointed in Tim's choice for a wife.

The routine was always the same. Tim's mother was an amazing cook. Every evening at five o'clock there was a cooked dinner, with vegetables and lots of gravy, ready for us to eat. Again, there was not much conversation. Once the dishes were washed I was allowed to help with drying up, which I welcomed as this gave me something to do and broke up the soul-destroying monotony and boredom.

As soon as the dishes were finished, mother-in-law would start preparing a big tray of sandwiches which were cut in identical triangles. These were very tasty. They contained fish paste, meat paste, all sorts of different spreads which were all

181

new to me. She did not stop piling the triangular sandwiches on to the tray until there were almost too many. The tray was placed on the coffee table, next to the uncomfortable three-seat Ercol settee in the front parlour. A pot of tea, with a crocheted cosy, a little jug with milk and a sugar bowl would take their regular space on the table, plus three mugs, of course. This offered non-stop cups of tea, and the mountain of sandwiches which I never thought could be eaten. I was wrong. They would be gone by ten-thirty in the evening. Nothing broke the monotony except the occasional necessity when Tim or his mother took turns to refill the teapot with fresh hot water.

The routine was repeated day after day. My belly was growing and so was my boredom and fear for my future. Tim didn't have much to say for himself and I resented deeply the way his brother and mother spoke to him as if he was a servant, the lowest of the low in the hierarchy of his family.

As soon as Tim had exchanged his smart air force uniform for civilian clothes he left his self-esteem behind. He had changed, sadly not for the better. I overheard a loud conversation, more of a telling off by his mother.

'What on earth possessed you to marry this girl? She has obviously never done any housework. She can't even cook! Just look at her long nails! I even had to give you the money to buy the engagement ring. Now she is pregnant. Are you sure the brat is yours?'

I heard all of those words. I could feel the tears running down my cheeks. I am not sure if I was sad or outraged. All I know is that I opened the door where the 'conversation' was taking place, removed my engagement ring from my finger and hurled it at Tim.

'Yes. The "brat" is Tim's, unfortunately, but don't worry, I'm sending a telegram to my mother asking her to send me a return ticket home. I know I'm not welcome here, nor is my baby. I will be out of here as soon as possible.'

Neither of them knew how to answer. I didn't hang around to find out. Tim ran up the stairs, following me. He pleaded and begged me to stay. He told me he loved me and couldn't live without me. He would do anything to make me not leave him. He said he would look for a new place for us to live. None of that changed my mind. I was determined to go back to Cyprus.

From that moment on I hardly left our bedroom and I didn't eat with them. I couldn't bear to spend a single moment in a place where I was so unwanted. I lived on cream crackers and sandwich spread, which I would buy next door at the little grocery store.

I was eagerly awaiting the postman to bring the letter from my mother with the return ticket. As I heard the postman knocking on the front door, I rushed from the bedroom. The prospect of getting the letter and the ticket was overpowering. I was so excited. I lost my balance, and fell down the flight of stairs. As I landed I started to bleed. The blood was gushing out of me. I was six months pregnant. I couldn't move and the pain was excruciating. The ambulance was called. I was taken to the nearest hospital which was in Nottingham. I was taken to the maternity ward. The bleeding couldn't be stopped and the pain got worse and worse. The ambulance man put some kind of mask on my face. I awoke in the operating theatre surrounded by doctors and nurses. Somebody was holding my hand.

I heard a female voice: 'I'm so sorry, my dear. You lost your little baby boy. We could not save him. We did try. He was very tiny and you are very young. Don't worry. You will have as many babies as you want.'

All the talk and what had happened to me did not register in my head. I cried, both from the pain and the sadness that my baby boy had died.

I spent a few days in hospital where I was bombarded with kind advice from the other ladies. They all thought I was fifteen years old and felt very protective towards me. They didn't realise that I was nineteen, and married! I couldn't help weighing up the situation and thinking perhaps this was a decision from a higher power which was telling me not to become a mum too early. What kind of a future could I have offered my son here? But all the reasoning couldn't stop me mourning the little boy I had been carrying for the last six months.

It was a relief to find that on being discharged from the hospital an envelope, with my return ticket to Cyprus, was waiting for me. I was still very weak, physically and emotionally. I only packed one suitcase with my personal things. I took the first available train to London; went straight to Heathrow airport and boarded the first plane flying out to Cyprus.

After much misery and pain I was the proud owner of a British passport, the most precious possession of my life. I had a choice of where to travel. I could choose which university I would enrol in. I had offers from Zurich University and from Munich University. After much consideration I decided to choose Munich. Having spent nearly a year in Augsburg with my step-grandparents my German was almost fluent. Munich and Augsburg were only one hour apart, which added a bit of security in my mind.

SCHWABING, MUNICH

I had been to Germany before: the Bavarian town of Augsburg. At that time I was fifteen years old and had no passport. I was travelling on a document issued by the German Embassy in Istanbul. What a different reception I was given by the German authorities upon showing my British passport at Munich.

The university had a list of student 'digs'. I looked at a few but none of them were what I was really looking for. The first accommodation I stayed in was in Schwabing with a grumpy old landlady who had two old, overfed Dachshunds. These dogs were so fat that when they waddled along, their stomachs polished the floor. My room was very small and dark. It had a little coal heater and it was so very cold. I did not have enough money to buy coal so in order to keep warm I stayed in bed as much as possible. I even wore gloves to stop my fingers from freezing. I was not offered cooking facilities. What completely put me off that miserable place was when I discovered that the landlady was bathing the fat dogs in the same communal bathtub as the students. That was it.

Schwabing was the Bohemian part of Munich. It was full of little jazz clubs and bars. There seemed to be music everywhere. Just the place for me. I felt like I was in paradise. The most amazing jazz sounds could be heard at one of the clubs, called Nacht Keuzchen. I was drawn like a magnet to go inside, almost like I sleep-walked my way in. I was with a small group of students who took it upon themselves to introduce me to the night-life.

The band that played inside Nacht Keuzchen consisted of four young, amazing musicians. After my first glass of wine I could hardly wait to ask the band if I could join them and sing a song. They agreed. After just one song, they realised I was not just another walk-in customer who thinks she can sing. The proprietor approached me and offered me a job to sing there. He told me he couldn't pay me much, but he offered me a hot meal every night and a small percentage from the door takings. That evening I had one of the best meals I had ever had in Munich. After only spending one month in Munich I had a job.

After hearing about my terrible digs, one of the band members, Martin, the drummer, gave me the address of his girlfriend, who was looking to share a flat. She was a young woman called Gretchen who owned a shop that sold designer hats. Gretchen was a typical young Bavarian – a jolly, blonde, full-figured twenty-three-year-old who owned her own business. I was twenty, slim, dark haired, and didn't even know how to boil an egg. We were opposites in both personalities and looks, which seemed to attract us to each other. We struck up an instant friendship. Gretchen made me feel at home from the first day onwards.

My room was large and sunny, like one of today's bedsits. We shared a kitchen and a bathroom and I was permitted to bring friends home. The flat was left to Gretchen when her mother moved out to live with her new boyfriend. This was the reason Gretchen needed a flatmate – for company and to share expenses.

I wanted to show off my independence so I invited my grandparents from Augsburg to cook a meal for them. I thought Grandma would be so proud when she saw all her hard work, teaching me how to be a good housewife, had paid off. Roast chicken with roast potatoes, and cucumber salad with sour cream. The only thing I bought was a lovely chocolate cake. It would have been pushing my luck to claim I had made that! I did everything, as far as I could remember, that my grandma had taught me regarding a roast chicken. I used tweezers to remove any remaining feathers. I cut off its head and feet, washed it in warm water, then I rubbed it with salt. I placed it in a baking tray, covered it with cooking oil and put it in to the preheated oven, making sure I turned it every twenty minutes in order to cook it evenly. I remembered that I had to boil the peeled potatoes first and only when it was easy to push the fork into the potatoes were they ready. I placed them around the half-cooked chicken in the baking tin to give them a nice brown colour, the same as the chicken. I ensured the browning was even by frequent turning.

I was very surprised that the longer the chicken was in the oven the more it started to smell of fish rather than chicken. As it was the first time I had ever prepared a meal like this I was not sure how a homemade roast chicken should smell. I opened a window. I set the table beautifully and my grandparents arrived in good time.

The four of us sat around the table. The chicken and roast potatoes looked perfect. With my oven gloves I managed to place the magnificent sight in the centre of the table. I passed a carving knife and fork to my grandmother, showing her the necessary respect. I couldn't help noticing her nostrils twitched a bit but she made no remark and was ready for the carving ceremony. As soon as she opened the chicken up the smell became strong and unbearable. It soon became obvious I had missed out one of the most important tasks. My grandmother pointed out that the smell was due to me failing to clean out the giblets from the chicken. It had never even occurred to me there would be something to remove from inside the chicken. I had never seen a chicken not served up by a waitress.

Of course I cried because I was so embarrassed. I so wanted to show Grandma my appreciation for all the hard work and time she had put in trying to make a perfect house-frau out of me. Both her and Grandpa just shook their heads and laughed until the tears rolled down their cheeks. Grandma put her arms around me and stroked my hair, assuring me it was a good thing I'd made the mistake when she was here, impressing on me it was a very important lesson in life as it would never happen to me again.

* * *   * * *   * * *

I enrolled in the language department of the university. My subjects were English, international law and interpreting. I interpreted from English to German and from German to English. It was very strenuous to be on time for lectures and to stay awake during lessons because I spent most nights singing in the jazz club which left only a few hours for sleep.

At university I befriended Christian, a very attractive young man who was four years my senior. He was tall, handsome and extremely intelligent. He already had two doctorates, one in journalism and the other in history of art. I became his protégé. He introduced me and educated me in a cultural life which I hadn't had the opportunity to pursue until then. He took me to see exhibitions by Kockoshka, Chagal, Degas, Picasso and Van Gogh, and many more painters. He took me to debating societies which I found very difficult at first. I learned that other people had the right to an opinion, which was an eye opener for me. We went to many parties. The 'Fasching' carnival was especially nice because people would dress up. Christian was perfect. He introduced me to a whole new world which I soon felt a part of, from 'Karnival' to 'Oktoberfest'. I realised how much I had missed.

* * *   * * *   * * *

Although my mother helped to support me, I subsidised my expenses by earning money through my singing. I soon became well known on the jazz scene. Offers to sing started to come my way. I'd started by literally singing for my supper but it had quickly escalated.

I secured a contract to sing in an American NCO club with a nine-piece band. There was no comparison between the high quality of the musicians in Germany and the previous musicians I had worked with. As far as the fights were concerned nothing had changed. The drunken American soldiers fought each other just as viciously as the sailors in Piraeus. The only difference was the colour of the uniforms. Instead of white these soldiers had khaki uniforms. Every time a fight broke out, which was more than once per night, the band would play 'When the Saints Go Marching In', which was a signal for the M.P.s to rush in to the club, truncheons in hand, to break up the fights. When that happened I had to be ushered in to my dressing room and bolt it from the inside for my safety. When the fights were over, the tables and chairs that were not broken were put back in to place, the broken glass was swept up and we continued playing and singing as if nothing had happened.

The price of popularity was already becoming clear to me. On New Year's Eve I was booked well in advance. The pay rose astronomically. In Germany New Year's Eve, combined with the American servicemen's celebrations, was one of the biggest events of the year. I sung in an Officers Club with a twelve-piece band. The sound of popping champagne corks was non-stop. There was smooch dancing, great jiving and endless requests for songs. The atmosphere was electric.

Come midnight people were hugging and kissing and wishing each other a happy new year. I was not only included in the Happy New Year wishes but became the centre of them as a big mob of well-wishers surrounded me. Unfortunately their eagerness burst into a large fight. I was not prepared to be pulled around like a rag doll for each and every one of the soldiers to kiss me on the lips and force their tongues down my throat. To me it felt like a lynching. Members of the band came to my aid and had to pull these kissing and groping machines off me, but twelve musicians against a group of fifty or so GIs was not a fair contest. The musicians who were not involved in defending me started to play 'When the Saints Go Marching In' to give the signal to the Military Police for help. Luckily the management had also alerted them and six big M.P.s, with truncheons ready, came to my aid. They quickly escorted me to the security of their jeep. On the way to the jeep a waiter handed me a white tablecloth which I wrapped around myself as there was very little left of my beautiful evening gown. My dress was torn to shreds. Parts of it were kept as souvenirs by the crazed fans.

The next day the management of the club gave me a big bouquet of flowers and a letter of apology. They arranged for two Military Policemen to be there at all times while I was performing and even arranged guards for my dressing room which was often invaded by unwanted visitors. It was a frightening and memorable period of my life.

The money was good and I had contracts offered to me to tour American clubs for a year in advance. It was getting too difficult to work until 4am and then to study while falling asleep during lectures. Some of the lecturers even had to wait for me before starting at nine o'clock because I was frequently late. My lateness became a joke. As singing was my life and my ultimate ambition, I had to weigh up my options. Did I want to become an interpreter to a high-ranking politician, or a professional singer? I recalled the advice that Stella, the House Madam, had given me and realized that as an interpreter if my boss pinched my bottom I couldn't complain for fear of being fired. As a singer if somebody pinched my bottom I could slap them around the face! I had the privileged opportunity to fulfil my childhood dream, singing and performing, and would even be paid for it. In my mind there was no competition. I accepted every contract that gave me an opportunity to further my singing career.

* * * * * * * * *

Working in clubs in Germany was nothing like being a dancer in the Middle East. Here I was appreciated and respected as a singer, as had always been my aim in life. The gropers did not disappear but I now had the freedom to choose who I could be groped by, and I was very choosey indeed.

There were many singing competitions to join big bands. I entered as many as I possibly could and I won several. The prizes varied, from a bunch of flowers to a bottle of champagne. If you were really lucky an agent would be listening and you could get offered a spot with a famous band or on a radio station. It was all good experience. I entered one of the bigger competitions that were run by a very famous band leader whose name I shouldn't mention. I was voted the winner by the public and the band leader complimented me on my voice and timbre. He suggested I 'keep my day job' because whilst I had an amazing voice, with a nose like mine there was very little chance of me ever becoming a star. Without realising it that man actually made me into a star. He gave me the strength to pursue my dream even more vigorously. I felt gutted by his comments. It was one of the biggest put-downs I had ever experienced; especially as he announced his opinions through the microphone. The audience booed him. I told him then and there, whilst I appreciated his advice, I would prove him wrong.

That was another big turning point in my life. I could have taken his advice. I remembered all the times when I was a little girl, frightened, hungry and hiding, when my singing had kept me alive. Who was that fat red-faced monster to rob me of my lifetime dream? I had proved I could sing because people paid me to do so. No, he was wrong, I thought. If nothing else I would make him eat his words backwards and regret how deeply he had hurt me. I would be a star!

* * *   * * *   * * *

My twenty-first birthday was approaching, which brought big excitement and preparation. I was supposed to 'come of age'. My friends were arranging a big party for me. There wasn't a better place to have the party than the apartment I was sharing with Gretchen. I was permitted to invite a few people of my choice but apart from that the party was arranged by Gretchen and Christian. All I had to do was get there and celebrate.

Gretchen insisted on making a special dress for me for my birthday as one of her presents. We chose a thin, woollen blue material and in no time, after only two fittings, there it was! A unique and beautiful creation: a skin tight dress with long sleeves and a high neck collar. A zip was fixed on the back of the dress, running to well below my waist. Only with great difficulty could I be poured into this marvellous dress. With my dark brown, wavy hair which reached to the middle of my back and oversized earrings with turquoise gemstones, I made a perfect, stunning birthday girl. Not only did I like what I saw but Christian couldn't take his eyes off me either.

My life in Schwabing was great and seemed well-balanced. I lived in a beautiful apartment. Gretchen and I had become close friends. Having Christian in my life had given me stability and I felt secure in his company. Just thinking of him made my heart beat faster. He was very kind and thoughtful. I never felt that I needed to protect myself from him in any way because he had proved himself over and over again. His love and care towards me was never selfish. He was my best friend. Although Christian and I were extremely close and had a sensual and passionate relationship, we never became 'lovers'. We were responsible people who couldn't justify the consequences so we always stopped ourselves just in time...

Everything was prepared with so much care and good taste. Flower decorations, sandwiches, balloons and candles. My two best friends had created a lavish spread for me. The guests started arriving in couples and groups, each bringing a bottle or two. Music was playing on the record player and the candles gave the party a festive atmosphere.

By ten-thirty in the evening the party was well underway. Then the front door bell rang and Christian opened it. He approached me with a very serious expression on his face but he remained calm. He asked me to follow him to the front door, telling me I had a very special guest. There he was, dressed in a smart navy blazer with gold buttons, grey flannel trousers and highly polished shoes. He had his usual charming, somewhat shy smile plastered on to his face.

'Happy birthday, darling!'

He gave me a big hug. I couldn't move. I wished the earth would open up so I could disappear, but life is not so simple and obliging. I managed to wriggle out of his most unwelcome embrace and turned to Christian.

'This is Tim, my estranged husband.'

'I know,' Christian replied, 'he has already introduced himself.'

The three of us returned to the party. Luckily the loudness of the music and laughter made it easy for us to blend in without causing a big disruption. Only Christian, Gretchen and I knew who the new arrival was. To everybody else he was just another party guest. I really had no idea what to do. Having not had any contact with Tim for the last two years I simply could not understand how he had found out where I was. My happy mood was turned around instantly as soon as I saw him standing at the door. I could feel a strange tremble in my body and an overwhelming fear. What does he want?

Christian, once again, surpassed all expectations. He took over looking after Tim, as he spoke perfect English. They had no problem communicating. With his usual charm and calm manner Christian prevented me from jumping from the third-floor window out of desperation. I avoided every opportunity to be alone with Tim. Eventually he cornered me.

He handed me a beautiful twenty-two-carat gold Tissot wristwatch.

'This is for your twenty-first birthday, darling,' he said. 'You look even more stunning than I remember. A day hasn't passed since you left that I didn't think of you and wanted you back.'

I could see tears rolling down his cheeks as he spoke. Hardly anybody at the party was aware of what was happening. They were too busy having a good time. Tim showed no signs of wanting to leave.

Yet again it was Christian, my beautiful, lovely man, who saved me from the awkward situation by inviting Tim to stay with him in his home. This was not how I had wanted to spend my birthday night! In hindsight maybe it was just as well. Would Christian have stayed the night? Who knows?

On parting I asked Tim to grant me a divorce because I was not going back to England, nor did I want to be his wife. I reminded him of the arrangement we had made when he first asked me to marry him. He didn't answer. He didn't stop crying.

As the front door shut I thought to myself, 'Happy Birthday, Dorit!' At that moment, as I stood there wondering how Tim had found me, there was nothing I wanted more than to be safe in the arms of Christian.

Tim contacted me the next day and insisted we meet. To avoid potential altercations I ensured we met in a public place, a coffee house. To onlookers we appeared to be an average young couple enjoying coffee and cakes. The reality was quite different. Tim refused to agree to a divorce. I kept reminding him of our original agreement as nicely as possible. I repeatedly told him how grateful I was for him enabling me to get my passport and that I would always be in his debt for opening the doors to the world for me. I told him I would do anything to repay his kindness other than live with him as his wife. I tried to make him understand that I enjoyed the life I now had and if it was not for me falling pregnant I would not have followed him to England. I said I was still mourning and heartbroken about the loss of our son.

Tim didn't hear or didn't want to hear any of my reasoning. He kept on pleading, begging me to give our marriage another chance. He said he would never give me a divorce and told me if he couldn't have me then nobody else would. Our planned calm coffee and cakes did not stay calm for long. Tim grabbed my hands and fell to his knees, insisting that I was his wife and he had rights as my husband. I had to get away, not only from his strong grasp but also from the rest of the customers in the café who were gawping and gasping with open mouths at the big drama. I ran out of the shop, shaken.

He followed me out of the café. Neither of us intended to make a big scene for everybody to see. I was so surprised to see an outburst like that from a man I remembered as even-tempered, quiet, shy and withdrawn. I had never experienced this side of him before. We walked for a while. I felt I owed him an apology for not having been able to be his wife and fulfil his expectations of playing happy families, but we both should have known that it was not meant to be.

At least we parted in a fairly amicable manner. I again asked him for a divorce as there was no point being married and I was sure he could find somebody else. The last memory I have from our meeting that day is of Tim shaking his head, saying no to my request. Parting from him was emotionally painful for me.

I went and stayed with Christian for a few days in case Tim showed up unexpectedly at my apartment again. I was soon to realise, after this I had to look over my shoulder constantly, awaiting Tim's sudden re-appearance.

A week later it was the end of the semester at the university and all students of English language were required to go to England in order to perfect their English. Textbooks were not enough. I decided to go to England to perfect my English.

GOLDERS GREEN, LONDON

There was no problem with finding accommodation in London and I moved in to a private house in Golders Green where I had a large bedsit, sharing a kitchen and bathroom. The landlady was a nice middle-aged Jewish woman, a refugee from Germany. I found a job in Golders Green in a Dolcis shoe shop. I soon learned the tricks of the trade, selling handbags to match the shoes and cleaning materials. Selling both was a part of a good sales technique. My knowledge of languages was a real asset because Golders Green was a very cosmopolitan area. The management were so pleased with my selling ability that in no time at all I was promoted to work at the Piccadilly Circus store, which was a main branch.

I earned enough money to pay my rent and food. I even had enough to buy new clothes. London was full of clubs. I soon made friends through which I was introduced to London's nightlife. It was in a London nightclub just off Leicester Square that I met a very good-looking blond pianist. Not only did he play all the 'smooches' but his passion and dexterity when he played jazz was breathtaking. He noticed me and during a break came over to our table, introduced himself and asked if he could join us.

'My name is Paul,' he said.

After his first sentence I could hear that his accent was not English. With a cheeky smile and a twinkle in his eye, he shrugged his shoulders and said, 'I'm Hungarian.'

I felt that my heart had jumped out of my body. Spontaneously I got up and replied, 'So am I!' and we gave each other a big, long hug.

Naturally I told Paul that I was a jazz singer who had to come to England to learn English. After his short break he returned to his piano and unexpectedly announced over his microphone that it was his pleasure to welcome a well-known singer from Germany. He then asked the audience to give me a big hand as I was going to sing a song for them. I didn't need any more encouragement! I sang 'Lullaby of Bird land', 'Summertime' and 'Blue Moon'.

* * *   * * *   * * *

Meeting Paul opened up many opportunities for me to be able to pursue my singing. The club offered me a singing job. Paul and I became very good friends. He introduced me to a group of Hungarian students who regularly got together. They made me feel very welcome.

Paul had a car. He also had a motorcycle which he used more often than the car because it was easier to wind through the traffic. When we had a gig together he would pick me up. Sitting on the back of a motorcycle zigzagging through the rush-hour traffic was a hair-raising experience, especially when it was foggy or pelting down with rain. Protecting my evening dress on the way to a gig became an art form of its own! On such occasions I had to take my hair dryer with me and reapply my make-up because by the time I arrived I would often resemble a drowned cat more than a performer.

Paul had escaped from Hungary in 1956 with his younger brother and his cousin, Zsuzsi. They all shared a house in Maida Vale. It was a large house where Paul rented rooms out to other Hungarian students and refugees.

* * *   * * *   * * *

My life at that point was quite well organised. I kept my day job at Dolcis and at night I had the occasional singing gig, mostly with Paul at the piano. My social life was good until the arrival of a familiar and unwelcome visitor.

One Sunday morning there he stood, at my front door with a big smile on his face, giving the impression that he was expected. Mrs Cohen, the landlady, opened the door and let him in and seemed to be very happy for me because my 'lovely' husband had joined me.

'Mazeltov!' she declared. 'How nice for you my dear.' And with those words she shut the front door and I had no choice but to walk up to my room with Tim following. Again I was astounded. I was wondering how on earth Tim had found out where I lived.

We sat down and talked. He told me he had a job with a big heating and plumbing firm in Golders Green which was a permanent job giving very good wages. This time he was very plausible, convincing me we should try to live together for six months and give our marriage a second chance. He pointed out that in London we were away from all of the outside pressures and influences. He promised me that if I still felt the same in six months he would grant me a divorce. He was still handsome and attractive to me. Giving it a six-month trial seemed to be fair to both of us.

Tim had come prepared with his belongings in a sports bag. I wondered how he had been so sure that I would take him up on his offer. I surprised myself by agreeing but at least I now had the promise of a divorce out of him. Mrs Cohen was happy to let Tim stay with me. She only upped the rent by ten shillings per week, which seemed fair.

The arrangement worked quite well at the start. Tim left for work an hour before me and prepared breakfast for both of us.

When I arrived home I often only had a few hours to get ready for Paul to pick me up for my singing engagements, which became more and more frequent. Even if I did not have a job it gave me the perfect opportunity to get out of my house to ensure I spent as little time as possible with Tim.

The times Tim and I were together we would go out for meals or head to a cinema. Golders Green was full of little coffee shops and wine bars. It became more and more obvious how very little we had in common. We came from different worlds and that gap became more and more obvious day by day. Every time Tim touched me I could feel my skin crawl. I was afraid to fall asleep in case I was unable to push him away as he couldn't keep his hands off me. He constantly declared his undying love and passion for me. I frequently reminded him that the feelings have to be reciprocal. Whilst I liked him as a person and a friend I did not find him sexually attractive and I wanted to have the freedom to continue my studies. I was not ready to settle down. I didn't feel I was 'wife material'. Singing was my love and my life, to which nothing compared.

One evening when I came home after a tiring day at the shoe shop I found my clothes in shreds, scattered in a loose pile in the middle of my room. Tim was sitting on the edge of the bed with a razor blade in one hand. He was cutting his wrist. He had been waiting for me to come through the door the perfect moment.

The blood was gushing from his wrist. I was terrified. I picked up a part of my shredded clothes and used it as a bandage to try to stop the bleeding. I rushed to the telephone and dialled 999 for an ambulance. I was not sure which upset me more – my beautiful clothes being ruined or Tim slashing his wrist. The ambulance came in no time and took Tim away; his parting words to me were, 'I'll never give you a divorce.'

When Tim was released from the hospital a few hours later he was full of remorse and apologies. I accepted the money he offered to replace my garments. He looked like a lost child. The guilt I felt was eating me up. As I was only twenty-two years old I wasn't ready to play the role of Mother to a grown man. One who was only four years older than me.

For a while in order to try to put the dreadful scenes behind us we both pretended that nothing had happened. For two months we walked around each other as if we were treading on eggshells. The English weather became a very welcome conversational topic. Our daily routines continued. Each morning we went our separate ways, meeting back at the flat after work. Most evenings by eight o'clock I would be picked up by Paul.

Then a bombshell dropped again. As I was entering the bedsit Tim was sitting on the bed. He was once again holding a cut-throat razor. His eyes were red and it was obvious he had been crying. His shirt sleeves were rolled up. He shook his head and in a very pathetic and sad voice said to me, 'I know I lost you. I can't live without you. You have to promise you will never leave me or I will cut my wrists again.' He stood up, looked at me, pleading and threatening me simultaneously. I knew that whatever I said other than, 'Yes I love you too, let's live happily ever after,' would not satisfy him. I was petrified, sad and worried. Seeing the razor against the skin of his wrist made me unable to utter a single word.

I ran for the corridor, grabbed the telephone and dialled 999 for an ambulance.

'Please hurry! My husband is cutting his wrists again. Please hurry; I don't know what to do!' I pleaded.

I then dialled Paul's number. 'Come quickly, help me! I need your help!' I begged him. He told me he would come straight over.

Tim had followed me into the corridor. With horror I saw blood gushing out of both of his wrists. The razor was still in his hand. He was now waving it in my direction. I thought he was going to kill me. I ran panic stricken down the stairs, Tim followed, only a few steps behind me. I reached the front door, still running for my life. I bolted outside and reached the front gate.

I turned around and he was there, looking like a wild, demented animal. His eyes were bulging from their sockets. The same voice that only a few minutes before was pleading and begging me to stay had now changed into an angry, hateful threat. Foam sprayed towards me from his mouth as he shouted, 'IF I CAN'T BLOODY HAVE YOU NOBODY ELSE WILL! I WILL NEVER GIVE YOU A DIVORCE! I'LL NEVER LET YOU GO!'

I managed to get through the front gate and at that moment Paul's car pulled up. The passenger door opened but as I got in Tim managed to stagger in front of Paul's car and fell on to the bonnet, spreading out both arms and clinging to the windscreen wipers. His blood was still pouring from his wrists. Sickening red blood ran down the front window. To see the expression on Tim's face, a grimace, showing his teeth, his face red with rage, was shocking. Could it really be the same man I knew? The man who was afraid of his own shadow?

I could hear the sirens and through the blood-drenched windscreen I saw the ambulance arrive. Paul tried to reverse his car in order to escape from Tim. The two ambulance people peeled the bleeding, raging Tim off the car. They managed to restrain him and load him into the ambulance. Paul didn't hang around. He drove us away from there as fast as he could. I couldn't even look back. I was unable to move or to talk, almost as if I was in a catatonic state.

Paul drove us to his house and gave me a room there, one had just become vacant. I just knew that this chapter of my life had to be ended. I felt I couldn't return to my job or to the bedsit. The outrageous experience I had just had meant there was no way I could go back, for any reason. The idea of Tim returning, and finding me again, was too terrifying.

* * *   * * *   * * *

I quickly found another job, this time in a very fashionable restaurant-cum-espresso bar in London's Hanover Square. It was very close to a well-known studio where auditions for dancers and singers took place there. I auditioned most weeks and occasionally I managed to get a small dancing part in the chorus or a few singing gigs. I had to stick to my steady job at the restaurant in order to pay my bills. The gigs I still had with Paul didn't earn enough to keep me going.

I found new accommodation in Willesden Green. The landlord and landlady, Mr and Mrs Thompson, were Pentecosts who rented rooms out to students. He was a Pentecostal minister. They were an unusual looking couple. He was a small man. She was big in every way. There was, however, no question who was the boss in their house. When he aired his opinion she became like a little frightened mouse.

There was one English girl living at the house called Maureen, who was my age. She was very blonde with a slight pink tinge in her hair. She was very attractive. Maureen was a hairdresser who worked for Raymond Bessone 'Teasie-Weasie' the most fashionable hairdresser in London at that time. We each had our own comfortable bedroom and shared a kitchen and bathroom. Maureen and I had a very good understanding. The difference in our backgrounds made our new friendship more interesting.

I was fascinated by her stories about the hair salon she worked at. She even arranged a specially discounted haircut for me.

For my new restaurant job I needed to wear little white frilly aprons, preferably with large pockets for my tips to be safely placed. Every day I needed a fresh one as they became stained very easily. Maureen and Mrs Thompson helped me to create new aprons made from pillowcases that we cut in half. Mrs Thompson showed me how to starch them and we created frills in the material to make the aprons look really pretty. With my black skirt, black top, black stockings and black shoes, the starched, white apron stopped me from looking like a nun, or a French chambermaid. I had to wear my long hair in a chignon to ensure it did not end up in the customers' food.

One evening I was in a hurry because the restaurant was full and everybody was awaiting service. Just as I was ready to serve the beef stroganoff to an elegant lady dressed in pale blue, the serving platter slipped off the napkin, burned my hand and landed on the lady's suited lap! This created a most unpleasant scene. The lady was screaming and I was screaming because of my burned hand. The head waiter tried to calm things down and the owner, Mr Cohen, offered to pay to have the lady's suit dry-cleaned. Of course, I knew I would have to foot the bill which would be more than two weeks of my hard-earned cash. After work I was called to the office. Mr Cohen was a very dignified, polite, middle-aged gentleman. He sat me down and we had a long chat. He was the son of a German-Jewish refugee. They had escaped Germany just as the anti-Semitism started there. He was very interested to hear my story, his eyes swelling with tears as he learned about my life. He stretched his hands over the desk to take mine in his, squeezing gently.

'Don't worry, my dear. I will not fire you. Your job is yours for as long as you want it. Accidents happen,' he assured me.

He did not accept my offer to pay for the lady's damaged suit. At closing time, when all the guests had left and the staff were ready to leave, as Mr Cohen helped me into my coat Mrs Cohen burst in to the office. She was the complete opposite to her husband. She was loud and laden with tasteless jewellery. Her hair was obviously dyed. She had long painted fingernails.

'What the hell do you think you are doing Zack? Why on earth are you helping this waitress into her coat? You are treating her above her station! She is just a waitress, not a lady!' she shrieked. She had a most unpleasant voice.

He calmly looked at her whilst making sure my coat was comfortably placed.

'My dear,' he replied, 'Dorit, 'just a waitress' as you call her, is more of a lady than you will ever be, and I expect you to treat her as such from now on. You listen to me – you make sure you treat her well.'

The expression of surprise on Mrs Cohen's face was indescribable! It was clear she was not used to being spoken to in that way by Zack.

I had to run all the way to the Oxford Street Underground station that night to catch the last train to Willesden Green at midnight. There was only one other person in the carriage. I was petrified. For protection I carried a single brick wrapped in beautiful wrapping paper and decorated with a big bow. It looked like a box of chocolates. I placed it in a string shopping bag and took it with me at all times just in case I needed it for protection.

From the tube station to my digs would normally take about six minutes to walk. However, as soon as I stepped on to the street I ran all the way home and could make it in three minutes flat. I was driven by fear. The newspapers at that time were full of stories about 'the Kilburn Strangler' whose victims were mostly women. Kilburn was the next station along from

Willesden Green. The short journey was particularly frightening when it was foggy. The prospect of the murderer lurking behind a tree made it feel like something from a horror movie. I had to face this fear every night.

* * *   * * *   * * *

In order to make more money I took on an extra shift in the restaurant. It was in the espresso bar on the first floor. Being the little know-it-all I assumed it should present no difficulties. However, operating the brand new Italian espresso machine was a far greater task than I expected. It was an impressive piece of machinery which had to be kept sparkling at all times. I had only been in charge of the bar and this monster for a week when the machine started hissing at me. Steam was escaping and the dial had moved into the 'red' position. The coffee machine then let out incredible whistling noises. It resembled a steam engine that was about to shoot off!

I was helplessly standing there, not knowing how to stop it. As a last resort I shouted at the top of my voice, 'Everybody out! Everybody out! There's going to be an explosion!'

I followed everyone out of the coffee bar and just as I reached the front door the time bomb of an espresso machine exploded! Steam, water and coffee grind decorated the ceiling and everything around the machine. Somebody must have informed the fire brigade as they were there in minutes. I didn't stay to see the outcome. I simply ran. I caught the first available train home. I couldn't face poor Mr Cohen with yet another accident under my belt.

In hindsight perhaps somebody should have shown me how to release the steam before it exploded. I could not face going back to the restaurant again to apologise in person.

* * *   * * *   * * *

The 10th of January was approaching: my birthday. My mother sent me an open-ended rail ticket and an invitation to go and spend time with her in Hamburg, where she was now living. It was a very welcome birthday present. I asked Paul to drive me to the station. We got there just in time. The conductor was already blowing his whistle and we could hear the sounds of slamming compartment doors. I jumped on and Paul managed to throw my suitcase on to the moving train. I waved at him from the window. When I heard the sound of the last slamming door, I felt I was shutting the door on the traumatic incidents I had endured over the last year.

'Good luck, little one!' Paul called out to me. 'You deserve a break! Keep in touch!'

All of my hard work and the drama of Tim over the past year had taken a heavy toll on me. As my body hit the seat I felt an immense tiredness overcome me. The painful experiences had caught up with me. I felt both a physical and mental exhaustion.

The train slowly pulled out of the station and I thought to myself, 'Hamburg, here I come!'

I slept for the entire journey.

HAMBURG, GERMANY – THE NOSE JOB

It was wonderful to see my mum waiting for me at Hamburg railway station. We were both overwhelmed by emotion. I felt such relief when hugging her. I hadn't realised until that moment how much I had missed her.

She was not alone at the station. Her attachment was a tall, very distinguished-looking gentleman with grey hair. He was very polite and very attractive.

My mum introduced us. 'This is Andreas. Baron Von Christoff. We are work colleagues.'

Andreas drove us to my mother's flat. Mum and I couldn't stop talking. We cried, we laughed, we hugged and we cried even more. The tears were pouring out of both of us. We felt a need to share and to know that we were each understood and loved unconditionally.

My mother told me about her new job. She was in charge of the integrating students from behind the Iron Curtain who had escaped to the West seeking political asylum. Many of these students came from Hungary. My mother's native language was Hungarian and although she was in overall charge of the programme she had a particular brief to help the students who had escaped from Hungary.

As it was the tenth of January, and my birthday, my Mother had arranged a surprise birthday treat for me. She and Andreas took me to the number-one night club in Hamburg.

This was Gallery Twenty-Four, the German equivalent to London's Ronnie Scott's Jazz Club. They had reserved a table in the corner. It was in a perfect spot facing the six-piece South American Latin/jazz band. Andreas ordered a bottle of champagne. The atmosphere was electric. As most people smoked, the mixture of nicotine, perfume, aftershave and alcohol gave it a special smell, adding to the magic. I was very surprised that my mother had chosen that place because after our Middle East experiences she never went into any place that could remotely remind her of our past. This was different. The clientele was extremely smart. This was obviously the centre of Hamburg's night life.

The band was excellent and very versatile. One minute they would play South American tunes accompanied by maracas and bongos, the next they would play swing and blues playing trumpets and saxophones. There was a male Brazilian vocalist. I could hardly sit still in my seat. I simply wanted to get up and join them but I thought it would not have been appropriate. Andreas must have spoken to the owner of the club because to my delight and surprise the owner approached me, a slim man in his mid-forties with a dark beard, a moustache and smiling eyes. Gerhard wished me a happy birthday and asked me if I would do him the honour of joining the band. Before he had finished the last word I was already making my way over to the stage!

Gerhard introduced me to the band, told them I was a vocalist from England and said I was visiting Hamburg for my birthday. I told the piano player the song I was going to sing and in which key. After four bars of introduction I started with 'The Lady is a Tramp' followed by 'Lullaby of Birdland', 'Besame Mucho' and 'Autumn Leaves'. I finished with 'C'est Si Bon'. The band particularly enjoyed 'Besame Mucho'. Everybody was dancing on the little dance floor that surrounded the bandstand. I could see their smiling faces through the cloudy blue veil of smoke. The clapping of hands and the shouts of 'More!' filled up the whole club.

I sang two encores and then after shaking hands with the band members I returned to my table where my mother sat with tears in her eyes.

'Darling, I never knew that you were so good! I never realised how talented you are.'

When I had finished my next glass of champagne Gerhard pulled a chair up to our table.

He asked me 'When can you start working at my club? You are incredible!'

As he was talking a crowd of people came, congratulated me and told me how much they loved my singing. They also asked when I would be starting work at the club, which must have encouraged Gerhard further.

'It is the tenth of January,' Gerhard said. 'How about the first of February? That would give you enough time to pick up the rest of your suitcases from London and give notice at your present job.' He had assumed I was already working as a singer. I was so thrilled to be offered a job at such an amazing place that I forgot to ask how much I would be paid!'

It turned out to be the best birthday present I had received.

* * *   * * *   * * *

My mother told me I could stay with her for as long as I wanted to. Over the next week or so I frantically searched for suitable clothes to wear for my new singing job. I already had arrangements for the songs I would sing, suitable to be played by a six-piece band. I organised a few rehearsals before starting at the club. It was a mixed-nationality band. The pianist and the alto-saxophone player were both German and first-class musicians. The bass player was Italian and the rest of the band was Brazilian. It was a most outlandish group of musicians but surprisingly they worked very well together. There was scope to mix jazz and Latin. Whilst I sang as part of the band I also had three or four solo spots during the night. Many of these songs were special requests. I started work at eight o'clock in the evening and worked to the early hours of the morning.

To my surprise there were spot checks made by police officers in plain clothes, strip-searching members of the band to look for drugs. They were taken discretely to the gents toilets. Even in those days people were heavily into substance abuse. They were mainly searching for needle marks. I picked up a whisper between two musicians. The pianist said to the bass player, 'I was lucky again. They looked everywhere but couldn't detect the needle marks in my heels. Ha! Ha!'

On another occasion, at two o'clock in the morning, the club was raided. Ten policemen in uniforms took the entire band into two waiting police vans. They also took Gerhard, the club owner. When we arrived at the police station we were greeted by dozens of reporters, which, at that time of the morning, was very surprising. I was unsure about the purpose of the raid – could it be another drug-related raid? It was very frightening to be 'picked up' by uniformed German police although I felt a little bit better when I was not singled out.

But that was the best publicity I could have had. The next day the newspapers told of a talented new singer called Dorit being taken to the police station after a raid on a night club. Photographs of me littered the pages. My name and face were suddenly stirring up curiosity. That night the club was heaving. There were long queues of people outside trying to get in to see me and hear me sing.

The night club was like a magnet to anybody who was involved in the entertainment business. It was there that I met Gräfin Von Richthofen. She was a tall, aristocratic, stunning, elegant and sophisticated lady who was not only eccentric in her attire but also in her mannerisms and behaviour. She was the widow of German fighter pilot, Gräf Von Richthofen: with a pedigree like hers I could not have asked for a better supporter.

Her black-rimmed designer hat was so oversized that nobody could sit on a seat alongside her for fear of having their eyes poked out. She had long, dark-red painted fingernails and glittering diamond rings on her fingers. Judging by the size of the diamonds they looked like they had come out of a Christmas cracker. She held a long silver cigarette holder between her fingers which she would regularly place between her bright red lips, draw deeply and blow smoke out sensuously, closing her eyes to indicate the pleasure it gave her. She had a deep, husky voice and when she laughed it sounded like a gurgle. Everything that she did was meant to impress.

She took a shine to me. She was very direct and very friendly.

'I like you, Dorit. May I call you Dorit?' she asked me. 'The name suits you. You may call me Sigrid.' I could see by her face as she gave me permission to use her first name that I was expected to feel very honoured by this.

Sigrid continued, 'I am going to take you under my wing. I will make you into a star. You have everything going for you. Your eyes, your lips, your voice is fantastic and your stage presence is excellent. But we need to do something about your nose! It does not do justice to the rest of your face.'

She said this with such charm, with no malice at all. There was so much warmth and caring in her words and I knew she was right.

Without interrupting her flow she had taken a little notebook out of her handbag. 'I'm going to make you an appointment to see the most prominent plastic surgeon in Germany. Give me your phone number and I'll call you when the appointment is made. I'll come and pick you up with my driver.' Her commands were not open for discussion. 'Once we have the nose job out of the way I will introduce you to Lotar Olias. He made Freddie Quinn.' Neither name meant anything to me.

She handed me her visiting card and said, 'Any time you need anything don't hesitate to call me. I will be in touch. That I promise.' Then she picked up her glass of champagne and continued to talk to the rest of the people at the table.

She was the most fascinating woman I had ever met. By the expressions on the faces of the people around her, I assumed everybody felt the same way.

* * * * * * * * *

Only a few days later I received a phone call from Gräfin Von Richthofen. She picked me up in her black chauffeur-driven limousine and we drove to a most impressive white villa along the Alster River. It was a stunning place, stood in its own grounds with its own sweeping driveway which took us to the front of the house. We were expected. The doors opened and the receptionist ushered us to the surgeon's office.

The surgeon, Doctor Sommer, was a small man in an elegant grey suit. He had neatly brushed dark hair and wore rimless glasses above a slightly hooked nose. He greeted the Gräfin by kissing her hand. He looked at me as he spoke to her, 'So this is your protégé, Dorit?'

He took a long look at me. I could feel his dark, piercing eyes focused on my nose.

Most of the conversation took place between Doctor Sommer and the Gräfin. She explained to him, 'Sitting here is a star waiting to be born. She has the voice and the talent but it is up to you to create the image that she deserves.'

I could almost feel him sculpting my face with his eyes. He asked me to get up and stand in front of a white screen. He took various pictures of my profile.

He placed his hands on my shoulders. 'Dorit,' he said to me, 'You have the most beautiful eyes and the sexiest lips. Life is so unfair to have given you this beak! I will change this for you. I have heard your voice on the radio and I must say that the Gräfin is right. I will do everything possible to give you the face that your voice deserves. I cannot wait to get you under my knife.'

I could feel my knees shaking. If I had not been able to sit down straight away I would probably have collapsed. The excitement and fear was almost too much for me to control.

Whether I would agree to the surgery was not questioned. It was a foregone conclusion that it had to be done and the sooner the better. I asked the doctor how much it would cost. I was aware that this sort of surgery was very expensive and well out of my reach. He just looked at me with his head slightly tilted and smiled, rubbing his hands together. 'My dear, Dorit, this will be my biggest challenge and a true pleasure. How about you pay me when you can? I would like to have your first signed record and your permission to use your "before and after" photos as advertising material.'

Without waiting for me to agree he looked at his calendar and asked, 'How about tomorrow afternoon at three? Bring your nightie, slippers and wash bag.'

I did not sleep that night. I did go to work, however, and had to tell Gerhard that I would not be able to sing for the next few weeks. He did not take the news very well and wanted to fire me on the spot, but when I explained the reason to him he was very understanding and wished me good luck.

As instructed by Dr Sommer I packed a little suitcase with a nightdress, dressing gown, comb, toothbrush, toothpaste and other little necessities that I would need. The next morning I arrived at Dr Sommer's sanatorium. I was starving because I was not allowed to eat before the surgery. I was greeted by a nurse in uniform who accompanied me through a corridor to find my room. I changed into a gown and was told to wait. My heart was pounding and I was suddenly overcome with fear and panic. The nurse gave me two pills to swallow with a glass of water.

'This will make you a bit drowsy,' she told me. It was a pre-med.

Thankfully I was not given much time to think or worry as Dr Sommer personally came to my room and, holding my hand, guided me down a flight of stairs to the operating theatre. It felt as though my legs were jelly and I found it difficult to walk straight or focus. The pills must have started to take effect.

The doctor pointed for me to sit on the operating table with its back elevated into a sitting position. I had to lean back. The lights in the operating theatre were so bright, seemingly equalling the ones I was used to on stage. Dr Sommer asked his assistants to leave the room.

I could see a syringe with a long needle in his right hand. With his left hand he was pulling my upper lip upwards. He administered numerous injections on both sides of my upper gum and inside my nostrils. I lost count of how many because everything seemed to be numb and my awareness was rapidly fading. I could hear the doctor's voice coming and going as I drifted in and out of consciousness.

At one time I must have regained a few seconds of clarity because to my amazement there was Dr Sommer, sitting on my chest, rubbing his hands together and laughing gleefully. The anaesthetics must have distorted the sounds because to me he sounded like the evil witch from Hansel and Gretel!

'I will make you beautiful!' he cried out.

I surely must have been hallucinating as a result of the drugs. As soon as the doctor realised my eyes were open I received another injection. I could hear the sound of sawing, like a branch of a tree being cut. Simultaneously I felt a heavy pain across the bridge of my nose.

I do not remember much more but I do recall two people dragging me up to my room. I must have then slept for hours because when I opened my eyes it was dark outside. The first thing I saw was my mother standing there looking at me. She had her hands clasped under her chin and was sobbing.

'What have you done, my child?' she asked.

I couldn't breathe through my nose and was forced to breathe through my mouth. I could taste the blood trickling down my throat and feel it dribbling from the corners of my lips on to the white gauze I had been given to wipe my mouth. The smiling nurse gave me a hand mirror. The image that looked back at me resembled someone who had just gone ten rounds with Rocky Marciano. I had hard white plaster stretching from the middle of my forehead down to the end of my nose and side to side covering my cheekbones. My lips were like thick sausages. What wasn't covered by plaster, like my eyelids and under my eyes, were bruised dark blue. I couldn't open my eyes properly because they were so swollen. Both of my nostrils had been stuffed with gauze and blood was still seeping through. I was not a pretty sight.

There were two large cushions placed tightly on either side of my face to prevent me from turning my head and destroying the plaster. I felt sick but the nurse urged me to hold back so as to not encourage internal bleeding. I was allowed to take small sips of water through a straw.

The next day Dr Sommer appeared again, accompanied by a nurse. He placed a kidney-shaped dish under my chin.

'Good morning, Dorit. I have come to remove the bandage from inside your nose which should ease your breathing.'

With a forceps in each hand he proceeded to pull the gauze first out of one nostril, then the other. I was astounded to see how many metres of bandage had been shoved up my nose. He repeated the procedure for my other nostril. It was a very strange feeling. The smell of stale blood was vile but hooray, I could breathe again.

With the aid of a little torch Dr Sommer inspected his work and nodded. He was very pleased with himself.

'I am amazing!' he declared. Then he ruffled my hair – thankfully on the only part of my head that didn't hurt.

Over the next few days the navy blue bruising became green then yellow. My face resembled a rainbow. The swelling on my eyelids and lips was eased by repeatedly applying ice cubes. I could only eat soft food as my jaws also hurt.

The big day arrived to take the plaster off. Mother came with me, as did Gräfin Von Richthofen. A bottle of champagne in an ice bucket was waiting for us. Then the moment came. Dr Sommer, in a very ceremonial manner, eased the Elastoplast that was stuck to the gypsum from one side of my nose, then the other, then my forehead. Slowly, slowly, he eased the mould away from my nose.

Then he steered me towards a large winged mirror so that I could see my nose from the front and sides without turning my head. All of us stared at the mirror with our mouths open. Even though my nose was still very swollen I looked like a changed person. I couldn't believe my eyes. The bruising and swelling were almost gone. I had expected to see some stitches but they were all concealed. Dr Sommer's special technique meant he applied the stitches from the inside.

'Well, my dear?' he questioned.

I couldn't stop my tears. Both my mother and the Gräfin cried. Even Dr Sommer had a tear trickling down his cheek. It was a very emotional unveiling indeed. The Gräfin, who was a head taller than I, said, 'Dorit, my dear, from now on your path is cleared and there is nothing that can hold you back from becoming the famous star that you deserve to be.'

Once the swelling had gone it made my nose even smaller. It almost halved in size. For a month after my nose job I slept with two little hand mirrors to check my nose from every angle, ensuring it hadn't returned to its original size and shape. It became almost an obsession to go to bed with two mirrors and perform regular inspections.

I was no longer 'The great singer with the long nose.' I was suddenly 'The singer with the beautiful voice.' From then on I was referred to as 'The Voice'.

HAMBURG, GERMANY –
CREATING DORIT OLIVER

That afternoon I was due to be introduced to the famous songwriter Lotar Olias, the legend of the German pop scene. He had made Freddie Quinn the leading star in Germany and beyond. The Gräfin picked me up, as usual, in her chauffeur driven black limousine, to take me to meet him. I was very nervous.

The crackling noise of the pebbled driveway came to a halt. The chauffer opened our doors and there was Lotar Olias outside his front door. He had a smile on his face and his arms open, walking towards the Gräfin.

'My dear Gräfin,' he said to her, 'You look as wonderful as always!'

Then he turned to me, eyeing me up from top to toe, and said, 'So this is Dorit, your protégé. If her voice is half as good as her looks, she will be my next star!'

I could feel the blood rushing to my head. Whilst I was used to getting compliments for my singing this was the first time anybody had complimented me for my looks. I must admit I liked it.

Lotar Olias was a man of medium height but it was obvious he liked his food. He was in his late fifties with receding dark hair and an open face. He had a welcoming smile. His skin looked as if he had spent most of his time in the south of France lying on a deck chair, sunning himself.

We proceeded into his studio. After the usual polite formalities he sat down at his grand piano and tinkled a few scales to warm up his fingers. Lotar gave me some sheet music.

'Can you read music?' he asked me.

'Yes, of course. Doesn't everyone?' I replied.

'That is great,' he said. 'There are so many wannabe singers who cannot read music.' He nodded with approval.

The title of the song was 'Du Bist Gut Zu Mir'. Lotar accompanied me on the piano as I sang the song. I was pleasantly surprised to hear what a catchy, swinging little number it was and I felt straight away that it was my song.

Lotar loved what he heard. He said, 'Well Dorit, how would you like to record this song? Of course we have to work more on it, so this will be the A-side. Now we have to look for a B-side. I understand that you like the Latin rhythm.' I nodded in response. I was surprised he knew about my style. My curiosity got the better of me and I asked Lotar how he knew I liked Latin rhythm.

'Ahhh,' he replied. 'Don't you think I did my research before I decided to write a song for you? I have been going to the club every night to listen to your singing and hoped nobody would snatch you before I had the chance.' He smiled.

There were two piles of Lotar's compositions scattered on the piano. The smaller pile contained titles he had composed just for me, with the lyrics written by Kurt Shwabach. We rummaged through numerous titles but I particularly liked 'Bongo Boy'. It had a calypso rhythm and lots of bongo sounds. We both decided it would make a good B-side.

Lotar was a very good pianist and when two musicians get together there is often a bonding which only musicians understand. He asked me about my favourite songs. It gave him an insight into the range and quality of my voice. With ease I could reach three and a half octaves.

Once Lotar and I had decided on the two songs to use he called in two formally dressed gentlemen. They had been patiently waiting to listen to the chosen songs. One man was the producer and the other was the director of Fontana Records, part of the Philips Recording Company.

Inside Lotar's elegant lounge, coffee, cake, sandwiches and a bottle of champagne had been prepared. The Gräfin was sat there in her full glory while the butler was walking around pouring champagne into glasses.

Before we could raise our glasses to toast our successful partnership, Lotar put his hands up and with his charming personality he stopped everybody.

'Halt!' he ordered. 'Now we have to decide on a proper stage name. Then we can properly celebrate our future.'

The name I was using was not that of a budding 'star'. All of us agreed that 'Dorit' was good but we needed an international sounding name which could be used without fear of mispronunciation in every country. I had to have a name that would be remembered. 'Dorita Ramon' and 'Dorita La Habana' were too Spanish sounding. I had used those names while dancing with a Spanish dancing troupe but they were not suitable for the international singing star I was poised to become.

We kept returning to another suggestion: 'Dorit Oliver'. The more we repeated the name the more I felt it was the right name for me. It felt just right. It was short, memorable and simple. It was me.

Lotar stood up. He raised his glass and announced, 'Here's to Dorit Oliver!'

I almost had to pinch myself. It was like a movie with me as the leading lady.

The producer pulled a contract out from his briefcase. He was offering me a chance to record exclusively for two years with Fontana Records. I did not have a solicitor with me. I was completely unaware that it was a must-do when signing a contract. I was so overwhelmed with the offer and opportunity that I was afraid that if I didn't sign it then and there, they might change their minds. I asked the Gräfin to read it and give me her advice. She must have seen more contracts in her life than I ever had. She nodded with approval and encouragement so I signed it using my new name, 'Dorit Oliver'. I was so nervous that the signature looked more like a scribble from a three-year-old child.

Each time the glasses were filled up with champagne we toasted our future success again.

There was a lot of planning ahead, including professional photographs for publicity.

The next morning the real work had to start. At ten o'clock in the morning I had to start rehearsing with Lotar Olias. I was greeted with coffee and toast with jam. Lotar guided me into his studio where his big piano was. Just being in that room made me happy, relaxed and yet excited. The room was in the back of the house with French doors leading to well-designed landscaped gardens. The room was like a gallery of famous stars. Photographs covered the walls. The bookshelves were laden with all sorts of sheet music. Many of the songs were Lotar's own compositions. I hoped that someday I would be among his gallery of fame.

Lotar must have guessed my thoughts. He remarked, 'Dorit, soon your picture will be added to my gallery of success.'

We started with 'Du Bist Gut Zu Mir' and after a lunch break we continued with 'Bongo Boy'. By about five o'clock we ended the rehearsals. I thought that was it but I was told to return the next morning at the same time to do it all over again. While I wasn't present Lotar had rehearsed the music with the band, preparing for the recording which was to take place the next day. Only when he was satisfied with the sound was I called to the recording studio.

I arrived at the recording studio at ten o'clock the next morning. It was the first time that I had been in a recording studio.

I entered the reception area and as I approached the desk a very smart receptionist asked me, 'Can I help you?'

I had to think before I told her my name, 'Dorit Oliver' because it was the first time I had officially used it. I proceeded to the lift and headed to the first floor, to studio number three. I opened the door and the sight before me was just like studios appear in films.

After some polite chit-chat Lotar and I entered the soundproofed room. It was like a hexagonal glass contraption. I heard a voice through the loudspeaker, 'Put the headphones on, Miss Oliver.' They were black and large with each side almost the size of a saucer. In front of me there was a microphone, equally oversized. There was a glass of water on a little table.

A voice spoke in my earphones. It said, 'We will run through the first track. Listen to it. If you hear anything that you are not happy with please just nod.'

Then I heard it, for the very first time, 'Du Bist Gut Zu Mir' played by the orchestra. Wow! It already sounded fantastic. I listened to the music twice. I was asked if I was ready to start recording. I quickly had a sip of water, cleared my throat, glanced at the words and then nodded.

Then the music started again. After four bars it was my cue. I didn't need to look at the words or the music at all. I sang. I hit the first note in perfect pitch. The rest of the song was equally perfect. No interruptions and no faults. There it was, my first recording! I only needed one take.

They played back the complete record. I was completely speechless. It just sounded so good. When I took my headphones off I saw people standing and clapping. Lotar Olias and the producer both had big grins from ear to ear. They congratulated me. Everybody was very happy with the A-side.

That evening they all came to the club and we celebrated my first record. Lotar, the Gräfin, the director and producer from the recording company were all there. The champagne flowed and there were photographers.

The only things still required were publicity pictures, which meant photo shoots. My new image had to be created. My first photo session came and a professional team of make-up artists were waiting in readiness to transform me into a glamorous star. As I arrived at the studio there was a group of people waiting for me.

My hair was arranged under a net to ensure that my face was free for the make-up team to do as they wished with me. While the make-up artists were busying themselves creating my new image I kept my eyes tightly shut. I had no idea what they were doing to my face and hair. The studio make-up smelled very different from the type I normally used.

Udo, the very camp hairdresser, could not help himself. He gave advice to the make-up artist, Googi. She was a blonde, blue-eyed, slender, almost imp-like young girl. She gave a very calm impression but the atmosphere in the entire studio was electric. Udo was also slender. He wore jeans which were far too tight and a black T-shirt which dazzled because of the glitzy pair of scissors motif. His hair was short and streaked with various colours. He was very funny.

Udo took charge of my hair and treated it like his private possession. I was not allowed to suggest how I would like to have my hair done. To be honest I wouldn't have known what style would suit me best anyway. Up until then I wore my hair a bit longer than shoulder length and naturally wavy. Occasionally I would wear it in a plait or chignon. All I had to do was run my fingers through it and shake my head a few times and I was set up for the day.

When I heard the scissors my heart stopped for a moment. By then it was too late to say anything because a large chunk of my hair was already lying under my feet. I didn't dare to look out of fear of Udo's reaction.

In unison, both Udo and Googi exclaimed, 'Oh my God! Open your eyes, Miss Oliver!'

Looking at myself in the big mirror left me speechless. My eyes filled with tears but I had to control my emotions because if the black mascara had run it would have been catastrophic. Googi quickly came to my rescue and saved the situation by dabbing tissue paper on my tear ducts in the corner of my eyes. With a bit of retouching it looked amazing once more.

The photographs turned out to be absolutely stunning. The photographer complimented me and told me I was a 'natural', whatever that meant. I was encouraged to look into the camera but to choose different poses and facial expressions in whatever way I felt comfortable. It was hard to believe that they were photos of me. That was the first time I had heard the word 'photogenic'.

The night I returned to the jazz club people could not keep their eyes off me. They looked, and they looked more, including Gerhard, the owner, and my colleagues in the band. They knew about my nose job but were sworn to secrecy. The public just thought I had different make-up and a different hair style.

My performance had to be carefully planned. For my signature tune I chose 'The Lady is a Tramp'. I love this song. It swings and puts the audience in the mood for more. At the end when the song finishes with the words, 'that's why the lady is a tramp', I changed the last words to make it my own by singing 'that's why they call me', and then I whispered seductively, 'Dorit Oliver!' This was always applauded and created enthusiasm and curiosity.

I was lucky to be in great demand. I was fully booked for a year in advance. I even had a role in a movie called *Mit 17 Weint Man Nicht*. It was only a small part but I made a great impression. I played a sexy private secretary to the managing director. I sat on a desk with my legs crossed. I wore high stiletto heels and a much-too-tight jumper. In a very husky voice that sounded more like deep breathing than speaking I had to answer the telephone, breathing the words, 'Yes? How can I help you?' It was the smallest part in the film but nevertheless my name was on the cast list. Many more offers followed, particularly voice-overs promoting various products.

My first record was released. My song was put on air on the major radio stations and given prime-time slots. The radio announcements were flattering: 'A new star is born. This is the voice of Dorit Oliver.' I was played on the radio all over Germany. I was even played on Radio Luxemburg. It was unimaginable to consider how many people could be listening to me sing.

My record, 'Du Bist Gut Zu Mir', reached the top ten within the first week of its release.

My life changed overnight.

The offers for singing engagements were flowing in. Fontana's PR department was very good. Inga, the woman in charge of the department, became a very good friend to me. She was a big admirer and supporter. She accompanied me to several concerts.

The programme director of N.D.R, 'Norddeutscher Rundfunk',

the German public radio and television broadcaster, asked me if I would be willing to record a couple of songs with a big band for his radio station. I thanked him politely but I had to hold my excitement back. I wanted to jump up on to a table and scream with delight! He invited me to his office the next day to discuss the songs and the contract. I couldn't sleep that night.

One of the songs we chose was an old beautiful evergreen 'Es-war Einmal Eine Liebe' ('There Was Once a Love'). The other was 'See the Pyramids around the Nile' translated into German as 'Du Bist Nie Alein'. To record live and with a thirty-six piece band was very different and the experience of a lifetime.

We needed two takes to get it right and when we were finished the band stood up to applaud me! I wasn't used to such appreciation and I felt extremely honoured. The band leader and producer congratulated me and hugged me.

They took me to a smaller studio and we listened to the recording. It was different to hearing my own voice through speakers when singing. It sounded so much better than I could have ever imagined. I couldn't stop my tears from flowing.

Television shows and newspaper articles followed. I never looked back.

I also had a main part in a television show called *The Seventh Man*, filmed in Berlin. I had a double role in this musical comedy. I played a Hungarian dancer dancing a *czardas* in Hungarian national costume and red boots. In the movie, the trombone player in the band didn't turn up so I had to double up as a replacement for him to stop him from losing his job. I had to dress up as a man with a moustache stuck over my top lip. Playing this double role was supposed to be really funny but I thought it was pathetic. However, it was well-paid work and it was a television show. Even bad publicity is better than no publicity at all.

TOURING + JAN + HAVING DESI

Living out of suitcases was not new to me. Except now my suitcases were bigger, cost more, were matching and made out of pigskin. I had a little red Karmann Ghia with a Porche engine, a sporty little car and I loved driving it.

I chose to make my home in Hamburg. I simply loved it. It was a beautiful city full of interesting places and I felt I was welcomed. My mother was working in Hamburg and for a while we shared a flat. I was not there very often because my new life took me all around Germany. My favourite place to sing was the jazz club where I first started. Each time that I came back to Hamburg I would have a job to come back to and was made to feel very welcome. One night as I was in the middle of a song, I felt a pair of eyes looking at me, looking straight into my soul. Everybody looked at me. But this one made me feel most uncomfortable. Neither of us was going to be the first to stop looking. This was the nearest I can describe as love at first sight. We seemed to be mesmerised.

This man was tall, had dark hair and very pale blue eyes. When he smiled at me, I felt that my heart was beating double time. I do not know whether anybody else noticed but to be truthful suddenly everybody else disappeared from this crowded place. It was as though only the two of us were there.

I had never ever experienced this kind of feeling. Having met many men in various clubs and theatres, nobody had ever had this effect or stirred up this kind of feeling in me. So far we had not spoken to each other, verbally that is. When I finished singing I went over to the bar, I needed a drink. And so did he.

He introduced himself: 'My name is Jan.'

'And mine is Dorit, as you have guessed by now.'

'Yes, I know,' he replied. 'I have been coming here to listen to you ever since your first appearance, but I sat at the very back table listening and admiring your singing.'

My question was, 'So, what made you stand so close to the stage now?'

'I just could not resist any longer. I had to have a closer look at your eyes.'

I had vodka on the rocks, one of my favourite drinks, and he had a glass of beer.

'So, what is your story?' I asked him. He seemed to be a bit perplexed by my straight question but I have never been a person to beat around the bush.

His voice was soft and melodious. 'Where shall I start?' he said. 'I was married to a famous actress, we had two little boys but sadly both of them died shortly after birth. They were both Rh-negative. Our marriage only lasted two years; losing two little boys did not help much towards keeping the relationship going. I am a designer. I design exhibitions. I studied art in Berlin where I was born. I broke up from a long-standing relationship about six months ago, and now it looks as though I have just started my new relationship.' He looked me in the eye and put his hand on mine and gave it a slight squeeze.

If I had not found him so attractive, I would most probably have been sick from this kind of an answer. I hated very few things more than men who were presumptuous or full of themselves. However...

I do not think we said much after this. This magnetism was new to me. This overwhelming feeling frightened me but at the same time I could not let go. I could hardly wait for the next evening; I knew he would turn up again. In a very short time we became close but it had already happened at the first glance. We were inseparable.

My career and the success I was experiencing at that time was more than I could have ever hoped for. I had worked towards it ever since I could remember. But meeting Jan was so unexpected. Every young girl dreams of falling in love, but I had had a few bad experiences and tried to keep my love life and my career as far apart as possible. My feelings towards Jan were almost uncontrollable. Nevertheless, my singing and my career had to come first. At times it was very very hard to find the right balance. We spent every moment I was not on stage or rehearsing together. He was just everything one would read about in fairy tales of how a man should be. His manners were impeccable, he was an excellent dancer and I was proud to be on his arm wherever we went. He just looked fantastic. I thought I was the luckiest girl on earth.

I moved out from the flat my mother and I were sharing and rented a beautiful top-floor flat in the house of a local doctor. Jan moved in with me and helped me design and decorate my first flat. The excitement of choosing the colours for the wall, the carpets, the sofa and of course the bed; all this was an experience which, again, I had never had before. I started to save up for a bigger flat. We made plans for when we would have children. We made plans about the kind of a place we would like to live in. This was what people in love do.

Between rehearsals we would go for wonderful walks. I can still remember walking in the park with Jan and carving our initials onto the bark of a big tree. Under our initials we carved 'forever'. I cannot remember how long we sat under that tree. All I do remember is that I wanted this feeling to last forever. I did not dare to move, I breathed as slowly as I possibly could, so to make it last longer. And if I had had to die then and there, I would have died happily with a smile on my face.

On one occasion when I came out of a TV studio in Hamburg, after singing with the Dutch Swing College, a famous jazz band from Holland, when I got to my car it was filled with at least a hundred red roses. Jan was a romantic man. I was very touched.

Often when I came home in the early hours of the morning after a show, there would be red roses on my bed, in the bathroom, everywhere. Breakfast time was always very special, because most of my rehearsals started after lunch. So this was a good chance to enjoy spending time together. One morning, Jan put his hand on mine and with a serious expression on his face, he said, 'I have something to tell you, Dorit. But there is nothing to worry about, all is under control. Tanya, my ex-girlfriend asked me to meet her, she had something important to say. We had coffee together and she told me that she was eight months pregnant with my baby. Needless to tell you I was absolutely speechless and I asked her why she had not come to tell me before. She knew I was living with you, why did she not say anything earlier?'

As I was listening to his matter-of-fact explanation, he never stopped chewing on his toast or drinking his coffee. He told me this completely matter of fact. As if he had gone to fill up the car with petrol and they gave him the wrong change. I on the other hand felt as if every drop of blood had drained out of my body. Finishing my breakfast was the last thing on my mind. In 1960 having a child out of wedlock was not exactly acceptable, especially not in the society she came from. Tanya must have been beside herself. I could not stop wondering why in the last six months did she not say anything to Jan or, if she did, how come that he never told me anything? So, I asked him, 'What are you going to do about it?'

'I really do not know,' he answered. 'She has had six months to work out the way and try to find the right solution, but from the moment we finished with each other, I have never heard from her, nor seen her. So you can imagine what a shock this was to me when she told me that she was eight months pregnant.'

'Well, this is not the baby's fault,' I replied, 'And it does not deserve to be illegitimate, nobody deserves that, poor little child. As far as Tanya is concerned, she cannot change the situation now. I have a solution. As I am still married to Tim and he is refusing to give me a divorce, you and I cannot get married yet. So, why don't you marry Tanya? It is only four weeks before the baby is due. At least it will be born legitimately. After the baby is born, you get divorced and then we can continue to push for my divorce and then you and I can get married. My conscience will be clear.' Jan dropped to his knees, put his head in my lap and was overwhelmed by my offer.

The day was set for the wedding. I loaned him my car as he did not have one at that time. I even gave him some money to pay for the wedding because he was, as ever, broke. After the wedding lunch he came home as if he had been out for lunch with some friends. Not to such an important event. I met up a few days later with Tanya for coffee and she held my hands and thanked me. Tanya was the same age as I, very similar in stature and a nice girl. She came from a lower-middle-class family. Her father worked on the railway as an inspector. She was extremely pretty and I felt very sorry for her. She had a kind of innocent look about her. Perhaps that is a special look only pregnant women get. But there she was thanking me again and again for this generosity, something she never ever knew existed. We talked for quite a while. She promised that after the baby was born, they would get a divorce. I assured her I would never stop

Jan seeing his child and there would be no need for him not to be a proper father to his child, even after we were married. We parted crying and hugging and I knew I had done the right thing.

That night Jan was more loving and attentive than I had experienced so far. Having lost two boys so early must have been very painful for him and to be given another chance to have a child was a wonderful gift. Hopefully it would be a little girl. Then the Rh-negative would not be applicable.

The following morning I set off for Stuttgart to take up a month's residency. After that I had a month's contract in the Hilton Hotel in Berlin. I was also engaged, whilst in Berlin, to taking part in filming *The Seventh Man*.

I travelled straight from Stuttgart and Jan travelled from Hamburg and stayed with me during the whole time whilst I was working in Berlin. He showed me around the city which he knew very well as he was born there. By coincidence, during this trip to Berlin, Jan celebrated his birthday.

Once back in Hamburg I encouraged my agent to choose engagements as near to Hamburg as possible because I did not like to be apart from Jan too long. This was not always possible. By now I had parted company with Fontana records and signed a new contract with Ariola. I was due to cut a new record in Munich and at the same time I had a contract to sing with a big band in Munich.

I was very much in demand. However, I never became complacent about my success or my popularity. Each and every time I walked onto the stage, no matter how big the audience, I felt truly privileged to be able to sing and that people had paid good money to listen. No matter how many autograph cards I signed, no matter how many fan letters I received, each and every time I was very excited and happy. I never became big headed or stuck up; I always stayed the person for whom music was the most important thing in life... until now.

Except the occasional weekend flying visit back to Hamburg, I had spent the last three months in Munich. Busy with recording sessions, radio interviews and engagements with the big band. By now I was six months pregnant, but it hardly showed. I was getting a letter every day from Jan. We were also talking on the telephone daily. But I never mentioned my pregnancy, because I wanted it to be a surprise. Jan's greatest wish in his life was to have a baby with me. We would give this baby all the love, care and security in the world. Our baby would never want for anything. After my final show in Munich I left immediately for Hamburg. It was four o'clock in the morning, but I just could not wait to leave, which under normal circumstances I would have done. I wanted to give the good news to Jan as soon as I could. There was no time to be wasted.

The journey took me a few hours on the autobahn. Luckily in those days there was no speed limit. I arrived at about seven o'clock in the morning, ran up the stairs two at a time. I opened the front door and rushed into the bedroom only to find that the bed was empty, the bed cover was completely untouched and unruffled. I put my hand under the duvet to feel whether it was warm. However, the sheets were stone cold and had obviously not been slept in.

Without any hesitation I drove my car to Tanya's house. I parked my car where it could not be seen from the house but where I would have a clear view of the front door. This was just a hunch and I sat and waited and waited, my eyes glued firmly on the front door. At eight-thirty the front door opened, the handsome tall figure of Jan appeared followed by petite and dark-haired Tanya dressed in a long, pink dressing gown with a tiny baby in her arms. Jan put his arms around the both of them and they stayed in a lingering embrace which not long ago I had experienced myself. He walked away a couple of steps and then he walked back to kiss her again and kiss the baby and as he was walking towards the gate his right arm was waving. He turned towards the bus station.

I could not move. I was glued to the seat of my car, as were my hands to the steering wheel. I did not cry, I do not remember breathing. Neither do I recall moving or even being alive. I really cannot tell how long I was there in that catatonic state. Some part of me died then and there. Eventually, as if in a trance, I drove back to our flat. This time my steps were not hurried. I walked up the stairs as if I weighed a ton.

I opened the front door and this time Jan was just coming out of the shower with only a bath towel wrapped around his body. The bed was ruffled up, as though it had been slept in and in the vase were twenty-five long stemmed red roses. He ran towards me, picked me up, twirled me around, hugged and kissed me, 'Darling I could not sleep all night, I was lying awake waiting for you. How every day we are not spending together is too long. I never knew that I could love anybody as much as I love you. You must not go away again. This torture of being apart is just too much for me.'

I did not know what to say. Suddenly those words which had once been the most beautiful sounds ever, now sounded like an insult. Every word cut me as if a sharp razor had slashed every part of me. I heard my own voice coming out of my mouth, 'You bloody liar! You lying shit!' and I slapped him hard across the face. 'You did not sleep here last night, I watched you coming out of Tanya's house and the way you were hugging and kissing each other did not look anything like a platonic encounter. Get your things and get out of my flat, now!'

He could not deny it and for the first time since I had met

him he was speechless. He didn't ever know about this child in my belly, this good news, news he would have wanted to hear. I could not bring myself to tell him. He did not deserve such wonderful news. Now this child is mine alone. I still could not cry, I just felt empty, hurt, betrayed, angry and full of hate. Without any arguments he packed his belongings. Then he sat down next to me and said, 'Let me explain, it was not what it looked like.'

'Even you cannot talk yourself out of the situation,' I replied, I stood up, opened the front door and as he left slammed it behind him. My whole body was shaking. I was sick.

The next few days the ringing never stopped of either my telephone or my front door bell. I did not answer either of them. Wherever I went, I found him standing waiting for me. The landlord reported Jan was sleeping in the doorway and that he had to call the police to have him removed. I took the next engagement I could out of Hamburg; I recorded two new songs which turned out to be exceptionally good. As I was recording them I was thinking of Jan and this deep, sad emotion could be detected in the tone of my voice. Even now after so many years when I listen to the record, I can still remember the pain that I had.

I accepted every engagement outside of Hamburg I was offered. I did not want to keep bumping into people at home and keep having to explain myself. I needed to make as much money as possible as I had no idea how soon after the birth I could work again. I had to design my own outfits for the stage trying to hide the fact that I was pregnant. For the last few weeks of my pregnancy, I stopped travelling, working only in my usual club in Hamburg.

During this time a chain of events was triggered that would eventually destroy my recording career. It was all to do with Mr

Wagner, the club owner. One night Mr Wagner joined me at the table after the show. He was a small rotund middle-aged man, very friendly, full of life and interested in everything. He wanted to know as much as he could about me and my past. He openly admitted he was proud to engage me as I filled up his club nightly. 'You can stay as long as you want,' he said to me. During the conversation when I mentioned the word Cyprus his eyes opened wide. 'Did you say Cyprus?'

'Yes, Cyprus.'

'Well, this is very interesting, Dorit,' he said, 'I am trying to find a company in Cyprus who could start a business or partnership with me. I want to start a canning factory to put fresh oranges into cans. Part of the supply of oranges would come from Israel, part from Cyprus and as they deliver the oranges by boat they would be put into the cans immediately, whilst they are still fresh.' It was well known that he was a businessman and that this night club was only a hobby of his run by his mistress.

'This is so exciting,' he said, 'let us have a bottle of champagne!' He wanted to know all about the company that I started at the age of nineteen when I married Tim.

I started this company as a gift to Werner who was such a good step-father to me. He could not get permission to start a company in Cyprus because he was a German citizen; I on the other hand was a British citizen having married Tim. Werner's export-import engineering firm was mine only on paper. I signed the papers and gave power of attorney to Werner, giving him full authority and permission to do with the company as he wished. At that time Werner was a civil engineer and he worked for an Anglo-American company. He had the knowledge and the connections to make this business a success. Sadly only a few months after we set it up he became ill. He had contracted asbestosis and developed lung cancer. As a result he spent the last five years of his life in a sanatorium in Agra, Switzerland. After five years of excruciating suffering he passed away. I was grateful to him for so many things. He taught me so much. Things which I appreciate even more, now.

As he was listening to my story Mr Wagner became more and more interested and excited. He insisted on setting up a meeting with his solicitor as soon as possible. He also insisted my mother had to be present.

I made it completely clear to all parties that I had never had any interest in the company and that I did not wish to have any part in any of the deals which were about to be arranged. 'I am a singer, a performer and now a mother to be. I have no interest whatsoever. Please make sure that it stays that way.'

My mother's enthusiasm and sudden interest in the company came as a big surprise to me. If it was not for Mr Wagner mentioning his plans I most probably would not have ever thought about the Mediterranean Export and Import Company again. As my mother was still working with the students and had a pretty well-paid job, I was amazed and surprised she would start the joint venture with Mr Wagner. With hindsight this was an opportunity for a new start with her boyfriend, the Baron.

They were to rekindle the Mediterranean Export and Import Company. Mr Wagner was going to send out one of his employees, Mr Strahle, and my mother and her boyfriend, the Baron, were also to go to Cyprus as business partners of Mr Wagner. To handle certain aspects of the new company they formed a sub-company.

* * *   * * *   * * *

Whilst Mr Wagner, my mother and the Baron were busy making the necessary arrangements for the new business, I was preoccupied with the preparations for having a baby. The doctor had told me I needed a caesarean as my hips were too narrow to give birth normally.

On the morning I was scheduled to go to the hospital, I rang the bell of my landlord, asking him to order a taxi because I was too far gone to drive myself. He was himself a doctor and looked at me with terror in his eyes, 'How dare you,' he yelled at me, 'you are having a baby? I will not allow a baby in the flat.'

'What do you mean you will not allow? This is my flat, I have a contract and it is nowhere written that I cannot have a baby.'

'It is!' He slammed the door in my face, refused to order me a taxi. The entrance to the house and the pavement beyond were covered with thick black ice and in order to get into my car without slipping, I had to go down on my hands and knees and crawl to my car. My hands were numb from the ice. I managed to squeeze myself and my oversized tummy behind the steering wheel. Here I was, all alone, driving my car into an unknown future for my baby and myself.

The journey took me longer than usual because of the black ice and I found it very difficult to drive with my big stomach, trying to reach the steering wheel. When the porter came out to help me from the car, he called for a wheel-chair to take me up to the maternity ward. He was completely shocked to see I was driving myself instead of arriving by taxi or ambulance. They wheeled me to my room.

I do not remember much about the birth as they put me to sleep before I reached the theatre. When I woke up a sister came through the door holding a little bundle: 'Here you are, you have a little daughter.' With this she placed the perfect looking little person into my arms. It was the sixth of January 1961. She was wrapped from her tummy down to her legs in a bandage on top of which was a little blanket. The first thing I did is start to count the little fingers on her hands and the tiny little toes on her feet, over and over again, just to make sure that nothing was missing and that she was perfect. I learned that many mothers do that. The nurse turned, telling me, 'I will leave you for a little while with your beautiful daughter.' And there we were the two of us completely alone, and yet not alone. We had each other.

There was nobody to sit there to hold my hand. Nobody to be proud of me or to say congratulations for having given birth to a beautiful little baby. I could not take my eyes off my little daughter. She was so perfect, no wrinkles, as though as she could have been carved from white marble. She even had eyelashes and hair. Her little chest was going up and down which told me she was alive, she was breathing. I had never held a baby before. I knew nothing about babies or baby care. The few motherhood books I had read made no sense at all to me.

The next few days I was kept busy. The nurses had to teach me how to bathe the baby. How to make sure the water temperature was right by dipping my elbow in the water. How to put the nappies on and how to clean the baby's bottom. I did not realise that there was a difference between how to clean a baby girl and how to clean a baby boy. I learned what a joy it is to hear your baby burp and how important it is for the baby's wellbeing. I had to learn how to put cream on her little bottom, how to prepare the formula of the milk, how to test the temperature of her food on the inside of my wrist.

When they brought my daughter to me on the fourth day she had three little anemones squeezed tightly in her miniscule little fist. The nurse had a smile in her face as she passed the baby to me: 'Happy birthday, Mummy!' This was the tenth of January. This was the best birthday present I had ever had, my beautiful little daughter and the three anemones. Who needs big bunches of flowers? Not I!

I was kept in the hospital for two weeks as the stitches on my tummy were very painful. Just before I left the maternity ward the nurse who looked after me most of the time sat down on my bed.

'Have you chosen a name for your little girl?'

'Yes,' I answered. 'You see, my father was killed when I was a little girl and I thought in his honour I should name my daughter after him. His name was Desider, Desko for short. So Desiree. Yes, Desiree, after my dad. And she will be Desi for short.

* * *   * * *   * * *

Walking down the corridor towards the car, each step that I took was still very painful. The carrycot I had bought fitted perfectly into the back of my little sports car. The roads were all covered with white snow. I drove very slowly and carefully back to the flat; I had to take extra care because I was carrying this very special, precious little passenger. At last, arriving back at the house, I opened the big front door and walked up two flights of stairs slowly. The carrycot, with the baby, seemed very heavy after the C-section. As I arrived on the second floor I had the shock of my life. My front door was boarded up and I could not get into my flat. I just could not believe it. I left the carry-cot on the landing and went back downstairs. I rang the landlord's bell and this red faced, pot-bellied man appeared.

'What happened to my flat?' I asked.

'Cannot you see? It is boarded up. I will not let you use the flat.'

I just could not believe what I had heard. 'Are you telling me that you will not let me and my newborn baby into the flat that I pay for? And you call yourself a doctor? What am I to do? Where shall I go?'

'That is not my problem, you should have thought of it before.' He slammed the door in my face, again.

Here I was, in the middle of January, freezing cold with a two-week-old newborn baby, homeless. I had no option but to drive to my mother's flat. She could not turn us away. Mother was not exactly welcoming when she opened her door. However, she did let us in. Next day I went to the police and complained about the landlord's behaviour. He stood firmly by his decision. Only after lengthy negotiations did he permit the policemen to go and collect my baby's clothes and to bundle up most of my clothes and a handful of my belongings. He would not even let me come back and collect the rest. In the state that I was in, nothing could surprise me anymore.

I stayed in my mother's flat for two weeks but then the neighbours started to complain about the baby's crying. At this time my mother was running the home for girls who had escaped from behind the Iron Curtain, countries such as East Germany and Hungary. There were about twelve rooms, each accommodating students. All the rooms were occupied. The only place Mother could offer me and my baby daughter was the converted loft room. It had an old iron bed with a mattress and bits and pieces of old furniture stacked up in the corner. This room was obviously used for storage. There was no heating but I was given blankets and a couple of pillows.

That first night I put the carrycot next to me without taking the baby out, as, inside of the carrycot she would be warmer. I was woken up by water dripping onto my face. Rain was coming through. I crept down the creaking staircase and found an umbrella. This I placed over Desi. I moved the bed away from the dripping rain. After half an hour trying to go back to sleep, shivering from the cold, I found this situation unbearable. I took the carrycot with my baby and settled in the empty common room. As the girls came down for breakfast and discovered us huddled up on the sofa, a few of them promptly offered to share their room with us.

Here again I realised how unfeeling my mother's action had been. What on earth possessed her to put me and my four-week-old baby in an unheated storeroom for the night? Surely she could have asked some of the students to double up and find a place for her own daughter and her grandchild.

* * *   * * *   * * *

By now my mother was all packed and her mind was preoccupied with the arrangements and excitement of her new life in Cyprus. It was clear to me that my problems were not one of her priorities. By the time Desi was six weeks old my mother and the Baron were on their way to the new business venture with Mr Wagner in Cyprus. I had not realised that this project had moved so fast. Nor that my mother and Mr Wagner had signed and sealed their business deal in such a short time.

Luckily I found a little one-bedroom flat in a nice area. Six weeks had passed and I remained overjoyed at being a full-time mom. I could not get over this new feeling which engulfed me. Being responsible for another human being who was so tiny and helpless and to feel so much love towards someone you have known for such a short time is not something that you can compare with any other emotion. Having created such a perfect little human was a real miracle.

My first outing with my newborn little baby was for a shopping spree into a posh department store near the Alster. I had put on a bit of weight so I needed some new clothes and of course some outfits for my baby. I was so proud pushing my pram; people stopped, looked into the pram and complimented me on what a pretty daughter I had. On my way out of this elegant shop, out of the blue, Jan stood next to me looking in the pram. 'And whose little bastard is this? No wonder you wanted me out of the flat so hurriedly! So, who is the happy father?' His voice was sarcastic, cutting straight through my heart as if he had used a razor; it could not have been more painful. I hung on to the pram, my knees and legs were like jelly and I honestly thought I would be sick into the pram. I did not know how to talk. This was the first time that I had had any contact with Jan for the last six months. He just stood there looking down on me with a sarcastic, and bitter expression, trying to make me feel that I had committed an unforgivable act. In a very quiet voice which surprised me greatly, I said, 'Even a selfish bastard like you should be able to count up to nine.'

As I was not prepared to enter into any kind of conversation I continued to push the pram, concentrating on putting one foot ahead of the other, not looking back, trying to get away from the shop as fast as I could to breathe in some fresh air.

I knew now that not trying to persuade him that Desi was his daughter was the right thing to do. This was not the man I wanted to spend the rest of my life with, nor have a family with. I made a decision then and there that I would never tell him he has a daughter. He did not deserve to share this beautiful little girl and neither did she deserve to have a father who was such a cheating, lying and sarcastic shit.

I had endless sleepless nights over this decision. Perhaps I should have given him a chance. Perhaps we should have found a way to share the parenthood. Not a day has passed by that I have not wondered whether I made the right decision. What kind of a life of deception might my child have had to go through?

* * *　* * *　* * *

My savings and my money had run out. I barely had enough money to pay the rent and electricity. My agent kept on phoning me and asking when I would be ready to go back to work and I kept on delaying. Eventually I accepted a concert and took Desi with me in her carrycot. I negotiated with the lady who was looking after the coats of the customers; she had a nice warm place in the club and she agreed to look after Desi whilst I was singing. I had prepared a little bottle for her and crossed my fingers hoping that this would work. Luckily my figure was returning to what it was before the pregnancy, so that I could fit into most of my clothes with a little alteration here and there. The show was a great success and I was offered a whole week of work. The hat-check lady was very happy and agreed to keep an eye on Desi. She was amazed what a good little girl she was – no trouble. In that week I made enough money to keep us going for a few weeks.

It became very hard for me as I would be working until two o'clock in the morning and Desi would wake up at about five o'clock. She was ready for her first feed but I had only slept for three hours and was tired and sleepy for the rest of the day. I had to find a solution. There was no question of my giving up singing because this was the way I earned my living. This was my job and I was very lucky I was still popular and had constant job offers.

The family paediatrician recommended a baby guesthouse. He knew about a retired midwife who had opened her most elegant house to accommodate babies who needed first-class, reliable, professional care. It was on the outskirts of Hamburg in a very smart, prestigious neighbourhood. Mrs Shnabel, the lady owner who ran this crèche, was very warm and caring. I explained my situation to her. I had interviewed several full-time nannies but none of them gave me the feeling I could trust my baby in their care. I needed to work and I wanted the best for my child. She recognised me and was very understanding and I felt that this was the woman that would give my baby the love and care she needed and deserved. She told me what the cost would be including all the food, the laundry and twenty-four hour care. Her fees were quite astronomical but I felt lucky to find such an amazing place where I felt my child would have the best.

She showed me around. There were two cots to each of the three nursery rooms. The babies varied in age and background. One baby's mother died at birth and the father could not look after the baby. Another one's mother was terminally ill and in hospital. Each and every one of these little babies had a tragic story and a very good reason to be looked after by Mrs Shnabel. There was one little boy, though, who was older than the rest. He was standing up in the cot. He was blond, quite thin and had a very sad look about him. 'Oh,' she said, 'he is little Peter. He is two years old. His mother brought him here and never returned. There is nobody who comes and visits him and I am making an application to adopt him.'

With this she picked him up and the little boy's face lit up and he put his arms around her neck and his face snuggled next to hers. I was really touched.

'As you see, I have a full house. Usually there is a long waiting list. You have no idea in what unbelievable situations people find themselves. I feel for you.' She put her arm around me. 'I will put an extra cot in the biggest room and you can leave Desi with me, and you, my dear, I will take to the guest room. You must have a rest and sleep. I can see you are just about to collapse.'

No sooner did I lie on top of the bed only having removing my shoes, than I was instantly asleep. I slept for four hours and if Mrs Shnabel had not woken me up and reminded me that I had to work, I, most probably, would have slept for the next twenty hours.

'How often am I allowed to visit my daughter?' I enquired.

'My dear, you can spend as much time as you want to with her.'

I had to work out a routine so that I could work and see Desi as much as I could. I left Desi in the hands of Mrs Shnabel and as I drove away I had very mixed feelings. This was the first time in three months we were separated from each other. One part of me wanted to turn back, snatch her out of the cot, say sorry to Mrs Shnabel, but I simply cannot leave her, but then the reasonable me took over: 'No Dorit, you are doing the right thing, you have to earn money.'

* * *   * * *   * * *

I got myself ready and felt a big sigh of relief. I had to admit it was much easier going to my next show without having to worry about someone in the night club looking after Desi while I was on stage. That evening I went to work with an easy heart and a clear conscience. When I got home from work I had my first night's proper sleep since Desi was born. Perhaps I had not wanted to admit it was very hard to work at night to look after a young baby without any additional help. However, I could hardly wait to go and see Desi.

When I arrived she was having a little nap as babies do after their meal. Mrs Shnabel had on a great big white apron and was busying herself with another little baby who needed her attention. There were two other women assisting her: one was a bit younger than her and the other one looked as though she had just finished college. She came close to me and winked, 'I will make sure I take care personally of little Desi. Although she has only been here for one night she is as good as gold. Miss Oliver, I must praise you for having looked after your baby perfectly. There is not one little pick-patch or any sign of nappy rash on your baby. She has been immaculately well looked after; such a beautiful little girl and so content. You must be so proud.'

Her words were like music to my ears. I asked her whether I could give a bath to Desi before her bedtime. She said, 'Yes, of course. Why don't you go and have a cup of coffee?'

Mrs Shnabel encouraged me to come back at five o'clock. As it was only two o'clock and there were three hours to bath time I got into my car, which was parked in her front garden, put the driver's seat into snooze position and had a very welcome, much-needed afternoon nap.

Desi loved the water. Her little arms were splashing and her legs were kicking as though she wanted to run. She smiled and gurgled, her big blue eyes sparkled. This was the best time of the day for both of us. I was allowed to dry her and get her ready for bed. Then it was time for the evening feed. I gave her the bottle and we were both happy and content with our new routine. Once she finished the bottle I placed her over my shoulder, as usual patted her little back and hey presto! She did what she had to do. Surprising what a loud, deep sound came out of this tiny little baby when she burped. Now she was ready to be placed into her cot and I could go off with a happy heart, to earn our keep and provide her with the best.

There were times when I missed her so much that instead of going home after work, which at times could be as late as four o'clock in the morning, I would drive out to Mrs Shnabel's establishment, park the car in her front garden and sleep until the morning, so that I could be there in time to give Desi her first feed. This gave us the chance to spend as much time together as possible. Mrs Shnabel and I became very close. She felt she had to look after me and when she knew that I slept half the night in the car in order to be with my daughter she would prepare a very healthy breakfast for me. She was very impressed at how dedicated, loving and caring I was. She also told me how many of the other mothers just leave the babies in her care and sometime they do not come to visit them at times for weeks or even months on end.

'Some people,' she said to me, 'do not deserve such precious babies. You are different. Please do not worry, I am taking good care of little Desi. Just look at her, how happy she is. If you get a contract which will take you further than Hamburg, do not worry, I will do everything in my power to care and to look after Desi.'

How did she know, I asked myself, I had just had an offer for four weeks work in Köln and I did not know if I should accept it or not. Four weeks seemed such a long time not to see my baby. However, the money was so good it would keep us for at least two months without my having to worry. They were opening a new club and wanted me to be their guest artist.

'Do not hesitate,' she said when I told her, 'take it, it will be good for you, not only the money but you will be able to sleep without trying to be here on time to be with Desi. Do you think that Desi would not get a bath if you do not come here? Do you think I do not know how to look after her? People are starting to think you are a member of the staff.'

249

She laughed and then gave me a hug and practically pushed me out of the front door. I quickly turned and ran up the stairs; I just had to give another kiss to my baby before I went off.

* * *   * * *   * * *

My suitcases were packed in no time. My stage clothes took up most of the space in the suitcases. I arrived in Köln and went straight to the very luxurious five-star hotel which the club had arranged. I had to be in the night club for rehearsals with the band at six o'clock in the evening. I was allocated the star dressing room, which was well equipped with its own bathroom and a chaise longue where I could rest between performances. This was my first big engagement since having Desi. It was wonderful to be back again. Once the radio station found out that I was in Köln, I was contacted by Dr Jazz and he invited me to join him at the studio.

I had very good reviews in the papers and numerous work offers. But I did miss my little baby so much. I phoned Mrs Schnable daily to check how Desi was. The club owner wanted me to stay a little longer. I rang Mrs Shnabel, asking for her opinion. 'You owe it to the public and you are lucky you are wanted. How many of your colleagues would wish to be in your position? You have to take the opportunity when it is given to you. Do not insult me by doubting my ability to look after your daughter.' She chuckled and hung up the phone. I was extremely busy for the next two weeks as I had several recordings with the radio station. I bought a lot of new things for Desi and a beautiful red crystal vase for Mrs Shnabel. She deserved it.

Once spring arrived and the weather got warmer, I used to take Desi for long walks pushing her pram. Sometimes I would put one of the other babies into the pram so that they too would benefit from the fresh air and sunshine.

My next big engagement was at a well-known variety theatre in Bremen. This was for a month with an option for an additional month. Now this was too long a time to be apart from Desi. As she became older she became more interested, more demanding and I really could not bear to be separated from her. Saying goodbye to Mrs Shnabel was an extremely emotional experience. In the last three months while she looked after my baby, we talked on a daily basis and had grown very close. As we said our goodbyes we both cried and to my greatest surprise she asked me if I could give her a signed record of mine.

'I never wanted to embarrass you by asking for a record but even before you came to me I used to admire your singing. I am a great fan and I like to believe that nobody knows you as well as I do because here I saw you as you really are. Here you were off stage with no make-up. Here you were just Desi's mom. If you ever need my help, I am always here and even if you do not need me, from time to time please come and visit me. I would like to see how Desi is getting on.'

We set off for Bremen. I kept glancing at Desi in my mirror and seeing how peacefully she was settled. And on the journey, my mind went back to the time Desi was born. I thought of Tim and of my mother. How they had helped or hindered me.

I was lucky I was still married to Tim when Desi was born. Nobody knew that she was not the daughter of Tim, my English husband. As soon as I had Desi I contacted Tim and told him I had just given birth to a little girl and would it be all right for me to register her with the British Consulate as his daughter, so that she could automatically become a British citizen. His reply was amazing. Not only did he agree and write a letter to the

British Consulate requesting his daughter be registered, he also wanted to adopt her to be her father as he still loved me. I was very grateful for his generous offer and had her registered. I thanked him very much for the offer but I was quite happy to bring my daughter up on my own.

I thought back to the time my mother popped in for a flying visit to see her first grandchild. My mother looked like a million dollars – all made-up and wearing one of her 'special' dresses, the one she always wore to impress. I was very surprised to see her like this. I could not think for a moment that my mother would go to all this trouble just to visit me in the hospital.

She took a glance at the baby. 'Oh, she is so beautiful and I am a grandmother!'

'Yes, but do not forget I am her mother,' I said.

I was really so happy to see her, but this joy was very short lived as my mother kept on fidgeting in her chair, kept on changing the position of her crossed legs from one to the other. So far she had only spent around fifteen minutes with us I could detect that she felt somewhat uncomfortable. Then all was made clear to me.

'I am sorry darling,' she said, 'but my taxi is waiting. I do not want to be late to the exhibition of Nan Cuz. I am opening the exhibition.' And with this she got up, gave me a peck on my forehead, turned on her heels towards the door.

'Please, Mother, just stay a little bit longer. Can you not stay?' I pleaded with her. 'Is this exhibition of Nan Cuz so much more important to you than your daughter? I need you, I am really so frightened.' This was the first time for ages that I really wanted my mother to be with me, just to hold my hand and make me feel that I was not alone, that she cared, that I mattered. But there was no point in my pleading. She would not stay. I again realised that I was not important, that my feelings did not matter. She never even turned around, just wafted out as though she could not get into her taxi soon enough.

At that time holding my daughter in my arms made me feel that, after all, I was not alone. We had a bond that could never be broken. I breathed in her smell, deep deep into my lungs, and the pain and disappointment of realising how little my feelings and my life meant to my mother eased.

'I will never do this to you, you will always come first and you will always be the most important person in my life.'

And so we arrived in Bremen.

JUGGLING MOTHERHOOD
AND SHOW BUSINESS

Having arrived a few days before I started my engagement in Bremen at the Astoria Variety Theatre, I put an advert in the local paper looking for a nanny for Desi. There were four candidates. The most important criteria were how Desi reacted to each one at the interview. Each girl had good references but I was watching Desi. There was only one girl who she smiled at. Although Desi was only six months old she already seemed to be a pretty good judge of character. So we made our mind up: it was Maria who got the job. She was an eighteen year-old buxom girl. I rented a beautiful two-bedroom ground floor flat which Maria shared with us. The flat was only ten-minute walk from the theatre. Nearby was a lovely park where Maria would take Desi. She had worked as a nanny to an American family with three children. The American family went back home and wanted to take Maria with them but she did not want to go. She wanted to stay near her family. She had a lovely personality and they took to each other straight away. This was a great relief for me and to my good fortune she knew more about how to look after a baby than I did, although I could not let her know this.

In Bremen I had a big fan club. They were very supportive and almost every night some of the members would come to the theatre. One evening there was a card in my dressing room pinned to a big bunch of flowers. This was an invitation for a visit to the best hair-dressing salon in town, signed by the owner Simon. Judging by the size of the bouquet, which could hardly fit into the vase, he was a very generous man. Or perhaps he just wanted to attract my custom.

The Astoria was a little theatre, seating around six hundred people. It had excellent acoustics and the sixteen-piece orchestra was just amazing. My first night it was a sell-out. After the show there was a knock on my dressing-room door. My private dresser answered and with a very polite voice said, 'Frau Oliver, Mr Simon would like to introduce himself to you,' and with this a smart young man stood there extending his hand to me. 'I hope you liked my flowers?' he smiled.

'I hope you are a good hairdresser,' I replied.

'Would you join me for a bottle of champagne,' he asked.

'Give me half an hour. That will give me time to change.'

He was a very pleasant young man, with impeccable manners, and I agreed to visit his salon the next day. My reception in the salon was spectacular. I felt very humbled by the extravagant treatment. He turned out to be a wonderful hairdresser. He would not accept any payment but declared he would be my personal stylist for the time that I was in Bremen. Every night before I went on stage he would wait for me in the dressing room ready to give my hair finishing touches. Although he was already the best known hairdresser in town, the fact I was his client gave him lots of publicity. I was unattached at the time and his invitations for dinner were very welcome.

* * *   * * *   * * *

Maria came back with us to Hamburg. My new little flat was perfect. Maria again shared a room with Desi and I slept on the sofa in the sitting room. She would care for Desi; give her a bath then breakfast, which was usually semolina pudding. After breakfast they would go out for a walk so that I could continue to sleep having worked into the early hours of the morning. At about eleven o'clock they would return and have a second breakfast with me. Here I took over my role as a mummy.

Desi had very fair curly hair, great big pale-blue eyes with long black eyelashes, and her two little front teeth were just peeping through. She was very proud of those because she kept on showing them. They were as sharp as needles. She kept on biting chunks out of my cheek and when I screamed out she thought it was very funny. She giggled out loud and kept on doing it again and again. Desi was a very contented child.

Unfortunately she developed bronchitis. Her cough became worse and worse. She was only a little girl, only nine months old. My paediatrician was a wonderful doctor and a good friend. He suggested to me the best thing would be for Desi to spend six months in a warm climate. Babies who are born in winter tend to develop bronchitis more than children who are born in summer, he said.

As my mother was running the Mediterranean Export and Import Company in Cyprus, with the Baron, her new boyfriend, it was a perfect solution for us to go and visit her. I booked a passage onto the ship that sailed out of Hamburg to Cyprus. I stopped all my engagements, sent Maria back to Bremen and paid her in full for the two months that I planned to stay away. The journey on the cruise ship was really a godsend. I did need a break as I had worked non-stop and only by not going to work did I find out how tired I really was.

The ship anchored just outside of Limassol. We had to get into a little motorboat which took us to the harbour. Mother and her boyfriend were waiting for us at the quayside. Mother lived in a nice little three-bedroom bungalow only a few metres from the sea. She hired a Greek nanny who would come to look after Desi, under her supervision. I did not like this arrangement at all but my mother insisted that I needed a rest and as she was my mother she had every right to look after her daughter. I discovered that I quite enjoyed this change of heart. For years I longed to be spoiled by my mother. So, under protest, I accepted the Greek nanny. I still bathed and fed Desi but I did welcome the help when I went down to the beach for a swim.

Whilst Maria had been a quiet, pleasant young woman, Sula, this middle-aged Greek nanny, was loud and bubbly. She would sing in the most unpleasant voice but it made Desi laugh. So did the bouncing on Sula's knees. Desi obviously enjoyed herself and after only two weeks her cough had stopped and her lungs were clear. This climate obviously was perfect for her. After four weeks I was ready to go back to Germany with Desi, but on the last visit to the local doctor I was told that taking the child back so soon would not be advisable as the bronchitis could return. By now my mother had tried to convince me that I should leave Desi with her in Cyprus as it would be good for Desi's health and that she really enjoyed being a grandmother and giving her all the love and attention that she could not give to me.

There was a contract waiting for me to go to Sweden. This contract was very tempting. It was for the most prestigious night club in Göteborg. The money was amazing. Not having worked for a whole month, my savings had gone down. I was persuaded by my mother to take this contract as leaving Desi in Cyprus for a bit longer was the right thing for her health.

It was very strange to be separated from Desi. She was part of me, like another limb. Surprisingly, learning how to be a mother was nothing like I thought it would be. It was the most natural feeling in the world. I learned how to put the nappies on, give a bath and burp her. I had to learn how to make semolina pudding and later mashed potatoes. I did miss her. I phoned every day to see how she was. Sometimes when I was lucky I heard her giggle or blow a kiss through the telephone. I was so afraid that she might forget me.

* * *   * * *   * * *

This club in Göteborg had a unique arrangement. The top floor was a very stylish coffee house. On the ground floor there was a restaurant where the speciality was fish – all kinds of fish – from bouillabaisse (French fish soup) to lobster. Giant prawns was the main delicacy in Sweden. This was served on chunks of ice. The restaurant had such a good reputation, people had to book weeks in advance.

Downstairs was the night club, with a shiny dance floor in the middle of the room, about twenty round tables with dark red velvet chairs, white tablecloths and a small vase with flowers on each table. There was a small podium where the five-piece band played. I had a microphone with which I could walk around among the customers.

Before I started, I was asked what time I would like to take my meal, before or after the show. As I was wearing skin-tight costumes and I could not sing on a full stomach I always had my meals after the show, but I never expected such star treatment. On my first night when I got back to my dressing room, after the show, there was a small table with a white tablecloth and a single red rose in a vase waiting for me with a little note: 'Dinner will be served in 15 minutes'. I quickly got out of my stage clothes and put on my dressing gown. I did not know what to expect but then three knocks on my door and the chef brought in a tray with the most amazing delicacies. My first course was the bouillabaisse. I can easily say that this was the best I ever tasted. The next course was lobster thermidor with a glass of champagne, followed by lemon sorbet. I was over the moon. All this time the chef was standing there watching me enjoy his creation. This treatment was repeated every night.

When I arrived back in Cyprus I could not believe how much Desi had grown. I was only five weeks since I last saw her. When she saw me she opened her arms and kept on repeating 'mommommommom'. I knew it straight away, this was my mother's teaching. Desi had the most smiling eyes I had ever seen. She was as happy to see me as I was to see her. It was obvious how well she had been looked after. I had never seen my mother being so warm and loving as she was with her granddaughter. I found out my mother told everyone that she was her child. She felt she was too young to be a grandma. I felt very jealous and upset. I thought she would be happy to be a grandmother and not try to muscle in on my right to be called 'mommy'. At the same time I was very touched and grateful at how well she had looked after my baby. I stayed for another two weeks. Then it was time to go back to Germany.

* * *   * * *   * *

Arriving back in Hamburg was comforting. The weather was much cooler, but opening the front door to my own little flat was just wonderful. Desi was a very heavy child and refused to walk. She propelled herself with amazing speed sitting on her bottom and working with her legs like a paddle. Occasionally she pulled herself up on parts of the furniture or a chair but she was not very happy to walk. By now she was eighteen months old. I just loved it when there was just the two of us.

She was a very intelligent little girl. It was no trouble to take her to restaurants as she was used to them from the very beginning. She could even use chopsticks, thanks to the Chinese gentleman who owned the Chinese restaurant next to the club where I was working. As it was so near and both of us loved Chinese cooking we ate there every day. The owner of the restaurant and his wife completely fell in love with my little daughter and as soon as we entered the restaurant they took her out of my arms, set her on a high chair and taught her how to use chopsticks. It became the special attraction of the restaurant: the customers watching a little European child, so young, eating with chopsticks. Whenever we went to a Chinese restaurant this was Desi's party trick.

One evening I was just about to give Desi a bath when the doorbell rang; two policemen stood there.

'Are you Miss Dorit Oliver? We have a warrant for your arrest.'

WHAT NEXT?

Arrest me? I could not imagine why they would want to. Seeing two policemen at my door with a warrant for my arrest was baffling. I had done nothing.

'We have a warranty for your immediate arrest. Please get ready.'

I just cannot go, they must wait. I told them. I was just about to give a bath to my baby daughter. I just cannot go to the police station as I have nobody to look after my child. I was panicking.

'There is nothing we can do, these are the papers and you have to come with us.'

I pleaded with them, trying to explain it must be a mistake. Why would I need to go with them to the police station, it must be a misunderstanding. The policemen showed me the documents and it clearly said 'Dorit Oliver'. I negotiated with them to give me a ride to Mrs Shnabel who would look after my daughter. She was the first person that came into my mind. I was permitted to pack a few things for my baby.

We drove out to Mrs Shnabel. The surprised look on her face as she opened the door; seeing Desi and me accompanied by two policemen was the most unexpected sight. I handed Desi over to Mrs Shnabel, explaining to her I had absolutely no idea what had happened. She said, 'Do not worry, I look after her', and she said she would contact a very good solicitor who was a friend of hers. I was in such a state of shock I did not believe I would need a solicitor but I was thankful she did the thinking for me. Then I sat in the police car and was driven to the prison in the middle of Hamburg.

At the imposing prison door they rang the bell and a female

prison officer came to get me. We had to go through three different locked doors made out of thick round metal bars. I was handed a blanket and a pillow and was taken to a small cell which contained a thin and narrow bed and a toilet with no seat. There was also a small sink with a single water tap. From a small square barred window I could see, in the distance, a crane on top of a roof. I was still in shock as the prison officer locked the cell door behind me. I was petrified. In a very short time a very pretty prison officer unlocked the door, sat next to me on my bed, brought a cup of coffee and a couple of biscuits and I asked, 'Why am I here?'

She said, 'Later on the prison warden will come and explain what you have to do. Then she looked at me and said, 'You are Dorit Oliver the famous recording star. As you were walking through the corridor they recognised you and so did I.'

I nodded, I wanted to say 'I am innocent' but there was no point as I did not know what I was in the prison for in the first place. By now it was meal time; the rest of the prisoners went into a dining place whilst I was brought some food in my cell on a tray with a cup of coffee and a glass of water. I heard voices calling from different directions: 'Hello Dorit Oliver, welcome! Do not be afraid!' All these little messages came. These were very encouraging. Although I could not see anybody I heard these friendly voices.

I do not remember how long I was lying there on this hard bed. I just could not fall asleep. Eventually I must have dozed off because the next thing I knew somebody was shaking my shoulders. 'Wake up, wake up! The prison warden is ready to talk to you.' I was accompanied by the same prison officer who came and sat with me last night. I was allowed to keep on my own clothes the ones with which I came in. The prison warden seemed a very stern, straight-laced woman in her mid-fifties, with her dark hair brushed into a bun on top of her head, no make-up. She had small piercing eyes. She did not seem to be a woman with whom you would want to have an argument. I was not offered a seat while she was sitting behind the desk.

'Are you Dorit Oliver?'

'Yes.'

'Have you got a solicitor?' she asked.

I said, 'I hope somebody will come.'

'I hope so too, otherwise we will recommend one.'

I asked, 'Why am I here?'

'You are here as surety for the debts of the company.'

'But I do not understand, I do not have a company, I am a singer.'

'All I can tell you is that you have been brought here for surety. A great sum of money is owed and you have to stay here to make sure the money is repaid.'

'What money?'

'That is all I have in my notes.' With this I was taken back to my cell not knowing what would happen to me. As I was approaching my cell along the lengthy corridor I could hear my record being played 'Du bist gut zu mir'. That was my very first record. As I was walking the inmates were clapping and asking me to give them an autograph. This cheered me up. Quite ironic to have such a friendly reception in the prison.

At about eleven o'clock the prison officer opened my cell door: 'Your solicitor is here.' With this she turned and made me follow her to meet 'my solicitor' who I had never met before.

He was a tall, very slim man in his seventies. White hair, gold-rimmed glasses, well-shaped lips and cigarette-stained teeth. He wore a dark grey suit which was hanging on him. It seemed as though he must have lost a lot of weight. He had a very nice and warm look in his eyes. He coughed a lot and each time he took

263

out a big white handkerchief and put it in front of his mouth. He was very calm and very nice, had a quiet, melodious voice. From his briefcase he took out two bundles of documents which he passed on to me and told me to read them. He asked lots of questions and he made endless notes. Mr Wagner was suing me personally for the expenses and the loss of money which had been incurred in Cyprus by the Mediterranean Export and Import Company of which I was the sole owner. The sum was thousands and thousands of pounds and I was arrested to stand surety until such time as this money is paid back. The solicitor, Mr Rotstein, said, 'Start from the beginning. So I did, telling him, I had signed away all rights. When we met with Mr Wagner's solicitor they signed a paper assuring me that I had nothing to do with any part of the company. I had given power of attorney to my step-father, explaining how it happened.

'Did you sell him the company?' he asked.

'No, how could I sell a company that was not mine?'

He made endless notes, pages and pages. His calmness rubbed off onto me. I could feel how he believed what I said and I had confidence that this man could help me.

'The first thing,' Mr. Rotstein told me, 'I have to get you out of here as soon as possible. It may take a few days but this is not a place for someone like you. Are they treating you all right?'

'Yes. Surprisingly they are playing my records and I have many requests to sign my autograph.' This brought a smile to his face.

Two days later Mr Rotstein returned. I was called to the director of the prison where Mr Rotstein was already waiting for me. He produced some documents which we both had to sign. Mr Rotstein signed the guarantor paper saying he would take all responsibility that I would not run away. With this I was released from the prison. I was only in prison for four days but it seemed much longer. Stepping out from behind those prison gates was wonderful. To be forced to stay behind locked doors is very intimidating and frightening. Mr Rotstein drove me back to my flat but on the way he stopped at a restaurant and treated me to a big meal. I was starving.

'I suggest you have a hot bath and a good night's sleep. Try not to think of what has happened to you. Do not answer any phone calls, do not open or answer the door. Just relax and leave everything to me. I will pick you up tomorrow morning at ten o'clock. I will ring the bell three times. Then we will go to my office to discuss what we are going to do.'

To have a warm bath and sleep in my own bed was such a luxury, especially after four days having been in prison for something that I still had no real idea about. As soon as I had checked with Mrs Shnabel that Desi was alright I sank into a warm bath, with luxurious oils, for hours not wanting to come out. I went straight to bed hoping to catch up with the sleep I had missed.

* * *   * * *   * * *

The bell rang three times at ten o'clock. Mr Rotstein was exactly on time. His offices were on the first floor in a highly prestigious and elegant building with wood-panelled walls and lots of Persian rugs scattered on the parquet floors. Sitting at the reception desk was a slim, middle-aged lady in a dark navy suit and a white blouse. As soon as we entered the office she got up and swiftly walked to Mr Rotstein's office and opened the door nodding '*Guten morgen, Her Rotstein.*' She took his hat and navy overcoat which was folded over his arm. Mr Rotstein stopped: 'Two coffees, please' – and just as he was walking to his office he quickly walked back and instructed Fraulein Stein, 'Can you please go over the road to the bakery and bring up a nice selection of their best cakes. This young lady needs feeding. Instead of the two coffees make it one coffee and one hot chocolate.'

The papers from my hearing seemed to have been all prepared and were waiting on his desk. He told me that he had known Mrs Shnabel for over twenty years and he had looked after her and her husband's dealings. The knocking on the door came as a big relief for both of us. There was Fraulein Stein with a big tray with a pot of coffee, a long glass with hot chocolate and a big cake tray with lots of wonderful cakes, two plates and two serviettes. I must have been very hungry and I remember how my mother taught me always to leave a little bit of food on the plate; this was for the fairies. But I was so hungry that I forgot all about etiquette and if the plates were not made up from china I suppose I would have also eaten them. I had hardly been able to eat anything for the last four days.

Now we came to the second part of our meeting and he read me the papers which had been served on him by the Court and the copy of the letter from Mr Wagner's solicitor. There were all sorts of papers there, some of them which I remember seeing when I met Mr Wagner's solicitor. But the most important document was the agreement we both signed where it was declared I had passed on all rights and authority to my mother and Mr Wagner and that I will not have any kind of moral or material responsibility whatsoever with anything concerning the Mediterranean Export and Import Company. This document was nowhere to be found. I assumed a copy of this must be in my mother's possession. It stated further Mr Wagner was holding my mother responsible for the losses which occurred during their partnership in Cyprus, and as my mother was not in the position to fulfil those obligations, he was holding me responsible, as the original owner and registered Managing Director of the company. He asked the courts to sign over all the rights to my royalties from my recordings, all my income from my shows. They had already confiscated my car. In other words, he would completely destroy my livelihood until the monies were repaid in full.

In Mr Rotstein's opinion he must have disposed of the original signed papers. He explained that I needed to sign these documents passing over my royalties and possessions to him as stake holder, if I wanted to stay out of prison. This was temporary until I appeared in court. Meanwhile, all I was allowed to keep were my costumes for the stage, but these had to be kept in Mr Rotstein's possession and he had to accompany me to each of my shows with the two or three stage clothes which I would wear during my show.

Mr Rotstein used to sit in my dressing room waiting and after each show I had to return to him my clothes which he had to take home with him until my next show.

At least I was out of prison and was able to work and earn some money. As soon as I possibly could I got in touch with Maria, sent her the train tickets and within about two days she arrived. We picked up Desi together from Mrs Shnabel. What an amazing friend she turned out to be. I noticed that Desi was not sleeping in one of the rooms allocated for clients but she had a big cot in Mrs Shnabel's own bedroom. So Desi was obviously looked upon as a member of the family.

My case was unique. They had sent the police car to arrest me even though I was not charged with a criminal act. This was not supposed to happen. Their excuse was that I was constantly on tour, often out of the country and they had to catch me before I absconded.

Nobody could prove that I owed anybody money as my

signature was nowhere to be found. The document they provided, I had never signed; although the signature looked like mine. This must have been a forgery. Mr Wagner was a very rich and influential man. He knew full well that my records were selling and my income from my shows was very lucrative, and he was determined to get his hands on my money by hook or by crook. This court case seemed to be endless. I had no answers to the charges. How could I? I had nothing to do with the company.

Mr Rotstein had achieved through lengthy negotiations that my royalties and income should go into his own company account from which he could then pay me a certain amount which would cover my daughter's and my daily living expenses. The rest that was left over would then go towards paying Mr Wagner's demands. This was of course a better arrangement than having to give all my income to Mr Wagner. At least Mr Rotstein made sure that I was not starving or short of money. Every now and then I had a few gigs where Mr Rotstein winked at me and let me keep the money.

Out of the blue, my mother arrived at my little flat. Her apologies were endless. She assured me that she knew nothing about it and that it was a lie that she owed money to Mr Wagner. How he had left her and the Baron in debt. Not paying for the rent of the bungalow, not paying the rent for the offices and not paying for the machinery that was ordered for the orange juice factory. He was supposed to be responsible for the finances. The Baron and a German, a Mr Strahle, were running the Export and Import Company while my mother was doing all the negotiations. The machinery arrived, the workers were employed. But Mr Wagner had not paid for any of it. Mr Strahle disappeared back to Germany and from what mother told me she and the Baron were left to face the debtors.

According to my mother, Mr Wagner accumulated thousands of pounds in income but never paid any of it out. The company got into serious trouble in Cyprus. All the machinery was repossessed and mother and the Baron had to make an urgent exit back to Germany. Mr Rotstein explained to my mother and the Baron, at a meeting which he arranged in his offices, that there was a possibility to sue Mr Wagner. But this was pointless as we did not have enough money to pay for the legal fees. The damage had been done. Mr Rotstein was very upset with my mother and he did not make any secret or hide his feelings. He simply could not understand how she could let this happen to her daughter who had tried to help her to start a new future at the same time as she was struggling to establish herself with a newborn baby. No matter how much Mother tried to persuade him that she knew nothing about the situation and how sorry she was for all this to have happened, somehow Mr Rotstein did not believe her.

* * *   * * *   * * *

Now there were four of us squashed into the small one-bedroom flat. I worked at night, Maria and Desi shared the room and my mother slept on the sofa in the lounge. I slept on the sofa during the day when my mother went to work. The government gave Mother back her job in charge of the Hungarian students who escaped from Hungary for a better life in Germany. She was very apologetic to me and tried to go out of her way to show how sorry she was. I was very disappointed and hurt. I did not want to believe that my mother would have let all this happen without knowing full well the consequences. But she was my mother and I always found a way to forgive her. Each time this forgiveness lark seemed to be harder and harder, but then I always forgave her no matter what.

Eventually Mr Rotstein, through the courts, was able to negotiate a settlement. I never received a further pfennig of royalties from my record sales but I could keep my income from performing and Mr Rotstein no longer had to bring my stage dresses.

* * *   * * *   * * *

Mother invited me to a concert which I knew full well would be very boring, not my taste at all. But if I had said no she would have taken it that I had not forgiven her for my arrest, imprisonment and loss of my record-deal income. As I expected the concert was deadly boring. The singer, Eva-Marie, was a talented soprano accompanied by a tall skinny piano player. From what I heard later on, she was employed by the Hamburg Opera. As I was sitting and listening somehow I felt there was someone staring at the back of my head. I turned to see a pair of eyes only two rows behind me that belonged to a young man who was visually very embarrassed to be caught out looking at me.

At the half-time interval we met up in the hall with some people my mother knew and behold there was this young man standing right next to me. He stood out from this German crowd. The first things I noticed were his brogue shoes, typically English. Also, he had a three-piece suit on. Germans do not wear waistcoats. He was very shy. He had a beautiful, dark, wavy mop of hair and a small moustache, a bit like Errol Flynn. This was Frank, Eve-Marie's cousin. He smiled at me and seemed pleasantly surprised by my English. He spoke perfect German. His family originated from Ludwigshafen before emigrating to England due to the anti-Semitism in Germany. At that time Frank was only six months old.

We were both very disappointed at the bell which ended the coffee break. All of us in the group were invited to Eva-Marie's party and we all agreed to meet in the foyer after the show.

I did not have a car. Frank jumped at this opportunity and volunteered to give me a lift with the excuse and a twinkle in his eye: 'I only have a two-seater sports car and there is only room for a very small, slim person,' and then he looked at me: 'Is it OK with you, Dorit?' They all smiled as it was not possible to give my mother a lift.

The party was quite a drive into the suburbs of Hamburg. As soon as we arrived I felt this too was not my scene. Most of the people seemed to be part of the symphony orchestra and classical musicians. The conversation was all related to composers and politics. My mother was in her element and I asked for permission from the hostess if it was all right to leave for half an hour as I had come straight from rehearsals and I had had no chance to have a meal. Luckily Frank felt the same way. The two of us could not get out quick enough. One of the guests said, turning to my mother: 'Zita, are you not worrying for your daughter? She is going out with this young man, she does not even know.' My mother smiled: 'No, my dear, I am worried for the young man.' And with this we escaped.

I was truly hungry. Since I had come out of the prison, I could not stop eating. Perhaps subconsciously I was afraid I would be locked up again and I wanted to have enough food reserves. I took Frank to my favourite restaurant in Hamburg, The Balkan Grill. The owner, Savo, was a good friend of mine. He was born in Novi Sad, like me. He escaped from the gas chambers as a young man. They caught him and beat him over the head with an iron rod which marked him for life. They left him for dead and that is what saved his life. I used to come for a meal sometimes after my shows when the restaurant was already shut. The chef and the waiters were all gone but he would prepare a meal for me to make sure I was not going home hungry.

It was about eleven o'clock at night when we arrived at the restaurant, which was completely full. He managed to squeeze in two chairs with a little table for us. He hardly ever asked me what I would like to have. He knew so well what I liked and he took it for granted that my partner would eat the same. A bottle of red wine was placed on the table. Our conversation flowed very easily. No strain, as if we knew each other for a very long time. Frank's eyes were dark blue with very dark, long eyelashes, almost as long as mine, except I used mascara. He spoke in a very quiet voice and he seemed shy. I told him I had six children and that I had been married three times. He did not blink an eyelid. Not a muscle moved on his face. 'You are trying to shock me, aren't you? But you cannot. Nothing can shock me.'

Savo did not let me pay but on the way out at the door he winked at me and whispered into my ear, 'He is nice.' We did not feel like going back to the party, so we went for a long drive along the water's edge. We found a lovely spot with a breathtaking view overlooking the Alster, now lit with the lights from the passing ships. He told me a little bit of his life, how his mother was a Catholic, his father Jewish. Frank's father had been a bank manager in Ludwigshafen and married his Catholic secretary, which in those days was considered outrageous. They lived in a big house, had servants but when Hitler decided that Jews and Christians could not be married and the children out of this union would be considered bastards, the servants one by one had to leave, as they were not allowed to work for Jews; they escaped to England. Frank was six months old when they made their escape from Nazi Germany. He had an elder brother, who was seven years older than him. Frank told me about the Blitz

272

in London and how he had to be evacuated as a five-year-old little boy to Dawlish to escape the bombs in London. I cannot explain why or how I just felt very safe and peaceful with this young man. I had the urge to tell him everything about my life, things that I never wanted to tell anyone, so many things I had kept locked within myself, never having had the urge to share with anyone.

By now it was four o'clock in the morning and we were sure that the party had ended. There is a famous flea market in Hamburg that starts between four and five o'clock in the morning. I often used to go there with members of the band. Not only did they sell everything you could imagine, there were restaurants, wine bars and coffee bars open. Frank had never heard of it. He was simply mesmerised. We stopped in front of this big bunch of bougainvillea which he wanted to buy for me. A really romantic gesture. He offered to pay with a very high denomination bank note for which the store holder could not give him change. I ended up buying my own bunch of flowers.

'Frank,' I turned to him, 'this is the first bunch of flowers I ever had to pay for.' Jokingly, I continued, 'And I will make you pay for it as long as you live.'

He just smiled and said, 'That's a deal.'

Frank stopped his car in front of the block of flats where I lived. 'When will I see you again?' he asked me.

'I will be back in four weeks' time. Tomorrow I am starting a job.'

'Can I have your phone number?'

Neither of us had pencil nor paper. So he opened the glove compartment of his blue TR3 and scratched my phone number onto the inside metal plate with a screw driver.

'You ruined your car,' I said.

'It does not matter. I will call when you are back.' With this he opened the car door, walked me to the house, gave me a little peck on my lips and sprinted back to his car.

What a nice man, I thought to myself. What a compact, unpretentious, well-behaved person he is.

* * *   * * *   * * *

Next morning I was picked up by an eight-seater Volkswagen van. Musicians and me. We had a month's contract in Travemunde. Knowing my mother lived in the flat supervising Desi was a great relief to me. Mother would tell Maria what to do and she was spending time with her little granddaughter. However, as soon as I finished my engagement and returned to Hamburg, Mother set off for America by boat. She had a friend who owned a freight line and had booked a cabin on the freighter.

I had only been back in the flat for two days when at eleven o'clock the doorbell rang and there was Frank standing at the door. I always made a point of not having any male visitors at home. I did not want Desi to meet various men. I managed to keep my professional life and my private life separate. As soon as the door opened, little footsteps appeared behind me and there she was, with her arms wide open, welcoming this completely strange man, who knelt down to her level, with a great big smile. She wrapped her arms around him repeating 'dadadadadada' as if she knew him. She would not let go. As he got up he carried Desi into the sitting room. I was very surprised and somewhat embarrassed because usually Desi did not take to people she had never met before. Especially surprising was such a friendly welcome to a completely strange man. Frank was absolutely amazing with Desi and Desi would not let go of him.

274

He took me out for lunch. He worked in Neumunster, which was about an hour's drive from Hamburg, and he said he would take me there to show me where he lived. Everything seemed so natural as if it was meant to be. He loved driving his pale blue Triumph TR3 which created huge interest in Germany. On the outskirts of Neumunster we drove into the garage, which regularly serviced his car, to get some petrol. When Frank was just about to pay, the man who owned the garage asked, 'Could you ask for an autograph from the young lady in your car?'

Frank was taken back and asked him: 'What do you mean an autograph? She is my girlfriend.'

'You lucky chap. What do you mean your girlfriend?'

'My girlfriend,' Frank laughed. He said to me: 'This funny man wants an autograph from you. Who does he think you are?'

I opened my handbag and took out a picture postcard of me, asking the man, 'Who do you want me to write it for?'

'Peter, my son,' he said.

Without hesitation I signed: 'To Peter, with love, Dorit Oliver' and gave him the card.

'My son is a big fan of yours. He has got all of your records. Thank you so much.'

Frank's mouth dropped open. 'Who are you?' He said to me.

The garage owner answered instead of me: 'She is your girlfriend. Do you not know? She is Dorit Oliver, one of our most famous recording artists.' The garage owner shook Frank's hand, patted him on the shoulder and congratulated him: 'How did you manage to get Dorit Oliver for your girlfriend? You lucky, lucky man!'

Still mumbling 'I had no idea, I had no idea', Frank shut the door and turned to me. His face still had this surprised expression: 'You never said?'

'I did not think it was important. I wanted to you to fall in love with me for the way I am, not for who I am.'

'I suppose it is too late now. I am deeply in love with you,' he said. 'If I'd known who you were when I first met you I would have run like hell. I would not have become involved with you. But now it is too late.' With this we drove off to pick up some papers from the Tannery where he worked. When the people from the factory discovered me in his car they all came to the windows waving and screaming and shouting my name. Lucky for Frank that he now knew who I was otherwise this kind of a demonstration would have given him a heart attack. Next day he was bombarded with requests for autographs.

* * *   * * *   * * *

Back in Hamburg Frank and I planned to visit a new Chinese restaurant. First we popped into the flat to make sure that Desi and Maria were OK. Desi was in my bed sleeping like a little angel. After a few hours Maria would pick her up and put her in her own cot. She loved sleeping in my bed and hugging my pillow. Maria was watching the late news on television with the most recent story about Marilyn Monroe's suicide, with newspapers and magazines leading on the same event piled up around her.

I was not working that night so it was not to be a quick meal in a hurry before my show. It was a good feeling to know Desi was being well looked after. Frank and I both liked Chinese food. This was a very elegant restaurant. Just before we finished the meal I had this funny feeling in my tummy. It was not because the food was bad. I just suddenly had this urge to go home. Something had happened to my daughter. We paid in a hurry and left. As we were approaching my flat we saw there were two fire engines parked in front. Firemen were just entering the building. I ran as fast as I could but the fireman stopped me:

'Sorry, you cannot go through, there is a fire in one of the flats.'

'But I have my little daughter in the first floor flat, number 11.'

'Oh,' he replied, 'that is where the fire is.'

I could see one of the firemen was preparing to break the door down just as I reached the front door. Instead I unlocked it. It was very hard to stay calm. There was smoke seeping from the gap under the front door. My first reaction was to get to the room where Desi was. The cot was empty and my bed was empty. By now I was shaking like a leaf. By a miracle Desi had rolled under my bed and was sound asleep. She must have rolled off the bed in her sleep. I passed the sleeping baby on to Frank who stood next to me.

I hurried into the sitting room where the other firemen were already pumping white foam over the scorched carpet. There was Maria lying on the floor amongst the newspapers with Marilyn Monroe's pictures and photos plastered all over the pages. The standard lamp must have been knocked over by her fall and the carpet and the lampshade caught fire. We discovered half a dozen boxes of empty aspirin containers and realised that Maria must have taken these pills because she had been sick all over herself. She was lying in her own vomit clutching an empty glass in her left hand. Also the telephone was off the hook lying next to her face.

The fire officer in charge informed me that he had had an urgent phone call from the fire brigade in Bremen. They contacted the Hamburg Fire Brigade which followed up the call immediately. He also explained to me that the Brigade had been alerted by a very prominent businessman called Mr Simon. If it had been reported by an anonymous person they would have taken it to be a hoax.

I accompanied the unconscious Maria in the ambulance to the hospital while Frank stayed to look after Desi who was completely oblivious to what was happening. It was a big struggle for the doctors to get Maria back to consciousness. They pumped her stomach out but she must have taken lots of pills in order to get into such a state. When she woke up she was crying bitterly and apologising. I had to hold myself back from doing her serious harm. There were police there asking her questions, wanting to know the reasons that possessed her to attempt suicide. It all came out. How much in love she was with Simon, the beautiful, famous hairdresser. But that he only had eyes for Miss Oliver. She already had the admiration of thousands of fans and now even had Frank, who was such a wonderful man. Reading Marilyn Monroe's suicide had made her realise that if a beautiful desirable woman like Marilyn Monroe could be spurned in love, what chance did she have to be noticed by Simon?

She rang Simon and plucked up the courage to tell him how much she loved him. It should be her he should look at because she was the one who loved him and not Miss Oliver. She told him this is her last phone call, as she cannot live, as he had eyes only for Miss Oliver. She still continued crying while the detective was writing all this down in his notebook. I never realised how she felt about Simon. From my point of view she was a well-balanced, good-tempered eighteen-year-old girl, who loved my daughter and felt very privileged and happy to come with me to various rehearsals, shows and restaurants. She was treated as a member of the family.

At this point I lost my cool. I got hold of her shoulders and started to shake her, shouting at her: 'I had no idea how you felt, but this is not the point. How dare you attempt suicide while you were looking after my baby? You were responsible for my baby. You could have killed her. She could have been burnt alive. What do you think I would have done to you then?' Both the police and the doctor tried to calm me down. But I was not ready to be calm. 'If you felt like committing suicide, for which I am very sorry, why did you not do it on your day off when you were visiting your parents? You have committed a serious crime. We are talking about my child's life. How I wish I had never trusted my daughter to your care.' All I could think of was what could have happened to my baby. I had never known so much anger and I had never realised how violent I could get. I just could not control myself.

When I got home Desi was sleeping in her cot and Frank had cleaned up the whole flat; including the vomit. I was amazed and very grateful. I could not stop crying. The whole place could have gone up in flames. I felt very relieved having Frank with me. His calm and cool approach to this catastrophic situation only made me realise even more that this is the man that I would like to spend my life with. I never saw Maria again.

* * *   * * *   * * *

It was unfortunate that this was the weekend when my mother, having returned from America, had decided to spend some time with her boyfriend. Had she been here, it would never have happened. In ten days' time I had a contract to go to Nice and then on to Monte Carlo to sing with a big band in the casino… I was the top of the bill. Now that Maria was no longer around my mother promised that she would look after Desi. I employed a part-time nanny and my mother would call her in if and when she needed her. However, I still had a major problem, for due to my mother's escapades I had no car. I needed to drive, with all my stage dresses and music, to the South of France. Frank offered to buy me a car to enable me to fulfil the contract. I could not accept it because any valuable possessions would be confiscated by the Court. As always I went to Mr Rotstein. This time Frank came with me. Mr Rotstein said, 'You obviously know the situation that poor Dorit has been forced into. This is the most generous and wonderful offer but the only way this can be done is for you to buy the car in your name and lend it to Dorit. Then she does not own the car and it cannot be taken away from her.

Frank bought me a brand new pale-blue four-seater Fiat. I realised how much I missed not having my own car.

Leaving Desi was hard but having my mother in charge was a great relief. The new girl, Karin, was a trainee nursery nurse and with my mother's supervision I was sure all would be well. I went off with an easy heart.

It took me two days and a night to travel to Nice. I arrived just after lunch at the guest house 'Pansionate'. This belonged to an old retired circus clown and the guests were solely artists who worked at the various shows at night. This was very convenient as everybody slept during the day. The atmosphere in this place was wonderful. We were allowed to use the kitchen as we pleased.

The night club was only a five-minute walk from the guest house, but I still drove as I did not feel safe walking at night after the show. Maxim's was an elegant night club. The majority of the performers were French. As I was the top of the bill this was a relatively easy job. I was on stage at eleven, by one o'clock I was back home and at about ten or eleven in the morning I went to the beautiful sandy beach, to soak up the sun, swim in the azure-coloured sea and enjoy the seafood that was served. In the afternoons I would drive around sightseeing.

I was offered a job to sing with a big band in the casino in Monte Carlo. I spoke to Mother and Desi every day. Frank had returned to England and had become an assistant sales manager in the export department of a leather tanning group near Croydon. Straight after Monte Carlo my next engagement was in Brussels. A long drive. Frank and I were also phoning each other every night at seven o'clock sharp. The people at the telephone exchange knew us by now and did not disconnect the phone even after the paid connection time was up.

Completely unexpectedly I received a telegram from my mother: 'Come immediately to pick up Desi. I am leaving for America in two days' time. I am very sorry to let you down. I hope you can forgive me.' I had to read this again and again, I simply could not believe the words that I was reading. After all she had put me through, forcing me to lose everything that I had, including the royalties from my records. Just when I had a chance to make a bit of money she was putting herself and her own interest first. I was so shocked and angry. I did not know what to do. I could not leave this job; I still had two weeks of the contract. And yet I could not leave Desi there with only Karin to look after her.

That night, after the show, I drove, through the night, to Hamburg. I was there by sunrise. My mother's suitcases were already packed. I could not bring myself to look my mother in the eye, let alone to give her a hug. I did not want to hear her apologies or her reasons, I just picked up a suitcase full of clothes for Desi and left without turning around to say goodbye. All I remembered telling my mother was: 'How could you? Again you let me down? How could you?' I paid Karin off. Then I left and slammed the door. I drove back to Brussels with Desi.

We arrived just in time for the matinee. I did not have time to go back to my hotel but had to go straight to the club. I had befriended a German acrobat husband and wife; they used to talk to me about their little daughter and how her mother was taking care of her while they were touring. I had no option but to ask them whether they could take care of Desi whilst I was on stage.

We continued this arrangement, for which I was very grateful, until the management found out. Somebody must have reported things to the boss. They asked me to leave straight away as it was a breach of contract to bring the child into the premises. I tried to convince them as there was only a week left. The couple also pleaded with them. Since I was the star attraction and they really did not want to lose me, I stayed.

I had no contract for a month after Brussels, so I decided to go and visit Frank in England. Frank knew I was coming but I was not able to tell him exactly when I would be arriving as I did not know which boat I would catch. I arrived at Frank's address. An elderly lady came to the door and when I asked for Mr Wolff, she turned and shouted in a loud voice: 'Mr Wolff, there is a coloured lady asking for you.' This bought a big smile to my face. Obviously because of my two months in the south of France sunning myself on the beach every day I must have acquired a healthy tan. When Desi saw Frank she was so happy and for me the feelings of upset, hurt and disappointment that I had had to endure because of my mother just fell from my shoulders.

Frank had a little flat on the first floor of this Victorian terraced house in South Norwood. The landlady, Mrs Michael, had no objection for us to stay for as long as we wanted. I did not know what to do. I had contracts waiting for me both in Sweden and France. There were two songs for me waiting to be recorded in Germany but it was so pointless for me to cut a new record. All the money, the royalties would go straight into Mr Rotstein's account, who would have to pass it on to Mr Wagner. It was breaking my heart to have worked so hard to achieve what I had;

to be amongst the top ten singers in Germany, to have bookings in advance for an entire year, and yet I could only keep a small proportion of my wages, just enough to pay for my upkeep.

Frank asked me to stay; he earned enough money to keep the three of us in comfort. For the first time in my life I felt secure. He also had some savings, sufficient to put down as a deposit on a little house. We both wanted to settle down together but this had come a bit sooner than we planned. I looked at my little daughter sitting and playing with her little teddy bear, so content. What could I offer to my little girl if I went back to Germany? The future that had looked so rosy and promising only a few months ago had been snatched away from me through no fault of my own. I had come to terms with bringing my child up by myself and I wanted to provide everything for her I promised her at her birth, all the things I never had. Now everything had changed and here was Frank, a real Mench (genuine person), who loved me for me, never tried to change me, accepted me, loved me and even loved my daughter. I decided this was a moment to start a new life. Having a home of my own, not having to live like a nomad, was a dream come true! Yes, I would make a proper home for us.

Mark, our newborn baby, had completed our perfect family. Mark was such a happy boy. Desi was very protective towards him and would not let anyone touch him or come near him. It was very hard being a housewife and a mother. To my greatest surprise I really loved being a mum. Being on stage singing was second nature to me. Being a mother of two and living a completely new life was the biggest challenge yet. Having to live such a complete change of life, and to be accepted, to feel part of British society, took much more effort than just mastering the English language! I decided to stay and make my home in England. I became Dorit Wolff.

ACKNOWLEDGEMENTS

There are many people who have provided enormous encouragement and help in the production of this book.

First and foremost my husband Frank, who has acted as reader, kind critic, chauffeur, and my best friend.

My children Desi and Mark. Thank you for giving me the childhood I missed out on.

Michael Fleming, who in helping with the first draft of the book, never allowed my own voice to be lost in translation. He too is a friend, supporter and critic who convinced me that less can be more.

Eliza, who kick-started me into writing chapter one.

Gareth, who gave up so much of his time in taking my dictation.

Rita, who spent countless hours typing up the manuscript (and in the process rejuvenated my Hungarian).

Iris, my telephone buddy.

My soul-sister Angela, for her constant encouragement and who lifted me when I began to doubt myself.

Anderida Writers Eastbourne, for their support, encouragement and constructive feedback.

Clare Christian, publisher at RedDoor. Thank you for believing in me.

Lastly, thanks to all those who helped me to survive.

I JUST AM

I come from Hiding, Sirens, Bombs, Smoke, Fear, Chaos, and Hunger.

I come from a long line of persecuted people.

Nazis, Swastikas, Star of David, Running, Air-raid Shelters,

Marching with pioneers, Dancing, Singing, Spotlights, Applause, Travelling.

Having babies.

Being a mum.

Remembering.

Remembering.

Where do I come from? I really don't know any more.

Does it matter?

I just am.

Dorit Oliver-Wolff

ABOUT THE AUTHOR

Dorit Oliver-Wolff was born Theodora Handler (Doriszka) in Novi Sad, Serbia in 1936. As an infant she survived the bombing of Belgrade before being cared for by the partisans in the forests outside of that city. She was taken by her mother to Budapest where they survived the persecution of the Jews, first by the Fascist regime of Hungary and later by the occupying German force which in 1944 instituted the mass arrest and deportation of Jews to concentration camps, under the personal authority of Adolf Eichmann. After the war's end, Dorit moved back to Novi Sad, then to Israel, then Turkey. Stateless, she had no option but to lead a double life: schoolgirl by day, and belly dancer by night. She toured the Middle East on an artist's visa working as a member of her mother's dance company. Dorit became an accomplished singer but was also keen to complete her education.

Dorit attended Munich University to study English from 1956–1958. She carried on performing during and after her time at university, appearing at many top hotels and clubs in cabaret throughout Europe. Dorit made many top-selling records which were released on the Philips-Fontana and Ariola labels. Her records are still being played and her folk songs in six languages are still regularly heard on the radio stations in Germany.

Dorit is an accomplished public speaker and is dedicated to educating others about the consequences of the Holocaust. She has appeared on numerous interviews on local and national radio stations including Radio 4, and was featured in a documentary for BBC One's *Inside Out* programme to mark the 70th anniversary of the Holocaust.

Dorit was nominated for the Lifetime Achievement Award in 2011 by Sovereign Radio Station and for the Resident of the Year in 2013 by *Eastbourne Gazette* and *Eastbourne Herald*. On Holocaust Memorial Day on 3rd February 2015, Dorit received one of the limited run of medals given out to Holocaust survivors by George Osborne, Chancellor of the Exchequer, for her work with the schools, colleges and communities across the United Kingdom that offer educational programmes about the Holocaust to their students. She was also the winner of the Services to Education category at the Eastbourne Achievers Awards in 2015. Dorit works closely with the Holocaust Educational Trust, which seeks to raise awareness and understanding of the Holocaust and its relevance today.

Dorit has two children and five grandchildren. She lives in East Sussex with her husband, Frank Wolff.

For further information on Dorit visit her website:
www.doritoliverwolff.com

For further information on the Holocaust Educational
Trust, please visit www.het.org.uk